PUTTING AI TO WORK IN DISCIPLINARY LITERACY

Putting AI to Work in Disciplinary Literacy

SHIFTING MINDSETS AND GUIDING CLASSROOM INSTRUCTION

Rachel Karchmer-Klein

Foreword by Amy C. Hutchison

THE GUILFORD PRESS
New York London

A Division of Guilford Publications, Inc.
www.guilford.com

Printed in the United States of America

This book is printed on acid-free paper.

For product and safety concerns within the EU, please contact *GPSR@taylorandfrancis.com,* Taylor & Francis Verlag GmbH, Kaufingerstraße 24, 80331 München, Germany.

Last digit is print number: 9 8 7 6 5 4 3 2 1

Library of Congress Cataloging-in-Publication Data is available from the publisher.

ISBN 978-1-4625-5944-2 (paperback) ISBN 978-1-4625-5945-9 (hardcover)

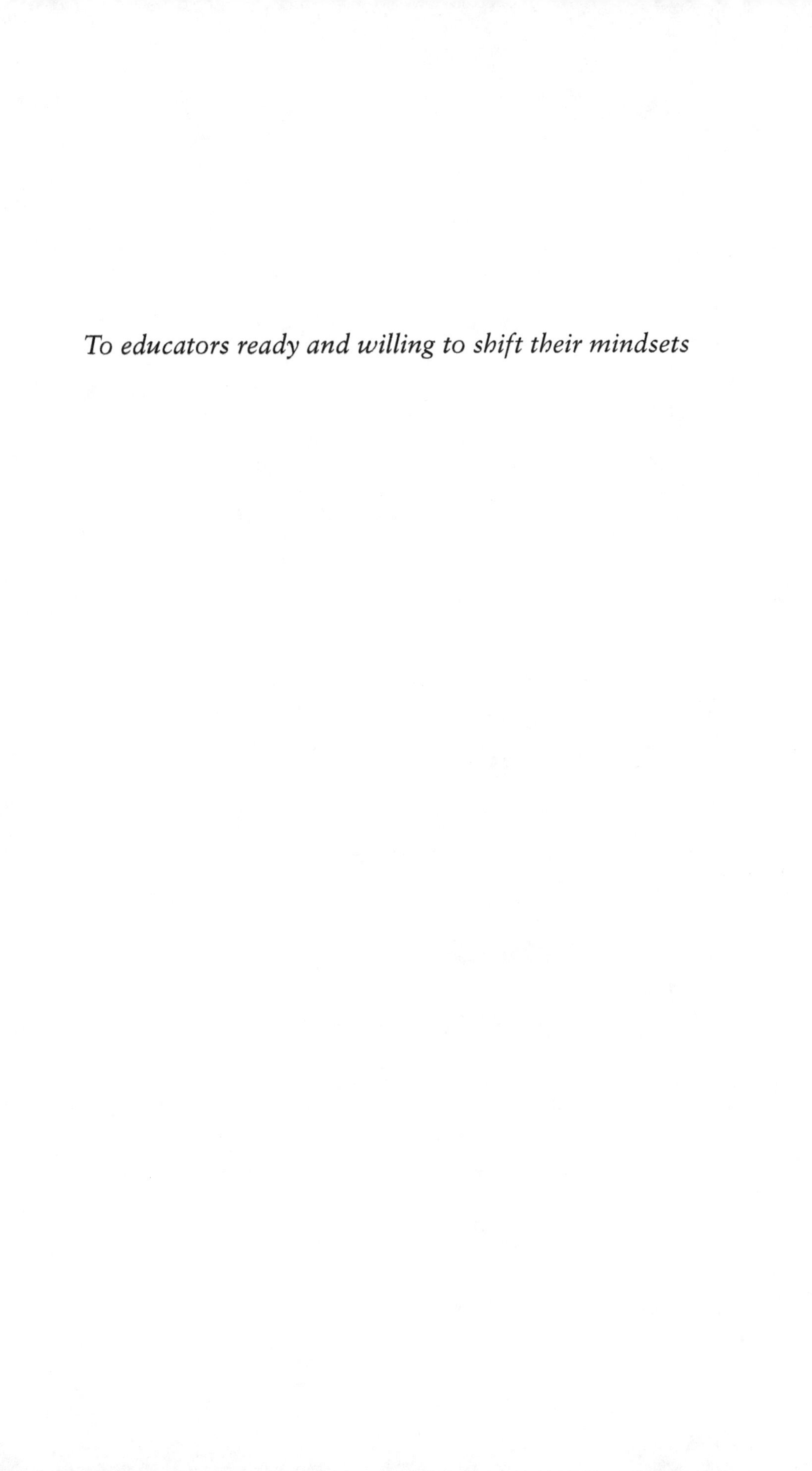

To educators ready and willing to shift their mindsets

About the Author

Rachel Karchmer-Klein, PhD, is Associate Professor in the School of Education at the University of Delaware, where she teaches undergraduate and graduate courses in literacy and educational technology. A former classroom teacher and reading specialist, her research investigates the intersection of literacy, digital tools, and instructional design. Dr. Karchmer-Klein explores how educators can create learning experiences that leverage technological affordances to support reading, writing, and critical thinking. She has published widely in peer-reviewed journals on such topics as online teacher education, multimodal literacy, and technology-integrated instruction. Dr. Karchmer-Klein's work is grounded in the belief that solid instruction—not technology—is the key to effective digital learning, and she aims to prepare educators to teach thoughtfully and adaptively in an increasingly connected world.

Foreword

In a rapidly evolving technological landscape, where artificial intelligence (AI) is transforming how we learn, work, and interact with information, *Putting AI to Work in Disciplinary Literacy: Shifting Mindsets and Guiding Classroom Instruction* arrives at a critical juncture. It's not just another contribution to the burgeoning collection of opinions and prognostications on AI in education; it's a timely and insightful guide to navigating the complex interplay between AI and its crucial connection to literacy skills. The integration of AI into education is no longer a question of *if* but *how.* This book provides an essential and timely guide for educators seeking to navigate this complex landscape and prepare their students for the future.

As a researcher who's embraced the transformative potential of digital tools for many years, I have imagined and witnessed firsthand how digital tools can transform learning experiences in the classroom and promote deep learning when applied thoughtfully. Despite my typically optimistic outlook on digital technologies in the classroom, I admit to having had reservations about the role of generative AI in classrooms, particularly when it comes to reading and writing. I have wondered if students will still learn to engage in deep, critical reading when they can ask AI to summarize an entire text for them and get a result in seconds. I have wondered if they will learn or retain the ability to generate a text consisting entirely of their own thoughts when AI can so quickly generate text on nearly any topic for them. After a lot of wondering, some experimentation, and thoughtful analysis, I have come to the same conclusion that I have come to many times before when considering educational technologies: Digital technologies are a tool, and it is up to us how we use them. It is the role of educators to find creative uses for these tools that require students to think deeply. Again, we must shift our instructional practices and approaches to assessment in such a way that assignments cannot be completed by simply generating a summary with AI. If we shift what we ask students to do, we can enhance, rather than detract from, their abilities to read and write critically by using AI as a thought partner. Karchmer-Klein's insights in this book mirror my own: a cautious optimism balanced by a creative exploration of AI's possibilities.

Karchmer-Klein's experience as a teacher and researcher provides a unique perspective, blending practical insights with a deep understanding of pedagogical principles. She masterfully addresses the anxieties and uncertainties surrounding AI integration in education, focusing not on the fear of disruption but on the potential for enhancement. She emphasizes the importance of not just teaching students *about* AI but empowering educators to *use* AI effectively to enhance teaching and learning. For educators who have valid fears about the use of generative AI, she offers suggestions that she calls "If you fear *this* . . . try this shift." Further, she provides practical insights for moving from fear to empowerment.

This book is predicated on the belief that the rise of generative AI necessitates a fundamental shift in how we approach digital literacy instruction. Karchmer-Klein helps us understand that traditional digital literacy skills, focused on navigating online searches, evaluating the reliability of existing sources, and composing multimodal texts, remain essential. However, the advent of AI-generated content, produced dynamically in real time by algorithms, broadens the scope of what it means to be digitally literate. This book offers a practical approach for navigating this shifting landscape and ensuring that teachers and students are prepared with the skills to be digitally literate in the AI era. This preparation requires developing new competencies, such as the ability to refine AI-generated outputs, identify inherent biases, and evaluate the credibility of responses based on their generation process rather than solely their origin. This evolving landscape calls for the cultivation of *AI digital literacies*: the skills needed to critically engage with and leverage AI tools effectively. Importantly, Karchmer-Klein calls for shifting mindsets to transform how individuals learn with generative AI rather than just accommodating AI in the classroom.

Through well-structured chapters and illustrative examples, *Putting AI to Work in Disciplinary Literacy* offers a clear path toward leveraging AI tools effectively. In this book, readers will find an emphasis on fostering critical thinking, problem solving, and ethical considerations in using AI. Instead of treating AI as a mere tool for rote tasks, Karchmer-Klein advocates for its use as a powerful thought partner that enhances, rather than replaces, human intelligence. The continual emphasis on real-world applications, hands-on learning activities, and the integration of AI into established pedagogical strategies, such as simulations and project-based learning, makes this a valuable resource for educators seeking to implement AI in meaningful ways. Karchmer-Klein places particular emphasis on the need to help students develop cognitive flexibility to avoid the pitfalls of AI and become active participants who critically evaluate AI-generated content rather than passive consumers of it.

Crucially, this book also highlights the critical role of students' disciplinary knowledge in evaluating AI-generated content. As Karchmer-Klein points out, since AI cannot participate in disciplinary activities, such as conducting experiments or troubleshooting methodological errors, students must be able to critically assess the validity of AI-generated hypotheses using their own expertise. This book empowers readers to leverage their experiences and disciplinary knowledge to refine and enhance AI-generated content, rather than feeling replaced by it. Further, it emphasizes the tremendous importance of leveraging AI for learning, not for convenience, and promotes an essential central principle: Generative AI should be leveraged as a scaffold for deeper literacy development, never as a shortcut that undermines the thinking process. With this principle in mind, Karchmer-Klein provides numerous evidence-informed approaches for AI-driven reading and writing instruction across several content areas. She has reimagined traditional approaches to reading and writing instruction and provides concrete examples of using generative AI for crafting evidence-based arguments, literary analysis, creative writing, and more.

Putting AI to Work in Disciplinary Literacy is not merely a guide for integrating AI into the classroom; it is a road map for preparing students and educators for the AI-driven future, and a "must read" for educators at all levels. Whether you're an experienced teacher seeking to refine your approach or a novice grappling with the complexities of AI integration, Karchmer-Klein offers invaluable guidance and actionable strategies to empower students with the essential skills needed to thrive in an AI-driven world. This is not a book about *resisting* the inevitable tide of AI but about *riding* it effectively, thoughtfully, and ethically. It is a guide to enhancing, not replacing, the very best of traditional education through the judicious and responsible implementation of AI.

AMY C. HUTCHISON, PhD
Fayard Endowed Chair in Literacy Education
University of Alabama

Acknowledgments

This was a challenging book to write, mostly due to the rapid pace of technological change. Just when I thought I understood a tool like ChatGPT, an update or a new version would emerge. These changes were significant, as they altered the tool's interface and required me to figure out new ways to integrate them into this text. Therefore, this acknowledgment serves as a thank you to the educators who supported me throughout my learning process (and continue to do so). Some of you I know personally, like Marissa Bongo, who began this journey with me, brainstorming ideas and sharing her lesson concepts and perspectives on generative AI (GenAI). Lauren Boulden, my constant collaborator and resident technology extraordinaire, always has an answer to my many questions. And Leigh Hibbard, a doctoral student whom I am fortunate enough to work with at the University of Delaware, assisted with a literature review so I was up to date on the most recent research in the field.

A second group of people who helped me on this journey are those I do not know personally. I share a heartfelt thank you to them. They are part of my ever-expanding professional learning network. They give their time and energy by posting videos and blog posts about these ever-changing digital tools so whenever I am stuck, I can search for answers, and I almost always find solutions.

And, of course, while these two did not help me write the book, they were certainly in the background, urging me to hurry up and encouraging me to achieve my goal. Joe and Ryan may not carry pom-poms, but they bring me hot water with lemon, clean up after dinner, and leave me in my office for hours so I can write. Cheers to Number 3.

Contents

Purchasers of this book can download and print the reproducible forms at *www.guilford.com/karchmer-klein-forms* for personal use or use with students (see copyright page for details).

Introduction

In January 2023, I began exploring generative artificial intelligence (GenAI) tools, mainly ChatGPT. As I always do when learning new technologies, I started examining how they fit into my daily life. I prompted ChatGPT to create recipes using the ingredients in my refrigerator and map out the most efficient train routes across three European cities for an upcoming family vacation.

I was impressed by the outputs. The recipes included the ingredients I provided, the necessary components I had not considered—flour, olive oil, salt, and pepper—and cooking times and temperatures. The travel routes were clear and concise, and they even offered alternatives if we chose to take different paths. However, GenAI could only assist us so much once my husband and I set out on the trip. Train delays, unexpected detours, and lousy weather required us to think critically, adapt, and verify information. The technology provided structure, but we were still responsible for problem solving.

As I sat on the train from Amsterdam to Bruges, it struck me that this was precisely the type of interaction students would need to have with ChatGPT, not as a tool that provides answers but as a thinking partner that supports *digital literacies*—an interconnected framework of skills that includes technical proficiency, problem solving, critical thinking, and reading and writing in digital spaces (Karchmer-Klein et al., in press). I turned to my husband and asked him this question: "If GenAI could anticipate my needs, fill in gaps, and organize information efficiently, what could it mean for classroom learning?"

At the time, GenAI in schools was seen as either an exciting opportunity or a disruptive educational force. Administrators banned GenAI outright, teachers felt unsure about how to respond, and conversations about ethics and academic integrity often overshadowed discussions about learning potential.

A Familiar Pattern: Resistance and Uncertainty in Education

Indeed, artificial intelligence (AI) has been an integral part of modern life for years. It powers online banking, Google searches, Netflix recommendations, and driver-assist features. These tools rely on traditional forms of AI that analyze data, recognize patterns, or make predictions. *Generative* AI, on the other hand, does something new. It creates original content—like text, images, or even full lesson plans—which raises very different questions for educators, especially when students can now use it to write essays or complete assignments in seconds.

At the time, I was still processing its implications for teaching and learning. The international conversation surrounding the technology focused almost entirely on academic dishonesty, with newspaper articles warning of students using ChatGPT to cheat. As a result, some of the largest school districts and universities around the world responded by banning it outright:

- "ChatGPT Banned in New York City Public Schools Over Concerns About Cheating, Learning Development" (Lukpat, 2023)
- "ChatGPT in Schools: Here's Where It's Banned—And How It Could Potentially Help Students" (Johnson, 2023)
- "Top French University Bans Use of ChatGPT to Prevent Plagiarism" (Reuters, 2023)

In the business sections of those same newspapers, though, there were plenty of headlines announcing the booming AI industry and the demand for AI-skilled workers:

- "AI Could Spur an Economic Boom. Humans Are in the Way" (Omeokwe, 2023)
- "Generative AI Is Already Changing White-Collar Work as We Know It" (Tarrant, 2023)
- "Jobs Are Now Requiring Experience with ChatGPT—And They'll Pay as Much as $800,000 a Year for the Skill" (Mok, 2023)

This tension between school reluctance and workforce innovation is not new to me. After 25 years of researching technology in education, I understand that integrating new digital tools is never just a matter of adoption or rejection. Every significant technological advancement, from the introduction of the calculator to the rise of the internet to the launch of a 1:1 iPad program, has been met with a blend of enthusiasm and hesitation. New initiatives bring challenges and opportunities, but their value should never be centered on the technology itself. The focus must always remain on learning objectives, with literacy skills serving as the foundation for deep learning of content across disciplines.

Fear of GenAI

Much of the fear surrounding AI in education stems from legitimate teacher concerns (Microsoft, 2023). There is the potential for increased cheating and becoming overly dependent on AI tools. Furthermore, the lack of clear, acceptable AI use policies means that educators are often left to navigate ethical dilemmas independently, creating uncertainty about when and how AI should be integrated into learning. Without well-defined guidelines, schools struggle to balance innovation with academic integrity, leaving both teachers and students unsure of AI's role in the classroom (Burleigh & Wilson, 2022).

Beyond these immediate classroom challenges lie deeper anxieties: Will GenAI widen existing achievement gaps, with some students having access to better tools and training than others? How do we protect student data and ensure the ethical use of AI tools that collect and analyze student information? Some teachers even fear that AI will ultimately devalue their expertise or replace them altogether.

These fears are understandable, especially given the lack of adequate training and support for teachers (Diliberti et al., 2024). Many educators feel unprepared to navigate this rapidly evolving landscape, lacking the knowledge and resources to leverage AI's potential while effectively mitigating its risks. The traditional emphasis on rote memorization in the classroom can make AI seem to threaten established pedagogical practices directly. However, these concerns often arise from a misunderstanding of AI's capabilities, viewing it as a replacement for human thought rather than a tool for enhancing it.

Traditional teaching approaches and assessments were not designed for a world where students have AI-generated responses at their fingertips. For example, a history assignment that asks students to list key events leading up to the Civil War or a science worksheet that requires students to define key terms can now be completed in seconds, with little effort, using GenAI.

Rachel Tobac is a former special education teacher, an expert in AI technologies, and the CEO of SocialProof Security, a company that trains employees to protect data from social engineering threats. She remembers a time when teachers warned students they would not always have a technology available. "You're never going to have a calculator in your pocket," she recalls, "so you have to learn how to do everything mentally, like mental math." Of course, that turned out to be false. She explained, "Today, we always have calculators in our pockets with the digital revolution of the iPhone or the Android phone. When we think about how AI is transforming the way that we think about teaching, we can kind of hearken back to this thought" (R. Tobac, personal communication, September 25, 2024).

For Tobac, the outdated warning of the calculator mirrors today's resistance to AI in schools. "Tools like ChatGPT are not going to go away. They will become more and more integrated," she explains. But instead of preparing students adequately, some schools are shutting AI out, banning ChatGPT from networks, and treating it as a shortcut for cheating rather than a tool for learning. "That's not useful for people," Tobac argues. "Because when they move into their career, they're going to have it in their pocket, and they're going to use it then."

She urges educators to take a different approach, not to resist AI but to teach students how to use it ethically and effectively. "If we can integrate it into how we communicate our curriculum at the middle and high school level, that will prepare students to use it appropriately as they go into college, as they move into their careers and beyond."

Tobac's insight emphasizes a central theme of this book: the shift in mindset isn't about whether students will use AI but *how* they will use it. Just as calculators didn't eliminate the need for number sense, AI won't replace critical thinking or problem solving. In fact, it will demand even greater application. Yet, if we don't teach students to use it responsibly, they will enter the workforce unprepared for a world where AI is already in their pockets, shaping how they learn, work, and navigate information.

Why Disciplinary Literacy Matters in an AI-Rich World

If there is one thing the field of literacy education is known for besides a love of reading, it is the tendency to define the same term in multiple ways. *Disciplinary literacy* is no exception. While definitions vary, my perspective aligns most closely with McConachie and Petrosky (2010), who explain that disciplinary literacy "involves the use of reading, reasoning, investigating, speaking, and writing required to learn and form complex content knowledge appropriate to a particular discipline" (p. 16).

Engineers do not just apply formulas. They design, prototype, troubleshoot, and optimize solutions for real-world challenges. Financial analysts do not only crunch numbers. They assess market trends, predict risks, and communicate insights through data storytelling. Attorneys do not just memorize laws. They analyze legal precedents, construct persuasive arguments, and anticipate counterarguments to advocate effectively. Cybersecurity specialists do not just install firewalls. They assess vulnerabilities, analyze cyber threats, and develop strategic defenses to protect sensitive information. Each discipline has distinct ways of reasoning, questioning, and communicating, and helping students master these discipline-specific literacy practices is crucial for deep learning.

GenAI has the potential to be a powerful thought partner in this process, assisting students in refining their thinking, solving problems, and engaging more deeply with disciplinary knowledge. Yet, it also demands that these very skills be used effectively. Without the ability to critically evaluate and question AI-generated content, there is a risk of misinterpreting information, accepting flawed reasoning, or failing to engage with the complexity of the subject areas. In this way, GenAI both supports *and* relies on the development of disciplinary literacy.

This book focuses on middle and high school disciplinary literacy because these are the years when the curriculum emphasizes discipline-specific ways of thinking. Students analyze conflicting primary sources, evaluate different perspectives, construct evidence-based arguments, design experiments, and troubleshoot errors. This period in education allows educators to explicitly teach students how to interrogate AI-generated content, refine AI-assisted research, and challenge AI's reasoning within their disciplines, preparing them for the demands of college, careers, and civic engagement life.

Shifting Mindsets in an AI-Infused Classroom

The rise of GenAI requires a fundamental shift in our approach to teaching and learning. GenAI should transform how individuals interact with information, construct knowledge, and engage in disciplinary thinking. To navigate this shift effectively, we must adjust our mindset. The following principles have been invaluable to me when considering how, when, and why to integrate GenAI into my teaching.

Instructional Design Must Be Intentional

There is a time and place for AI to perform rote tasks. However, they must be reimagined if most AI-integrated learning activities in your classroom can be accomplished without analysis, synthesis, or problem solving. This book provides practical strategies for redesigning assessments and classroom assignments to enhance learning rather than enable AI shortcuts.

AI Is a Tool, Not an Expert

AI generates information but struggles with verifying sources, forming original arguments, assessing ethical issues, and even basic math. Students and teachers are still the experts. A key pedagogical shift involves teaching students how to question AI-generated content, evaluate its validity, and utilize it as a learning partner rather than an authority.

Cognitive Flexibility Is Essential

Adaptive thinking is essential in an AI-powered classroom. GenAI does not provide fixed answers—instead, it generates responses that require interpretation, refinement, and evaluation. Students must learn to question AI outputs, adjust their inquiries, and apply critical reasoning to ensure meaningful engagement with disciplinary content. This book explores strategies for fostering cognitive flexibility so students can navigate AI-generated information with agility and intent.

AI Can Be Leveraged for Differentiated Instruction

GenAI's adaptability offers new opportunities for personalized learning in genuinely dynamic and responsive ways. While many teachers already differentiate instruction, GenAI enables real-time scaffolding, adaptive feedback, and personalized learning pathways that were previously unattainable.

Ethical AI Use Must Be Explicitly Taught

AI ethics encompass more than just plagiarism. AI-generated content poses biases, privacy concerns, and misinformation risks that must be addressed across all disciplines. Teaching AI ethics has become an essential part of disciplinary literacy. In this book, you will discover practical methods to incorporate ethics discussions into research, writing, and inquiry-based learning across various subjects.

AI Is Constantly Evolving

AI tools are evolving at an unprecedented pace. GenAI today is not what it was a year ago and will not be the same next year. While its capabilities continue to expand, the foundational literacy skills that students need—critical thinking, problem solving, and reading and writing in digital spaces—remain constant. This book explores how educators can prepare students for an AI landscape that is still unfolding.

Understanding AI Terms

As you engage with the ideas in this book, you will encounter key terms that are helpful to understand up front. Most important, I use the terms *artificial intelligence* (AI) and *generative AI* (GenAI) interchangeably throughout the text. While they are related, they are not the same. AI is a broad field of computer science focused on creating systems that can perform tasks requiring human intelligence, such as facial recognition on your phone. GenAI, by contrast, is a specific type of AI designed to create new content in response to user input. This book focuses on GenAI, though for simplicity I often refer to it as AI throughout the chapters.

Here are short definitions of some of the key terms used in this book. I pair each one with an example to help bring them to life in a classroom context:

Artificial intelligence (AI): A broad term for computer systems that can perform tasks on existing data and typically requiring human intelligence, such as recognizing speech, predicting patterns, or detecting faces in photos.

Example: Netflix uses AI to suggest shows or movies based on what you've previously watched.

Generative AI (GenAI): A type of AI that creates new content, such as text, images, music, or code, based on prompts from the user.

Example: A student uses ChatGPT to generate a summary of a science article before writing their own analysis.

Prompt engineering: The process of crafting clear, specific questions or instructions to guide what an AI tool generates.

Example: A teacher asks students to revise a vague prompt like "Write a story" to "Write a short story that includes a conflict between two friends and ends with a resolution."

Hallucination: When an AI tool produces content that sounds accurate but is actually false or made up.

Example: An AI tool generates a quote from a historical figure that sounds real—but was never actually said by that person.

Large language model (LLM): A type of GenAI trained on huge amounts of text data to generate human-like responses to prompts.

Example: Tools like ChatGPT are built on LLMs that can answer questions, explain concepts, or engage in conversation.

Training data: The large sets of text, images, or other information used to teach AI tools how to recognize patterns and respond to inputs.

Example: If an AI tool has read thousands of news articles, it can generate a mock article in a similar style using what it learned from its training data.

Book Organization and Unique Features

Once I began integrating GenAI into my teaching, it was important to me to help other educators prepare to navigate the necessary pedagogical shifts. To do so, I returned to three key questions that have shaped my work on literacy and technology throughout my career. These questions became the foundation for my systematic approach to designing GenAI coursework and now serve as the framework for this book.

Part I. How Does GenAI Intersect with the Literacy Skills Essential across Disciplines?

Part I lays the groundwork for understanding how GenAI influences problem solving, critical thinking, and reading and writing in digital spaces, skills that are more essential than ever in today's classrooms. It then addresses teachers' common fears and misconceptions when integrating GenAI into literacy instruction. It offers a realistic and research-informed perspective on what thoughtful use can look like in the classroom. Finally, it introduces a practical instructional design framework to help educators align GenAI tools with disciplinary goals, learning outcomes, and student needs. Chapters 1–3 together lay the foundation for intentional, ethical, and literacy-driven integration of GenAI in schools.

Part II. How Do We Reimagine Instruction for an AI-Infused World?

Part II outlines effective methods for integrating GenAI into instructional practices while maintaining rigorous disciplinary curriculum standards. The goal is not to modify lessons to accommodate GenAI but to strategically employ GenAI as a tool that enhances students' literacy skills and discipline-specific knowledge. The evidence-informed strategies encompass multiple disciplines, illustrating how teachers can leverage GenAI to strengthen students' problem solving, critical thinking, and ability to read and write texts to keep students actively engaged in the learning process.

Part III. How Do We Prepare Students for an AI-Infused Workforce and Higher Education?

Students will graduate into a workforce where GenAI is integrated into nearly every profession. Part III provides insights from professionals regarding the AI-related skills they seek in employees. It also examines the role of AI in higher education and how K–12 schools can prepare students for ethical and effective AI use in their future careers. A crucial aspect of this is the professional development available to educators to learn about new technologies during and after the school day.

Unique Features

This book is designed for teachers, providing practical tools and strategies that you can apply in your classroom immediately. Each chapter is structured to help you navigate AI integration with confidence and purpose, featuring:

- *Try It Out exercises.* Throughout this book, you will find "Try It Out" features designed to give you quick, hands-on opportunities to engage with GenAI tools in meaningful ways. These exercises are short, practical invitations to experiment, reflect, and think critically about how GenAI can support student learning and your own professional practice. Whether you're testing a prompt strategy, analyzing a student–AI exchange, or generating content to evaluate, these moments are built to help you experience the concepts in action and imagine how they might come to life in your classroom.

- *Teacher Reflection Questions.* Each chapter ends with reflection questions to help readers connect the content to their own teaching. These prompts are designed to encourage thoughtful consideration of your beliefs, goals, and instructional choices as you explore how GenAI can support literacy learning. Use them individually or with colleagues to guide meaningful conversations and professional growth.

- *Ethical Dilemmas and Discussion Prompts.* GenAI raises important questions: bias in AI-generated sources, academic integrity, authorship, and more. Every chapter includes real-world dilemmas with discussion prompts to help you, your colleagues, and your students explore these complexities and reflect on their impact on teaching, learning, and society.

- *Lesson plans for different disciplines.* The chapters in Part II provide ready-to-use activities designed for various subjects, demonstrating how AI can enhance learning without replacing critical thinking. These lessons guide students in refining arguments, evaluating sources, critiquing AI-generated texts, and engaging in disciplinary literacy practices that promote higher-order thinking.

- *Reproducible forms.* To make implementation easier, I have included a collection of reproducible documents you can use and adapt for your students. These ready-to-use resources are designed to help you bring the ideas in this book to life. You can copy them as is or modify them to meet your learners' unique needs.

- *Action steps for educators and schools.* The final chapter concludes with practical action steps for teachers and school leaders, offering clear guidance on moving forward with GenAI integration at different levels.

Whether you are just beginning to explore GenAI or already experimenting with it in your teaching, these features will help you apply it thoughtfully and purposefully while keeping student learning at the center.

Conclusion

I aim for this book to enhance education now and in the future, ensuring that students develop the complex and adaptable literacy skills necessary for success in an AI-driven world. I hope it promotes responsible, ethical, and intelligent engagement with digital information. Above all, I hope this book reinforces the power of disciplinary literacy and provides the tools needed to harness GenAI in ways that deepen student learning. AI is already changing education. Our challenge is to ensure that it strengthens, rather than replaces, critical thinking, inquiry, and authentic engagement.

PART I

How Does GenAI Intersect with the Literacy Skills Essential across Disciplines?

Chapter 1

GenAI Digital Literacies

EXPANDING BEYOND TRADITIONAL DIGITAL LITERACY SKILLS

I earned my PhD in reading education from Syracuse University in 1999. My dissertation explored K–12 teachers' perspectives on how the internet influenced literacy and literacy instruction in their classrooms. It was published in Reading Research Quarterly, if you'd like to read it (Karchmer, 2001). I became interested in this topic because, in the late 1990s, a growing body of evidence suggested that technological proficiency would be essential for our children's futures (e.g., Drucker, 1994; The New London Group, 1996). The global economy shifted toward an information-based model emphasizing quick, collaborative communication, requiring new literacy competencies beyond reading and writing traditional print texts.

Back then, the call was clear: Students needed to be proficient in problem solving, critical thinking, digital reading, and digital writing. These skills were seen as necessary for navigating digital landscapes, working collaboratively, and communicating effectively across formats and contexts.

More than two decades later, I am still researching, writing, and preaching about the same core literacy skills, but the context has now changed dramatically. The emergence of generative artificial intelligence (GenAI) has broadened the scope of digital literacies beyond foundational skills. Students are no longer just locating and evaluating information created by others—they are interacting with content generated in real time by algorithms based on patterns learned from massive data sets. This change introduces new complexities, such as refining artificial intelligence (AI)-generated responses, recognizing embedded biases, and evaluating credibility not based on who wrote it but how it was created.

While GenAI is a fundamentally different tool from the early internet, the literacy skills required to engage with it meaningfully remain strikingly familiar. What has changed is the need to extend those foundational skills—problem solving, critical thinking, digital reading, and digital writing—into new territory. As educators, we are not abandoning what we have long valued but rather expanding it to meet the demands of a new digital landscape.

Building Blocks of Deep Learning: Four Literacy Skills

Literacy skills are the building blocks for understanding and interacting with the world. They extend far beyond decoding and reading fluently to include problem solving, critical thinking, and reading and writing texts. These skills lay the groundwork for lifelong learning. Through literacy, individuals pose meaningful questions, engage in thoughtful discourse, and construct knowledge that transcends surface-level understanding.

Literacy skills do not function in isolation; they are deeply interwoven with how individuals engage in their fields of study and professions. A historian evaluates sources and builds arguments based on evidence, while a scientist examines data and communicates findings clearly. Professionals engage in persuasive discussions in business, and in law, precise language can influence a case's outcome. This perspective aligns with McConachie and Petrosky's (2010) definition of disciplinary literacy, which emphasizes that learning within a discipline requires students to read, write, think, and solve problems using the terminology of that profession. The teacher's role is to design intentional literacy instruction that is closely connected to disciplinary practices. The next section of this chapter explores each of the literacy skills mentioned above. It demonstrates how they can be effectively integrated into middle and high school teaching and learning.

Problem Solving

Students need problem-solving skills to tackle challenges, consider different perspectives, and formulate well-reasoned solutions. Research indicates that students engaged in inquiry-based learning have a greater capacity to adapt prior knowledge to solve new problems and develop stronger reasoning abilities (Glazewski & Hmelo-Silver, 2019). Instruction that includes problem solving goes beyond rote learning and prompts students to refine their thinking through iteration, questioning, and reflection.

Teachers can support problem solving by designing real-world challenges that require students to apply their knowledge in new contexts (see Table 1.1). Instead

TABLE 1.1. Classroom Applications: Problem Solving

Discipline	Classroom application
Environmental science	Investigate solutions for reducing plastic waste in a local community by analyzing current waste management systems and proposing actionable improvements.
Forensic science	Determine the most effective method for lifting fingerprints in an investigation.
Pre-algebra	Solve a real-world budgeting problem by calculating costs, comparing financial options, and determining the most cost-effective solutions.
English language arts	Rewrite the ending of a novel by analyzing character motivations, identifying narrative gaps, and proposing a solution that resolves conflicting themes.
Marketing	Analyze a struggling brand by diagnosing the reasons for its decline, researching consumer behavior, and developing a data-driven marketing pivot to improve its market presence.

of following step-by-step instructions, students benefit from open-ended tasks that allow for multiple approaches and solutions.

Critical Thinking

Critical thinking incorporates a range of cognitive skills, including interpreting, analyzing, synthesizing, reasoning, and evaluating information. Research consistently demonstrates that critical thinking can be explicitly taught and developed through instruction, encouraging educators to integrate it into their teaching practices (Dwyer, 2023).

Explicit critical thinking instruction provides structured opportunities for students to evaluate sources, test ideas, justify claims, and analyze reasoning (see Table 1.2). Strategies like structured debates, case study evaluations, and Socratic seminars encourage students to question assumptions and apply reasoning meaningfully. Embedding critical thinking into discipline-specific instruction helps students move beyond memorization, requiring them to analyze situations in relevant, authentic, and transferable ways across contexts.

Reading Texts

Reading comprehension is more than recognizing words on a page. It requires analyzing, synthesizing, and interpreting meaning within texts. Students must learn to navigate sophisticated material, identify key ideas, and make connections

TABLE 1.2. Classroom Applications: Critical Thinking

Discipline	Classroom application
World languages	Compare how cultural perspectives influence language by analyzing translations of idiomatic expressions, identifying shifts in meaning, and explaining the significance of linguistic nuance.
Music theory	Critically assess how a musical composition conveys emotion by analyzing the interplay of harmony, rhythm, and dynamics, and arguing how different interpretations affect the listener's perception.
Psychology	Critique psychology research studies by evaluating the experimental design, identifying ethical concerns, and determining whether the conclusions are supported by the data.
History	Assess the reliability of primary and secondary sources on a historical event by identifying author biases, cross-referencing accounts, and determining which sources provide the most accurate representation of the past.
Government and civics	Investigate the impact of media bias on public opinion by comparing news coverage from different political perspectives and evaluating the role of language in shaping narratives.

across concepts (Shanahan & Shanahan, 2008). Research shows that exposure to longer texts may build students' reasoning skills, deepen content knowledge, and strengthen their ability to synthesize information when scaffolds are put in place to help them remain on task (Reynolds & Fisher, 2022).

Explicit instruction in reading comprehension involves modeling close reading strategies, teaching disciplinary reading approaches, and guiding students to extract meaning from dense or technical materials (see Table 1.3). Strategies such as annotation, questioning the text, text-based discussions, and comparative analysis help students engage with challenging material and develop deeper transferable literacy skills across disciplines (Lewis & Strong, 2020).

Writing Texts

Writing is a powerful tool for learning and communication. Students who can clearly express their ideas in writing demonstrate a deep understanding of content, strong reasoning skills, and the ability to support arguments with evidence (Graham et al., 2018). Writing is not just a way to record information. It is a process that helps students refine their thinking, organize complex ideas, and engage in meaning making across disciplines (Bazerman et al., 2017).

Explicit instruction in writing involves teaching students how to construct well-organized, evidence-based, and discipline-specific texts. Strategies such as outlining, revising cycles, writing for different audiences, and effectively integrating sources help students develop stronger writing skills (see Table 1.4). When writing regularly, students build the capacity to explain their reasoning, analyze concepts, and communicate effectively in both academic and real-world contexts (Graham et al., 2018).

Applying Multiple Literacy Skills across Disciplines

Outlining each of the literacy skills above was meant to underscore their significance in student learning. However, each skill works in conjunction with at least one other skill, if not more. For example, when students are expected to think critically about content, they will likely engage with texts as part of the process. Similarly, problem solving often involves synthesizing information from various sources, connecting ideas, and effectively communicating solutions through writing.

Mehta and Fine's (2019) concept of deep learning applies directly to this literacy discussion. It is a powerful teaching approach that combines mastery, identity, and creativity in the classroom. For teachers, this means designing lessons that challenge students to use multiple literacy skills simultaneously. When students engage in these rich, multifaceted activities, they are not just memorizing facts but developing expertise, seeing themselves as capable learners in the subject, and applying their knowledge creatively.

Teachers integrating multiple literacy skills within a single lesson create a deeper, more meaningful learning experience. Students are more likely to retain

TABLE 1.3. Classroom Applications: Reading Texts

Discipline	Classroom application
World languages	Translate and analyze a literary text from another language by identifying cultural influences, recognizing linguistic structures, and comparing interpretations across different translations.
Music theory	Analyze a composer's written explanation of their work by identifying stylistic choices, comparing them to the actual composition, and evaluating how theory translates into practice.
English language arts	Compare the rhetorical strategies in two argumentative essays by identifying tone, structure, and evidence use, and evaluating the effectiveness of each argument.
Mathematics	Interpret a mathematical proof by breaking down each logical step, identifying assumptions, and explaining the reasoning in simpler terms.
Graphic design	Analyze a multimodal advertisement or artwork by evaluating how text, images, colors, and layout work together to convey meaning, influence perception, and communicate a message effectively.

TABLE 1.4. Classroom Applications: Writing Complex Texts

Discipline	Classroom application
Journalism	Write an investigative article on a school or community issue by conducting interviews, gathering evidence, and structuring a compelling narrative.
Anatomy	Write a research summary explaining how a specific organ system functions, integrating peer-reviewed scientific sources and real-world applications.
Engineering	Document the design process for a prototype, detailing problem-solving approaches, technical specifications, and iterative improvements.
Music and performing arts	Develop a critical review of a musical or theatrical performance, analyzing how different artistic elements contribute to storytelling and emotional impact.
Biology	Write an explanatory essay on the process of photosynthesis, using simple analogies and diagrams to communicate key concepts to a younger audience.

and apply what they have learned in new situations, which is the hallmark of true understanding. Table 1.5 provides cross-disciplinary examples of classroom applications to illustrate how to frame lessons incorporating multiple literacy skills.

Applying Literacy Skills in a Digital World

As literacy skills remain central to students' engagement with information, it is essential to consider how their application has evolved in response to digital technologies. Digital literacy instruction gained traction after the Common Core State Standards (CCSS) Initiative (National Governors Association Center for Best Practices & Council of Chief State School Officers [NGA & CCSSO], 2010) emphasized that, to be college and career ready, students in grades 6–12 must be able to read, write, and interpret digital texts and media.

Traditionally, digital literacy instruction has focused on skills such as navigating online environments, evaluating sources for credibility, composing multimodal texts, and engaging responsibly with digital content (Coiro, 2021; Smith et al., 2021). These competencies remain essential, but they are no longer sufficient.

With the rise of GenAI, students are no longer just retrieving and analyzing human-created content. They interact with dynamically generated responses produced in real time based on human-generated prompts. This presents new challenges: understanding how AI-generated content is constructed, identifying potential biases or inaccuracies, refining outputs, and integrating those responses thoughtfully into their own thinking and writing.

TABLE 1.5. Classroom Applications: Multiple Literacy Skills

Disciplines	Classroom application	Multiple literacy skills
World languages and geography	Students study a region where multiple languages are spoken, analyzing how geography influences language use and writing a bilingual travel guide incorporating cultural insights.	• Critical thinking • Reading texts • Writing texts
Business and psychology	Students research consumer behavior and create a persuasive marketing campaign based on psychological principles of decision making and advertising.	• Critical thinking • Problem solving • Reading texts • Writing texts
Science and journalism	Students conduct a simple environmental science experiment, interpret their results, and write a news article explaining the findings for a general audience.	• Critical thinking • Problem solving • Reading texts • Writing texts
STEM and ethics	Students investigate the ethical implications of artificial intelligence in healthcare, evaluating scientific reports, patient privacy laws, and medical ethics frameworks before drafting a policy recommendation.	• Critical thinking • Reading texts • Writing texts

Note. STEM, science, technology, engineering, and mathematics.

Digital literacy education must, therefore, evolve. Building on foundational skills, students must now learn to co-construct knowledge with AI tools and interrogate how generative systems function. Was a response shaped by biased training data? Does it reinforce stereotypes? How does it compare to human-authored content in the same discipline? These kinds of critical questions define AI digital literacy, a framework that helps students navigate AI's generative and iterative nature as both creators and critical thinkers.

Try It Out Investigating AI Bias through Image Generation

Try the activity described in Table 1.6 and see what you uncover when you prompt a GenAI to generate an image. My input was:

> Create an image of a farming conference with a room full of farmers listening to a speaker. The speaker stands at the front of the room, and the audience listens intently to the presenter's speech.

Figure 1.1 shows the image produced by Gemini. A closer look reveals several embedded biases: nearly all attendees are White males, the speaker is a White male, and the outfit of choice consists of jeans and a baseball cap.

The biases revealed in this single image highlight a deeper truth: engaging with AI tools requires more than technical proficiency. It demands a critical literacy mindset. As AI becomes more embedded in students' learning experiences, we must expand our understanding of digital literacy to account for how algorithms generate, shape, and present knowledge.

Table 1.7 illustrates how existing digital literacy skills are being extended and reimagined to prepare students for thoughtful, critical engagement with AI-generated content. When these changes are regularly integrated into instruction, students improve upon the skills necessary to critically engage with AI tools by questioning AI-generated outputs and utilizing AI for deeper learning.

TABLE 1.6. Investigating AI Bias through Image Generation

Step	Action	Purpose
1	Choose a GenAI image tool (e.g., Gemini, DALL·E, Bing Image Creator).	Familiarize yourself with a tool students may encounter or use in the classroom.
2	Use this customizable prompt: "Create an image of a [type of] conference with a room full of [type of people] listening to a speaker."	
3	Examine the generated image carefully.	Look for patterns in gender, race, attire, setting, and roles (e.g., who is speaking vs. who is listening).
4	Reflect on the following questions: • Who is represented? • Who is missing? • What assumptions might the AI have made? • How could you revise the prompt to encourage more inclusive outputs?	Begin developing a critical lens toward how GenAI constructs meaning—and how it can subtly reinforce social norms and biases.

FIGURE 1.1. Farm conference image generated by Gemini.

TABLE 1.7. Traditional versus AI-Digital Literacy Skills

Literacy skill	Traditional digital literacy skills	AI digital literacy skills
Problem solving	• Navigating search engines effectively • Identifying relevant online sources • Applying technology tools to solve content-related problems	• Prompt engineering (iterative refinement of AI responses) • Evaluating AI-generated solutions for accuracy and logic • Debugging AI-generated errors or inconsistencies
Critical thinking	• Assessing credibility of online sources • Recognizing bias and misinformation • Ethical considerations in digital spaces (digital citizenship, plagiarism)	• Detecting hallucinations in AI-generated content • Identifying bias embedded in AI models • Applying AI ethics in decision making (academic integrity, responsible use)
Reading texts	• Summarizing digital texts • Evaluating multimodal content (text, images, videos) • Recognizing an author's perspective and intent	• Analyzing AI-generated summaries for completeness and accuracy • Interpreting AI-generated multimodal content critically • Refining AI-generated explanations to align with disciplinary knowledge
Writing texts	• Organizing ideas through digital composition • Revising and editing using digital tools • Citing and integrating online sources appropriately	• Using AI tools for iterative revision and feedback • Developing AI-assisted outlines while maintaining originality • Fact-checking AI-generated research before incorporating it into writing

Cognitive Flexibility in an AI-Driven Learning Environment

Like the "ill-structured" digital environments of the internet (Coiro & Dobler, 2007, p. 246), GenAI tools do not operate within a fixed, linear system. Instead, they create a dynamic, interactive space where meaning must be assembled, negotiated, and critically applied. AI-generated responses are unpredictable and highly context dependent, varying based on how a question is framed, the specificity of the prompt, and the iterations made during refinement. GenAI content is shaped by algorithms rather than absolute truth—therefore, users must recognize when outputs plagiarize a source, reinforce stereotypes, or oversimplify complex information. More importantly, they must develop cognitive flexibility—"the ability to hold multiple elements of a task in mind and actively switch between them" (Cartwright, 2023, p. xv)—to adjust their approach accordingly. Without this adaptive thinking, students risk passively accepting AI-generated content without questioning its validity or ethical implications.

Developing cognitive flexibility is particularly critical in middle and high school classrooms, where students are expected to engage in higher-order thinking skills, such as analysis, evaluation, and synthesis. At the secondary level, disciplinary literacy demands more than basic comprehension. It requires students to engage in subject-specific reasoning that acknowledges multiple perspectives, conflicting interpretations, and evolving knowledge within each field.

For example, imagine a high school history student using GenAI to research the causes of the French Revolution. The AI-generated response may provide an overview of key events yet omit marginalized voices, oversimplify socioeconomic complexities, or reflect biases in its training data. A student lacking cognitive flexibility might accept this response uncritically, assuming history as a fixed set of facts rather than a discipline that requires analysis and interpretation. An AI-literate student, however, would recognize the limitations of the AI-generated content and challenge the reliability of its claims, seek additional sources, and critically evaluate how the AI constructed its historical narrative. Rather than refining their query, they would question the underlying assumptions embedded in the AI's response and consider how historical argumentation, evidence, and multiple viewpoints shape understanding.

This same need for adaptive reasoning extends to other disciplines. A science student using GenAI to generate a hypothesis for a lab experiment should assess whether the technology's reasoning aligns with scientific principles. Since GenAI cannot conduct experiments or troubleshoot methodological errors, students must apply their own disciplinary knowledge to determine the validity of AI-generated hypotheses. Similarly, in mathematics, AI-generated solutions may appear correct at first glance. Yet, students must justify their answers, verify steps, and ensure AI's reasoning aligns with mathematical methods rather than blindly accepting computational outputs.

Cognitive flexibility is especially important when students engage with AI-generated multimodal texts across disciplines. In today's classrooms, students increasingly consume AI-generated presentations, infographics, and interactive media. To critically engage with these texts, students must determine how different modes of communication (e.g., text, audio, visuals, animations) contribute to meaning. For instance, when analyzing an AI-generated environmental science video, they must ask:

- Does the spoken narration provide the most critical insights, or does the on-screen text emphasize key ideas?
- Do the images and animations influence how the event is perceived?
- How do the modes work together and present a balanced or biased view?

Without cognitive flexibility, students may over-rely on a single mode, misinterpreting key ideas or overlooking how different forms of communication interact to shape understanding (Karchmer-Klein & Shinas, 2019; Kress, 1998). Just as students must evaluate written sources for credibility, they must learn to decode, compare, and critique AI-generated multimodal compositions. This skill is essential as AI-generated media becomes increasingly prevalent in education, journalism, and other professional fields.

Classroom Application: GenAI Digital Literacy and Cognitive Flexibility

Effectively integrating GenAI into learning requires students to develop AI digital literacy and cognitive flexibility, skills that enable them to engage with AI-generated content rather than passively accept it critically. Digital literacy skills help students assess sources, interpret multimodal texts, and apply disciplinary reasoning. At the same time, cognitive flexibility ensures they can challenge, adjust, and rethink AI outputs when faced with inaccuracies, biases, or missing perspectives. Tables 1.8 and 1.9 illustrate lessons that emphasize cognitive flexibility in multimodal learning, increasing students' awareness of how meaning is constructed across various modes (e.g., text, images, audio). These activities do not require AI skills. Instead, their purpose is to home in on cognitive flexibility—in other words, the ability to adapt to digital environments. These lessons lay the foundation for more complex AI integration in later chapters by reinforcing essential literacy practices that prepare students to analyze and question more sophisticated AI-generated content.

TABLE 1.8. Lesson Idea for Building Cognitive Flexibility in English Language Arts

	Middle school English language arts: Evaluating AI-generated stories
Learning objective	Practice cognitive flexibility by determining which mode holds the most meaning of the story.
Activity 1	Students use Canva's AI Video Generator to create a book trailer for a novel they have read. The AI-generated trailer includes text overlays, images, music, and audio narration.
Activity 2	A classmate watches the AI-generated trailer and responds to the following questions: • Does the narration carry the most critical information, or do the text and visuals do more of the storytelling? • If the text were removed, would the visuals and audio still convey the story's tone and theme? • Are the different modes working together, or is one mode doing most of the work?
How this builds cognitive flexibility	• Builds awareness that digital texts are composed of multiple modes. • Builds awareness of the need for flexibility when interpreting and integrating meaning across different modes of communication.

TABLE 1.9. Lesson Idea for Building Cognitive Flexibility Using Documentaries

High school history: Analyzing authenticity and trust in *The Frozen Planet*	
Learning objective	Practice cognitive flexibility by analyzing how different modes contribute to meaning in a documentary Assess how editing choices can shape viewers' understanding
Activity 1	Students watch the scene from *The Frozen Planet* documentary depicting the birth of polar bear cubs, which was later revealed to have been filmed in a zoo rather than in the wild.
Activity 2	In pairs, students discuss the following questions: • How does David Attenborough's narration contribute to the sense of realism? • What role do the visuals play in shaping the audience's perception of the event? • Does the film's use of real and staged footage change how the event is understood? • How might a viewer's trust in the documentary be affected upon learning the truth about the scene's production?
How this builds cognitive flexibility	Encourages students to: • Analyze how multimodal elements interact to construct meaning • Recognize the role of editing in shaping perception • Question how trust is built (or broken) in documentary filmmaking

Conclusion

At their core, literacy skills—problem solving, critical thinking, reading, and writing—have long been essential for student learning across disciplines. These interwoven skills empower learners to ask meaningful questions, analyze information, construct arguments, and communicate clearly. This chapter has outlined that they are not simply academic competencies but the foundation for deep, transferable learning.

The rise of the internet introduced nonlinear, multimodal, and often ambiguous information environments. Students had to develop digital literacy skills to navigate online texts, evaluate credibility, synthesize sources, and compose across formats. This transformation also demanded cognitive flexibility: the ability to adapt their thinking to make sense of complex, ever-changing digital content.

Today, the emergence of GenAI represents the next major expansion in this progression. Students are no longer just evaluating static digital content. They engage with dynamically generated responses, co-creating content through prompts and interacting with tools that simulate human reasoning. These developments do not replace traditional literacy skills—rather, they extend and recontextualize them. Students must now apply their problem-solving, critical thinking, reading, and writing skills in interactive, algorithm-driven environments where knowledge is constructed in real time. And, cognitive flexibility remains essential in this AI-infused world. Students must learn to interrogate how AI content is created, identify embedded assumptions, and refine their thinking through iteration and critical reflection. This is what it means to be literate in the age of GenAI: to collaborate with AI tools thoughtfully, using them to deepen understanding rather than shortcut learning.

The following chapters build upon this foundation, exploring the intersection of GenAI literacy with disciplinary literacy practices. Through practical strategies and ready-to-use classroom examples, we examine how educators can guide students to become critical thinkers who are capable of problem solving and proficient in reading and writing using GenAI.

Teacher Reflection Questions

Use the questions below to reflect on your current approach to digital literacy instruction and consider how GenAI might reshape how students read, write, think critically, and solve problems in your classroom.

1. How do I currently teach problem solving, critical thinking, and reading and writing complex texts in my classroom? How are these skills integrated into my everyday instruction?
2. How might digital tools, including online platforms and AI-powered resources, influence students' ability to apply these literacy skills effectively? What benefits or challenges have I observed?
3. How do digital tools enhance or complicate my literacy instruction? What strategies can I use to ensure they support rather than distract from learning?
4. How comfortable am I with teaching digital literacies in my current context? What professional learning or support would help me grow in this area?

ETHICAL DILEMMA AND DISCUSSION PROMPTS

Ethical Dilemma: Choice or Confusion?

You have spent the semester teaching your high school students how to use GenAI tools to support their learning. For a culminating project, you offer them the option to use AI to help plan, research, and present their final argument on a controversial topic of their choice. Some students embrace the freedom, while others feel overwhelmed by the sheer number of AI tools and the constant decisions they must make.

- Which tool is best for research?
- Should they start with AI or draft their ideas first?
- How much should they edit AI responses before using them?

One student tells you, "There are too many choices. I don't even know where to start." Another says, "I just asked AI for everything. It was easier than figuring out what I wanted to say." You notice that some students thrive with the flexibility, while others seem stuck in analysis paralysis or, worse, defaulting to full AI dependence. You're torn. You want to give students agency, but you're beginning to wonder whether the freedom to choose tools, formats, and processes hinders learning for some students who lack the cognitive flexibility to manage complex tasks.

Discussion Prompts

1. How do we balance student autonomy with appropriate structure in AI-enhanced learning environments?
2. When does choice empower students and when does it overwhelm them?
3. How do we support the development of cognitive flexibility without asking students to juggle too many moving parts too soon?

Chapter 2

Addressing the Fears of GenAI in Literacy Instruction

My teenage son returned home from school recently and told me he was accused of cheating on his German midterm. The teacher suspected him of using ChatGPT on the essay portion of the exam. He told me he did not use GenAI, and I believed him, but I needed to hear more to understand the context of this very out-of-character accusation. It seems his teacher "knew" he had used the AI tool. I asked what evidence she had given him, and he said it was because he used the word *block* instead of the word *street* in his essay. She found the word choice unusual, which confirmed to her that he used AI on his test. Of course, I was ready to fight this battle, but I took a breath and reminded myself that high school is when you put down your armor and let your children fight for themselves.

Ryan spoke to his teacher and explained that he had spent considerable time in New York City, which led him to use the word *block* interchangeably with *street*. He was unclear about the issue with his word choice. However, his explanation was to no avail; the teacher remained adamant that he had cheated. Subsequently, he visited his guidance counselor, who clarified that while the school has an acceptable use policy that vaguely addresses AI usage, its application ultimately depends on the teacher's discretion. As a result, my son, who was in his third year of earning straight A's in German, received a C on his midterm due to a significant point deduction in this unfair situation.

GenAI has sparked significant debate in education, with teachers, parents, and students expressing concerns about its effects on student learning. Many of these concerns are valid. However, as my son's experience shows, we find ourselves in an AI "wild wild west" where some teachers adhere to school policies while others make snap decisions based on intuition rather than evidence. Some educators strive to integrate AI thoughtfully, while others hastily assume its misuse, occasionally lacking a clear understanding of how AI functions or tangible proof. This inconsistency traps students in a system where expectations vary greatly from one classroom to another.

Schools wrestle daily with what responsible AI use should look like, leaving many teachers to interpret AI policy independently. Some worry that students might use AI to write essays, respond to exam questions, and mimic writing styles, raising doubts about the authenticity of student work. Others fear that students will become overly reliant on AI tools, undermining their ability to think critically, write independently, and solve problems on their own. The potential for AI-generated misinformation and bias introduces additional complexity, as does the question of how AI could affect traditional reading and writing skills.

GenAI is here to stay. Therefore, the real challenge is not whether students should use it but how we can ensure they utilize it ethically, effectively, and as a means for deeper learning rather than as a shortcut. If we let fear drive the conversation, we risk making reactionary decisions that could hurt students more than AI itself.

Lessons from the Past: How Schools Adapted to New Technologies

The apprehension surrounding AI in education is not unprecedented. Throughout history, technological advancements have been met with initial skepticism, only to become integral to learning once educators familiarize themselves with instructional practices. The introduction of calculators, the rise of Google searches, and the turn from physical to digital textbooks were all met with similar resistance. Examining past innovations reveals how schools have navigated the tension between technological disruption and educational enhancement.

When calculators became widely available, many educators worried they would reduce students' basic math skills. This did not happen. For instance, Kastberg and Leatham (2005) found that fears regarding graphing calculator use were largely unfounded when these digital tools were effectively integrated into middle and high school math instruction. Success depended on three critical factors: student access, alignment with curriculum goals, and teacher pedagogy. Situations where calculators were thoughtfully incorporated into instructional design reflected achievement gains as students progressed beyond rote computation to deeper problem-solving and mathematical reasoning. The findings of this review also highlighted the importance of teacher training, as educators who were well prepared to integrate graphing calculators could utilize them as tools for conceptual understanding rather than automation.

A similar cycle occurred with Wikipedia. In its early years, teachers discouraged or outright banned students from using the online encyclopedia, fearing that its user-generated nature would spread misinformation. Educators were concerned that students might accept Wikipedia entries at face value without verifying their sources. Although this concern is valid, educators have become more lenient, recognizing that with purposeful instruction, students can edit and contribute to Wikipedia articles in ways that help them develop critical and academic writing skills (Konieczny, 2016). When they participate in creating and refining content, they gain a deeper understanding of the subject matter and learn to evaluate information sources critically. Moreover, instructing students how to use Wikipedia as an initial source and then cross-check findings to validate further may be the most effective use of the site as it is the first stop for many academics (*The Economist*, 2021).

Online translation tools, like Google Translate and Deepl, are a third type of digital tool that has encountered resistance when introduced to classrooms. Teachers have feared students might use these tools to avoid the cognitive effort required for language acquisition, relying instead on automated translations rather than developing language proficiency (Nguyen et al., 2025). However, over time, educators discovered ways to incorporate AI translation tools to enhance learning rather than replace it. Many now utilize these tools to help students compare grammatical structures across languages, improve their writing through iterative translation, and engage in real-world communication with native speakers.

Adapting to Change: Lessons from Other Professions

Resistance to new technology is not unique to education. Yet, while other fields embrace innovation to enhance expertise, education often frames new tools as a gateway to cheating.

Consider professional chefs. In the past, skilled chefs forged their own knives from raw steel, shaping and sharpening them by hand. Today, chefs buy high-quality blades crafted with advanced technology. Is this cheating? No, it is leveraging innovation to improve their craft. The skill isn't in making the knife. It is in how they use it to create something exceptional.

Similarly, architects once spent hours drafting blueprints by hand, carefully measuring and sketching every detail. Now, they use computer-aided design software to create precise, scalable models. Is this cheating? No. The value of their work isn't in manually drawing each line. It is in their ability to design structurally sound, innovative buildings.

Even in medicine, where precision is critical, doctors rely on AI-assisted diagnostic tools, magnetic resonance imaging (MRI), and computed tomography (CT) scans to identify illnesses more accurately and efficiently. Is this cheating? No. These tools do not replace doctors' expertise. They enhance their ability to make informed medical decisions.

Why, then, in education, are new technologies frequently met with suspicion? If a student uses AI to organize their ideas, refine their writing, or analyze information, is that cheating? Or is it simply using a tool to enhance learning, just as professionals do in their fields? Instead of viewing AI as a shortcut, educators should recognize it as an opportunity to develop critical thinking, creativity, and deeper engagement with content.

Just as calculators did not replace mathematical thinking but rather changed the focus of instruction, GenAI can enhance learning when used intentionally. The key takeaway is that technological tools must be integrated strategically, with clear instructional goals and teacher support, rather than feared or banned outright.

Moving Beyond the Fear: Addressing Common Concerns about GenAI in Literacy Instruction

In preparing for this book, I surveyed teachers to understand their most pressing concerns about AI in literacy instruction. Four key fears emerged. Rather than allowing these concerns to lead to reactionary policies or outright bans, we should focus on thoughtful AI integration that enhances, rather than replaces, student learning.

In the following sections, I outline the four most common fears teachers shared, explain why these concerns resonate, and offer practical strategies for addressing them. Whether teachers are new to AI or experienced users, these strategies provide concrete ways to help students use AI as a tool for deeper thinking rather than a shortcut.

At the end of each fear discussion, you will find a table titled "If You Fear *This* . . . , Try These Shifts," which presents specific mindset shifts and actionable strategies for moving beyond the fear. These tables are designed to help teachers reframe fears into opportunities, providing practical alternatives that encourage responsible AI use in literacy instruction. Following each table, at least one actionable strategy demonstrates an approach for engaging students in a strategy that directly counteracts the fear. These strategies serve as a starting point for integrating AI in ways that support student learning while maintaining academic integrity. For more detailed, discipline-specific GenAI-integrated lesson ideas, see Chapters 4–6 in Part II of this text.

Fear 1: GenAI Will Eliminate Original Student Writing

> If my students can type a question into AI and get a full essay back in seconds, how do I know if they're actually learning to write for themselves?
>
> —Seventh-grade English teacher

One of the primary concerns among the educators I surveyed is that GenAI will undermine student originality by making it too easy to generate polished, well-structured writing with minimal effort. If students can produce entire essays with a simple prompt, does this mean they will stop developing their own ideas, voice, and writing skills?

The fear is that writing will become passive, with students relying on GenAI to think instead of engaging in the creative and intellectual work themselves. This concern assumes AI is replacing writing rather than reshaping the writing process. Instead of viewing AI as a threat to student writing, we should recognize its potential as a writing development tool that can help students refine their thinking, strengthen arguments, and improve revision skills.

The key is intentionality: Teachers must design purposeful writing tasks where AI enhances learning rather than replaces cognitive effort. The real fear isn't that students will rely on AI. It's that their creativity and voice will disappear, replaced by AI-generated phrases and prestructured responses. If students see writing as simply copying and pasting from AI, they risk losing their sense of ownership over their words. Instructional design must shift to ensure that AI is a writing partner, not a replacement for original thought (see Table 2.1 for a subset of fears and mindset shifts).

GenAI can act as a thinking tool by helping students refine ideas, generate alternatives, and engage in deeper revision. These can all be done without taking away the cognitive effort that makes writing meaningful. Much like a peer reviewer or a writing coach, AI should be integrated in ways that support creativity rather than automate it.

TABLE 2.1. If You Fear *This* . . . , Try These Shifts

Fear 1: GenAI will eliminate original student writing.	Mindset shift
Students will let GenAI do all the writing for them.	Require students to include statements with their completed work describing how and to what extent AI was used to complete the assignment.
Students will not think critically about AI-generated writing.	Require students to compare GenAI versus human writing; rewrite AI responses in their own voice; and reflect on similarities, differences, and incorrect information.
Students will rely on GenAI to revise rather than improve their own work.	Teach students how to leverage GenAI tools as a revision partner, challenging students to interact with them to refine arguments and strengthen clarity.
AI-generated writing lacks personal voice and creativity.	Use AI to explore tone, style, and structure, and then challenge students to rewrite text with more personality and depth.
AI-generated feedback is too generic.	Teach students to evaluate GenAI feedback critically, deciding what to accept or reject.

TABLE 2.2. Fear 1: Actionable Strategies

AI versus human writing analysis

Objective: Before students start using AI, they need to understand the difference between AI-generated and human-written text. This activity teaches students how to identify what makes writing personal, original, and engaging.

Steps:

1. Provide students with two versions of a response to the same prompt—one written by a student and one generated by AI.
2. Students read both texts and analyze what makes the human writing unique (voice, creativity, depth of analysis, sentence variation, personal connection).
3. Students discuss the question *Does the AI-generated response sound generic or overly polished? Is it missing something?*
4. Students rewrite the AI version in their own voice, adding personal perspective and critical thinking.

AI as a revision partner

Objective: Many students struggle with self-editing because they do not know how to revise beyond fixing grammar. GenAI can act as a revision partner, someone to provide feedback like a peer or teacher, to help students strengthen organization, clarity, and argumentation rather than just correcting small mistakes.

Steps:

1. Students write an essay draft without AI.
2. Students input their draft into an AI tool and ask it specific questions, such as:
   - *How can I make my argument clearer?*
   - *Which sentences are too vague?*
   - *Are my paragraphs logically organized?*
3. AI will provide feedback, but instead of blindly accepting suggestions, students must analyze and decide which feedback to use.
4. Students will write a short reflection explaining which AI feedback they accepted or rejected and why.

Teachers can encourage this by requiring students to engage with multiple drafts before using GenAI, having students reflect on how GenAI suggestions influenced their writing, and asking students to compare GenAI feedback with human feedback to build revision literacy (see Table 2.2 for actionable strategies).

Fear 2: AI-Generated Content Will Lead to Misinformation

> AI just predicts words. It doesn't really know things. How do I make sure my students aren't believing everything AI generates?
>
> —Ninth-grade social studies teacher

One of the most pressing concerns in education is that students might accept AI-generated content as fact without recognizing its potential for errors, bias, or outright fabrications, known as AI hallucinations. And this is absolutely a concern. The most likely reason for this is that most people do not fully understand how large language models (LLMs) work. GenAI, such as ChatGPT, is powered by LLMs, which are trained on vast amounts of text data from books, articles, websites, and other sources. GenAI does not "know" things as humans do. It does not retrieve facts from a database or verify sources for accuracy. Instead, it relies on complex algorithms and probability-based models to predict the next most likely word or phrase based on the patterns it has learned from training data. It is not thinking or verifying facts. It simply assembles words based on patterns (Akgun & Greenhow, 2022). This is why it sometimes creates seemingly convincing but incorrect information, giving the illusion of credibility without actual verification.

Educators should understand how GenAI works so they can confidently explain this to students and prepare them to navigate and assess AI-generated content. If not, they can easily be overwhelmed by the sheer power of the technology. They may struggle to guide students in fact-checking GenAI content, determining when and how GenAI can be used responsibly in the classroom, or at risk of misinformation when using GenAI for lesson planning or research.

Teachers can build confidence and professional expertise by exploring how AI works, experimenting with tools, and practicing fact-checking AI-generated content (see Table 2.3 for a subset of fears and mindset shifts).

This autonomy will allow teachers to decide how much or how little GenAI belongs in their classrooms rather than feeling pressured by outside forces. The challenge is not preventing misinformation but teaching the skills to identify and counteract them (see Table 2.4 for actionable strategies).

TABLE 2.3. If You Fear *This* . . . , Try These Shifts

Fear 2: AI-generated content will lead to misinformation.	Mindset shift
AI will generate misinformation and "hallucinate" facts.	Explain how GenAI retrieves its information. Teach students to fact-check AI content using reliable sources and revise inaccuracies.
AI-generated content will reflect bias.	Have students analyze AI responses for missing perspectives and rewrite them to provide a more balanced view.
Students will accept AI content at face value.	Use AI to generate questionable claims and then require students to prove or disprove them using evidence.
AI cannot be used for research because it makes up sources.	Teach students to verify AI-generated citations and replace fabricated ones with real, reputable sources.

TABLE 2.4. Fear 2: Actionable Strategies

AI fact-checking challenges

Objective: Many students assume that if AI provides an answer, it must be correct. This activity teaches them to question and verify AI-generated content using multiple sources.

Steps:

- Provide students with an AI-generated paragraph on a topic relevant to your subject
- Students highlight statements that require verification (facts, statistics, claims).
- Require students to cross-check AI-generated claims with at least three reputable sources (e.g., academic journals, government websites, trusted news sources).
- Students revise the AI-generated response, correcting any inaccuracies or misleading information they found.
- Discuss the process: *Where was AI wrong? Why? How do we determine which sources are credible?*

Reverse engineering research with AI

Objective: Many students assume AI "knows" everything. This strategy forces them to test AI's credibility by fact checking its citations and sources.

Steps:

- Students ask AI a research question and request citations or sources for its answer.
- Instruct students to investigate:
  - *Do these sources actually exist?*
  - *Are they from credible publishers?*
  - *Are they properly cited, or did AI fabricate them?*
- If AI provides fake sources, ask:
  - *Why might AI have created them?*
  - *What real sources could we use instead?*
- Students rewrite the AI-generated response, replacing fabricated sources with real, verifiable ones.

Fear 3: Students Will Become Dependent on AI

I know students will use AI to write their assignments, but I'm more worried that kids will stop trusting their own ideas. If they think AI always has a better answer, I'm afraid they will stop thinking critically and making decisions on their own.

—12TH-GRADE BUSINESS TEACHER

A fundamental part of education is helping students develop confidence in their ability to think critically, read, write, and problem solve. Whether composing an essay, brainstorming a business plan, or tackling a real-world issue, students need to trust themselves and not just look for the "right" answer from an external source.

A top concern with GenAI is that it flattens the struggle of learning. If students can generate a well-structured response in seconds, will they still engage in the messy, nonlinear process of thinking through ideas? If AI always provides an instant solution, will students stop wrestling with complex problems and lose the

TABLE 2.5. If You Fear *This* . . . , Try These Shifts

Fear 3: Students will become dependent on AI.	Mindset shift
Students will use AI instead of thinking for themselves.	Implement decision-making exercises where students evaluate and critique AI-generated answers.
AI makes assignments too easy.	Design AI-resistant tasks that require deep thinking, explanation, and personal insights.
Students will default to AI without reflection.	Require "GenAI Use Journals" where students document and analyze how AI influenced their work.
AI will replace students' need to problem solve.	Have students debate AI, identifying flaws in its reasoning and arguing against it.

ability to navigate uncertainty? (See Table 2.5 for a subset of fears and mindset shifts.)

This issue extends beyond academics. Students will encounter complex college, career, and life situations where GenAI will not provide clear-cut answers. They will need to think critically, make independent decisions, defend their reasoning, and adapt to new challenges. If students become overly reliant on GenAI in middle and high school, they risk losing confidence in their own thinking, avoiding intellectual risks, and missing opportunities to develop essential problem-solving skills. Instead of strengthening their ability to analyze deeply and trust their own voice, they may defer to AI-generated responses, leaving them unprepared for real-world decision making.

This does not mean we should sidestep GenAI. Instead, the solution is to integrate it in ways that push students toward deeper engagement, not passive shortcuts. When used with intention, GenAI can scaffold students' ability to create ideas, evaluate arguments, and strengthen their writing while ensuring that the cognitive effort still belongs to them. We can do this by teaching students to trust their decision making alongside using the technology (see Table 2.6 for actionable strategies).

Fear 4: AI Will Widen Educational Inequities

> We already have students with different levels of access to technology. If AI becomes a normal part of learning, how do we ensure that students in underfunded schools don't fall further behind?
>
> —Eighth-grade science teacher

GenAI will exacerbate educational inequities unless we take deliberate steps to counteract it. While much of the discourse around GenAI and equity centers on

TABLE 2.6. Fear 3: Actionable Strategies

The "blind draft" method: Write first, AI second
Objective: To build writing confidence, students should first write independently before using AI for refinement. This reinforces the idea that their ideas are valid before AI enters the process. *Steps:* 1. Students write an essay, response, or argument without AI assistance. 2. Once they have a draft, they use AI to generate an alternative version or suggestions for improvement. 3. Students compare their draft to AI's response and decide: • *What was stronger in their own writing?* • *What did AI do well, and what was lacking?* • *Which version do they prefer, and why?* 4. Students justify what they kept, rejected, or revised based on AI's suggestions.
The "AI debate" model: Make AI a sparring partner
Objective: If students assume AI knows best, they will not challenge it. This strategy teaches them to argue with AI and prove its answers wrong—reinforcing confidence in their own critical thinking. *Steps:* 1. Assign students a controversial or debatable topic. 2. Students ask AI for a position or argument on the topic. 3. Students argue against AI by: • Identifying flaws or gaps in AI's reasoning. • Providing evidence AI overlooked. • Strengthening their counterargument with examples AI didn't include.

access to devices and internet connectivity, the issue runs much deeper than who possesses the technology. GenAI has the potential to amplify existing disparities in education, influencing not only how students are taught and assessed but also who controls their data, how their personal information is used, and how algorithmic biases shape the content and opportunities they receive.

Inconsistency and ambiguity of school policies around GenAI use are some of the most immediate concerns. Right now, AI policies are all over the place. Some schools ban it outright, and others embrace it without much structure, and many educators are left to make individual decisions without clear guidance. This inconsistency creates an unfair and confusing landscape for students. GenAI can be a powerful learning tool in one classroom, helping students brainstorm, refine ideas, and strengthen their writing. In another, students may be punished for simply experimenting with the tools, even if no clear rules were broken. Without a unified approach, students in the same schools but different classrooms receive vastly different messages about what GenAI is and how they should engage with it.

Beyond policy confusion, GenAI can also reinforce systemic biases in the content it generates. Many GenAI models are trained on data sets that overrepresent dominant cultures and underrepresent marginalized communities. This results in AI-generated content reflecting and perpetuating existing biases in historical narratives, language use, or the examples it provides. If AI tools are used to assist with writing, research, or even grading, how can we ensure that students are not exposed to biased, incomplete, or even harmful information? The risk is particularly high for students in underfunded schools, where AI tools may be relied on without adequate training in AI literacy and critical evaluation skills.

Perhaps the most concerning issues are data privacy and student surveillance. Many free AI tools collect and store vast amounts of student data, and schools with limited resources may rely on these tools without fully understanding how student information is being used. Who controls these data? How are they being utilized? Could student information be sold, tracked, or even used to predict future academic performance in ways that reinforce inequities? If more affluent schools can afford safer, more private AI tools while underfunded schools are compelled to use data-harvesting AI platforms, the risks extend beyond technological access. They concern student rights and long-term privacy (see Table 2.7 for a subset of fears and mindset shifts).

Instead of questioning whether AI will exacerbate inequities, we must recognize that they already exist. The real challenge is ensuring that all students, regardless of their background, have equitable opportunities to learn with and about AI, while being protected from algorithmic bias, privacy risks, and harmful disparities in implementation (see Table 2.8 for actionable strategies).

TABLE 2.7. You Fear *This* . . . , Try These Shifts

Fear 4: AI will widen educational inequities.	Mindset shift
AI will create a wider technology gap between schools.	Use low-tech AI strategies like printed AI examples and teacher-led demonstrations.
Some students will have more AI access than others.	Implement peer mentoring programs where tech-savvy students support those with less AI experience.
AI could replace human differentiation.	Use AI to support struggling learners (e.g., generate reading accommodations, language translation, or scaffolded writing).
Only well-funded schools will benefit from AI tools.	Advocate for AI literacy training, funding, and schoolwide guidelines to ensure equitable access.

TABLE 2.8. Fear 4: Actionable Strategy

Using AI to bridge educational gaps
Objective: Students will explore how AI can support diverse learners, provide access to resources, and promote inclusive learning experiences. *Steps:* 1. Framing the issue (class discussion and reflection) • Begin with a class discussion: *What does educational equity mean? Where do students see gaps in access to learning resources?* • Introduce AI's role in accessibility (e.g., text-to-speech for students with reading disabilities, real-time translation for multilingual learners). 2. AI in action—accessibility and personalized learning • Divide students into small groups, assigning each a specific equity challenge (e.g., language barriers, reading difficulties, lack of tutoring support). • Each group explores how AI tools could help address that challenge (e.g., using Microsoft Immersive Reader to make texts more accessible). • Students test an AI tool and document how it improves access for a specific learning need. 3. Presenting AI as a solution • Each group presents their findings, explaining: • The challenge they explored • How an AI tool addressed the issue • Any limitations or ethical considerations they noticed 4. The class discusses how AI can be used equitably and what teachers/schools can do to ensure AI helps all students, not just those with access to expensive tools.

Try It Out Reimagining the Task of Instruction

As this chapter has explored, many educators share four common fears about GenAI: that it will strip away student creativity and voice, lead to overdependence, spread misinformation, and widen educational inequities. These concerns are valid, but they are also invitations to reimagine instruction. If an assignment can be completed entirely by GenAI, it may not be pushing students to think, synthesize, or express themselves in meaningful ways. The goal is not to ban GenAI but to design tasks that make student thinking essential and AI a helpful tool, not a replacement. Let's try an activity that pushes you to reimagine your current instruction. Follow the steps below:

1. *Choose a task that you fear AI would undermine.* Select an assignment you have or are considering implementing in your teaching that feels especially vulnerable to GenAI as you think about your students. For example:
   - Summarize the plot of a novel.
   - Explain the steps of the water cycle.
   - Write a five-paragraph essay on a current event.
2. *Test it in GenAI.* Run your original prompt through a GenAI tool like ChatGPT. Review the responses:

- Would a student be tempted to submit this as is?
- Is it formulaic or surface level?
- What aspects of thinking or creativity are missing?

3. *Reimagine the task.* Redesign your assignment to invite student perspective, interpretation, or originality. Here are some creative twists across disciplines:
   - English Language Arts
     - Rewrite a scene from the antagonist's point of view.
     - Create a dialogue between two authors whose works you've read this year. How would they debate a modern issue?
     - Generate an AI summary of a poem, then critique what it misses about tone, symbolism, or emotion.
   - Science
     - Create a comic strip explaining the water cycle from the perspective of a water droplet.
     - Design a science myth-busting blog post that corrects a common misconception using evidence.
     - Ask AI to describe photosynthesis, then revise its explanation to make it more accurate and engaging for fifth graders.
   - History
     - Write a journal entry from the perspective of a historical figure not usually centered in textbook narratives.
     - Compare AI's explanation of a historical event to two primary sources. What does it get right or wrong?
     - Create a timeline infographic including significant events and your commentary on their impact.
   - Math
     - Solve a problem, then write a letter to a peer explaining your process and where mistakes could happen.
     - Ask AI to explain a math concept, then revise it to be clearer or add analogies a middle schooler could understand.
     - Invent a math problem based on your favorite hobby (e.g., basketball stats, baking, travel budgeting).
   - Other
     - Use AI to generate a script for a podcast intro, then rewrite it to reflect your actual voice and viewpoint.
     - Design a visual or multimedia piece (poster, comic, animation) that teaches your peers a key concept—then explain why you chose that format.
4. *Reflect.* Ask yourself: "How does this redesigned task support student thinking, voice, and purpose?"

Why It Matters

Our goal in school is to nurture independent thinking. When assignments are too generic or narrowly focused, GenAI can take over the process and produce polished responses that bypass the intellectual work we want students to do. However, when tasks are thoughtfully designed to demand interpretation, originality, and perspective, student thinking becomes central—and GenAI becomes a support, not a substitute.

By testing and redesigning one of your own assignments, you turned the lens on your instruction. You took a meaningful step toward safeguarding the core goals of literacy education: critical thought, meaningful expression, and student ownership of learning. In a GenAI-infused classroom, this intentional design ensures that real thinking remains the priority.

Addressing Fears: Moving from Uncertainty to Action

Reimagining instruction is essential for integrating GenAI into classrooms, but schools must also implement broader measures to address educators' concerns. Many worries regarding AI arise from uncertainty about its ethical implications, proper use, and potential effects on student learning. Most concerns are legitimate, yet they should not result in inaction or hasty bans. Schools and educators should take intentional, structured steps to foster trust, transparency, and confidence in AI as a learning tool.

When clear policies, structured training, and a culture of responsible GenAI use are implemented, they can help educators move past fear and toward empowerment. The following strategies illustrate how stakeholders can work together to ensure GenAI is used ethically and effectively.

Acceptable Use Policies and Ethics Courses

As schools begin integrating AI into classrooms, establishing clear and consistent policies is one of the most critical steps. The San Gabriel Unified School District (2024) is one example of a school system proactively using AI. Its Responsible Use Guidelines for Generative AI Tools document emphasizes the importance of ethical and creative engagement with AI, setting expectations for both students and educators to combat inconsistency in expectations among students, teachers, and administrators.

Inconsistency was exactly what Melanie Frey, a high school composition and world literature teacher at the Tome School in Maryland, encountered firsthand:

> As generative AI has become more widespread, integrating it into our teaching has proven challenging. High school students need guardrails to help them understand

> what is acceptable in a classroom setting. AI should be a way to begin the learning process, but never an endpoint. However, understanding where that line is requires explicit teaching, and that responsibility falls on us as educators. (M. Frey, personal communication, March 13, 2025)

Explicitly teaching students that line has been a long process in Frey's school, mostly due to the lack of consistency among teachers' interpretation and implementation of policies. She explains,

> . . . every teacher's acceptable usage line for generative AI is different. Some teachers prohibit AI entirely, while others allow it for brainstorming but not for writing assignments. Our school values consistency in rules and curriculum, so we've struggled as a faculty to create clear guidelines for students. (M. Frey, personal communication, March 13, 2025)

To address these challenges, Frey's school formed a faculty committee to develop an AI Ethics and Literacy course covering consistent messages about AI's capabilities, limitations, and responsible uses. Her school's approach is unique because before AI is integrated into any classroom, all students and faculty must first complete this course. This ensures that everyone, from teachers to students, understands AI's role, potential, and limitations. Once every student and faculty member has completed the training, teachers can then decide how to incorporate GenAI into their instruction. By prioritizing AI literacy before full implementation, the school establishes a strong ethical foundation that allows for more thoughtful and consistent AI use.

By implementing structured policies like those at San Gabriel Unified or developing AI education initiatives like Frey's school, schools can move beyond uncertainty and fear and toward intentional, informed AI integration. AI policies should not be punitive but educational, ensuring that both teachers and students understand how to use AI tools responsibly while maintaining academic integrity.

Empowering Students to Shape AI Integration

Schools that successfully integrate AI into learning environments recognize that students must be active participants, not just passive users. When given the opportunity, students can engage in critical conversations about AI ethics, responsible use, and its evolving role in education. Some schools have embraced this by creating student AI committees where they help shape AI policies, provide feedback to school leaders, and educate their peers on responsible AI use.

A powerful example of student-driven AI governance is located at McDonell Area Catholic Schools (2024) in Wisconsin. The school implemented an Honor

Council, where students take an active role in upholding academic integrity and AI responsibility. Rather than relying solely on teachers or administrators to enforce AI policies, this student-led council reviews cases related to AI misuse, plagiarism, and broader ethical concerns. Instead of punitive measures when classmates have been found using GenAI on schoolwork, the Honor Council emphasizes education and ethics, so that classmates learn how to engage with AI responsibly.

What makes this initiative particularly unique is that students themselves designed the school's AI Acceptable Use Policy. Initially tasked with creating AI guidelines, student committee members quickly realized that a static policy would not be enough. AI is evolving, and its policy needs to be adaptable. Through ongoing discussion, individual educators play a vital role in shaping its impact on learning.

Moving from Policy to Practice: Strategies for AI Integration

Schools need a framework that allows for structured AI integration to move forward effectively. While policies like the student-driven AI governance at McDonell Area Catholic Schools help set ethical expectations, schools must also provide practical support for teachers and students. The following recommendations outline key steps educators can take to ensure AI serves as a meaningful tool for deeper learning rather than a shortcut for assignments.

First, teachers can rethink assignments to prioritize deep learning. If GenAI can complete an assignment in seconds, it may not cultivate the critical thinking, synthesis, and inquiry we want students to develop. Educators must design assessments that require students to analyze, question, and personalize their work, using AI as a tool for deeper engagement rather than a shortcut for completion. A simple shift in instructional design can prevent AI from replacing student effort and ensure that learning remains active rather than passive.

Second, teachers can enhance students' AI literacy skills by guiding them to engage with AI responsibly rather than banning it outright. Since GenAI is now embedded in everyday learning, students must understand how AI generates responses, recognize its biases, and develop fact-checking abilities. These skills prepare students to use AI critically, rather than blindly trusting its outputs.

Third, educators must establish ethical and responsible AI use in the classroom. Students need clear expectations for when, how, and why they can use AI. Schools should adopt transparent acceptable use policies that clarify appropriate AI engagement and ensure students develop essential writing, research, and analytical skills. Teachers can reinforce these policies by setting guidelines that encourage AI as a support tool rather than a replacement for original thought.

Fourth, teachers can build their confidence through professional learning. Many educators feel unprepared to integrate AI effectively, which fuels apprehension. Schools must provide ongoing professional development that goes beyond technical training and focuses on AI's pedagogical possibilities. Supported teachers are more likely to embrace AI as an instructional tool rather than a challenge to overcome. Seeking AI workshops, peer discussions, and online courses can help teachers feel more comfortable integrating AI into their classrooms in meaningful ways.

Finally, educators should empower students as co-creators in the AI conversation. Instead of imposing AI policies from the top down, teachers can invite students to actively participate in shaping how AI is used in learning environments. This might involve student-led discussions on AI ethics, collaborative AI projects that require critical engagement, or opportunities for students to reflect on and critique AI's role in their work. When students feel included in these conversations, they develop a sense of responsibility and agency in how AI is used.

Call to Action: From Fear to Empowerment

Fears surrounding GenAI in literacy instruction are understandable, but they should not paralyze educators. Instead of viewing AI as a threat, teachers can see it as a catalyst for transforming literacy instruction—one that better prepares students for the complexities of the digital age.

To ensure AI is integrated ethically and effectively into teaching practices, I propose five key commitments in Figure 2.1. These are designed to help teachers confidently navigate AI integration while maintaining student engagement. Each commitment is accompanied by specific action steps that offer practical ways to implement AI thoughtfully in the classroom. Additionally, guiding questions are provided to help educators reflect on different dimensions of AI integration, challenge assumptions, and explore new strategies that align with their teaching goals. These components work together to support a balanced approach to AI, ensuring that it enhances learning rather than replaces essential skills.

By committing to these five key commitments, educators can move beyond fear and into a thoughtful, informed approach to AI integration, ensuring that AI enhances learning without replacing critical thinking and creativity.

Conclusion

The future of literacy instruction is not about choosing between *human* intelligence and *artificial* intelligence. Instead, we should focus on ensuring students develop the skills, confidence, and discernment to use AI as an asset in their learning journey. By integrating GenAI in ways that promote critical problem solving, complex reading and writing, and ethical reasoning, we prepare students to engage meaningfully with knowledge, both within and beyond the classroom.

1. **Rethink Assignments to Prioritize Deep Learning**

   Action step: Audit your existing assignments.

   Guiding questions: Does this task necessitate genuine thinking, problem solving, or creativity that AI alone cannot produce? How can I design assignments where AI enhances, rather than replaces, student effort?

2. **Strengthen Students' AI Literacy Skills**

   Action step: Teach students to critically assess AI-generated content by verifying sources, recognizing bias, and evaluating the accuracy of AI outputs.

   Guiding questions: Do my students understand how AI functions, including its limitations and potential biases? How can I assist them in developing fact-checking skills when using AI tools?

3. **Establish Clear and Ethical Guidelines for AI Use**

   Action step: Develop classroom AI guidelines that define when and how AI can be utilized, ensuring transparency and ethical engagement. Ask for student input.

   Guiding questions: What questions exist in AI for student work, and how can I clarify? Have I communicated clear expectations for AI engagement in my classroom?

4. **Build Teacher Confidence in Using AI Effectively**

   Action step: Participate in AI professional learning opportunities and advocate for schoolwide training to enhance confidence in AI integration.

   Guiding questions: How confident am I with incorporating AI into my instruction, and what support do I require? What professional development opportunities are available to boost my understanding of AI in education?

5. **Empower Students as Active Participants in AI Integration**

   Action step: Encourage student-led AI discussions, committees, and projects to ensure they have a voice in how AI is utilized in learning.

   Guiding questions: How can I ensure AI remains a collaborative learning tool rather than a passive replacement for student effort? What opportunities can I create for students to engage with AI and develop responsible practices?

FIGURE 2.1. Five key commitments and action steps to GenAI integration.

Teacher Reflection Questions

Use the questions below to reflect on how your current mindset, experiences, and school context shape your approach to GenAI in the classroom and how you might move forward with greater clarity and confidence.

1. How does my current approach to GenAI in the classroom align with the concerns and solutions discussed in this chapter? Does my school have clear GenAI policies, or have I been navigating integration on my own?
2. How have past technological shifts, such as calculators, Wikipedia, or online translation tools, influenced my teaching? How might those experiences help inform my approach to GenAI today?

3. What fears or uncertainties do I still have about using GenAI in literacy instruction? What steps can I take to address those concerns or gain more confidence?
4. How can I create a classroom culture where students feel comfortable discussing GenAI openly, ethically, and without fear? What routines or norms could help support that culture?

ETHICAL DILEMMA AND DISCUSSION PROMPTS

Ethical Dilemma: The Case of the Unverified Source

Mr. Anderson, a high school history teacher, assigns his students a research paper on global conflicts. To help them brainstorm ideas and structure their arguments, he encourages them to use a GenAI tool. One student, Mia, drafts her paper using AI and submits a well-structured essay with strong arguments and cited sources. However, when Mr. Anderson double-checks one of her AI-generated citations, he realizes it does not exist. A few other references in her paper also seem questionable. When he asks Mia about her sources, she admits she didn't verify them. She assumed AI had provided accurate information.

Now, Mr. Anderson faces a dilemma: Should he penalize Mia for including fabricated sources, even though she was unaware of the issue? How can he use this situation as a learning experience to teach all his students about verifying AI-generated content? How should educators approach AI-generated citations when students increasingly rely on AI as a research assistant?

Discussion Prompts

1. Should teachers create explicit policies regarding the use of AI in research assignments? If so, what key elements should be included?
2. How can Mr. Anderson turn this situation into a learning opportunity for the entire class to improve AI literacy and critical thinking?
3. What instructional strategies can be implemented to help students verify AI-generated sources before using them in academic work?

Chapter 3

Reimagining Instructional Design and Selecting GenAI Tools

In the acknowledgments section of this text, I commented that this book was difficult to write due to how quickly GenAI tools change. The focus morphed from the time I proposed the idea to my editor to the last word typed on the final page. My previous experience writing books on integrating technology in education (Karchmer-Klein, 2020; Karchmer-Klein et al., 2022) was built around hours of instructional design, student feedback, and a steadfast focus on pedagogy. Those books had clear frameworks. This one . . . didn't. The outline I developed a year before finishing the manuscript proved almost unrecognizable.

What I imagined this book would encompass stemmed from an earlier vantage point of GenAI before it offered individualized literacy tutoring, accurate text-to-image generation, or the ability to analyze handwritten work. Each time I brainstormed ideas, I discovered new tools or existing ones had changed so drastically that their instructional affordances had shifted entirely.

For example, ChatGPT-4 is my chatbot of choice. In just 9 months, the paid version's affordances expanded from limited, text-only capabilities to a broad, sophisticated set of features, transforming not just what AI can do but also what teachers and students can do with it. See Table 3.1 for a simple comparison of those updates.

But this chapter is not about the tools. It is about the decisions educators make around them. As I revised the outline of this book repeatedly, I kept returning to the same question I ask in my own teaching: What is the learning goal? The tool

TABLE 3.1. ChatGPT Affordances Comparison: October 2024 versus July 2025

Affordance	October 2024	July 2025
Text input and output	Text-based responses with limited context retention	Text responses are more accurate, nuanced, and responsive to complex instructions with larger context windows Supports dynamic, mixed-modal conversations that integrate text, image, and voice seamlessly; allows more intuitive back-and-forth exchanges in educational scenarios
Voice capabilities	Limited voice interaction through third-party tools	Real-time, natural voice conversation with expressive tone and language support Voice conversations are now more responsive and memory-aware; supports real-time co-reading, language learning, and verbal feedback on student work
Image understanding	Could generate images with DALL·E, but had limited ability to analyze visuals	Understands, analyzes, and discusses uploaded images, charts, and hand-drawn student work Improved accuracy with visual reasoning tasks (e.g., interpreting infographics, math problems); can now cross-reference images with text in multistep tasks
Document handling	Text-based input only; required manual formatting/export	Can generate, edit, and export to Word or PDF formats, streamlining lesson prep and assignment creation Offers structured editing suggestions, auto-summarization of student papers, and lesson plan formatting; improved compatibility with classroom templates
Memory and context	Could retain session memory but limited in scope and length	Can process and retain long-form content up to 1 million words for in-depth projects Expanded contextual memory across sessions allows for personalized instructional support over time; remembers classroom goals and prior student responses (if enabled)
Data and spreadsheet analysis	Basic file analysis in limited settings	Analyzes spreadsheets, summarizes trends, and provides insights with code interpreter support Enhanced ability to create data visualizations and simulations for classroom use; integrates with classroom grading tools and progress tracking dashboards

Note. This table compares ChatGPT's capabilities between October 2024 and July 2025, highlighting the rapid evolution of its features and instructional affordances for educators. These comparisons reflect the paid version of ChatGPT (ChatGPT Plus, GPT-4o) as of July 2025. The free version may still have limitations on features such as memory, voice conversations, multimodal input, and advanced document or data handling.

should never lead. The pedagogy should. That has been the core lesson of watching GenAI evolve in real time, and it is the message I share in this chapter and the remainder of this book.

Designing with Intention: Instructional Planning in the Age of GenAI

The most frequent mistake I see educators make with new technology is using it because it is available, not because it is appropriate. That's why, before exploring what GenAI can do, I would like to revisit what solid instructional design has *always* required: specified learning goals, evidence-based practices, and a focus on students. Drawing on my previous work (Karchmer-Klein, 2020; Karchmer-Klein et al., 2022), I advocate a planning approach grounded in reflexive pedagogy (Cope & Kalantzis, 2015). Effective teaching with GenAI does not start with features. It starts with learning.

Reflexive Pedagogy and GenAI

Reflexive pedagogy (Cope & Kalantzis, 2015) is a teaching approach that combines didactic and authentic instructional methods within a cohesive set of activities designed to achieve the same learning objectives. Didactic methods are teacher centered, where educators, as experts, impart knowledge to students through strategies such as lectures, teacher-led discussions, and worksheets. In contrast, authentic methods connect learning to real-world contexts, inviting students to explore concepts firsthand through activities like field trips, simulations, and maker spaces. Reflexive pedagogy positions teachers as intentional designers who make deliberate choices about guiding learning directly and when to open space for real-world exploration.

GenAI tools, such as ChatGPT, offer unique opportunities to enhance both didactic and authentic practices. They can support teacher-led activities for didactic methods by generating sample paragraphs, moderating discussions, and providing interactive worksheets that adapt to student responses. For authentic practices, GenAI can simulate real-world scenarios, create case-based instructional materials, and facilitate virtual guest lectures, making knowledge contextual and accessible.

It is important to note, many evidence-based practices validated in traditional classroom settings have not been extensively studied in digital environments (Price & Kirkwood, 2014). Therefore, when I share strategies in this book, I refer to them as evidence-informed practices (EIPs). These practices are grounded in research findings, student data, and educators' insights into effective pedagogical approaches for specific content areas (Malin et al., 2020). While we have substantial evidence that these strategies improve student learning in face-to-face settings, we lack comprehensive research on their effectiveness when integrated with GenAI tools. Nonetheless, it is reasonable to believe that if a strategy works well in direct teacher–student interactions or peer collaborations, it could potentially be effective when adapted to involve GenAI. For example, peer editing between a student and GenAI might mirror the benefits seen in traditional peer editing. By leveraging the capabilities of GenAI, we aim to enhance these EIPs within technology-integrated instruction.

From Purpose to Practice: A Process for Designing with GenAI

While GenAI offers new opportunities for personalization, simulation, and creativity, it does not change what good instructional design requires. The process I recommend begins not with a tool but with clearly articulating the learning goal. From there, teachers draw on EIPs to design activities that align with students' cognitive, developmental, and disciplinary needs. Only then should a GenAI tool be selected intentionally to enhance, not replace, the thinking that students must do. Figure 3.1 presents a visual of the instructional design process.

Pause and Reflect: Where Are You in Your GenAI Journey?

Before we explore specific categories of GenAI tools, it is worth pausing to reflect on your current level of comfort, experience, and understanding. Just like we differentiate for students, we need to differentiate for ourselves as educators. Where are you starting from? What feels exciting? What still feels unfamiliar? The self-assessment in Form 3.1 is not a test. It is a mirror to help you notice your strengths and growth areas so that the next section of this chapter is as useful and practical as possible.

As teachers consider how to integrate GenAI into learning, it's equally important to think about where students are starting from. The self-assessment in Form 3.2 can help students reflect on their familiarity, confidence, and habits when using AI tools. It also gives teachers valuable insights into what kind of modeling, scaffolding, and digital citizenship instruction might be needed before introducing a GenAI-powered task.

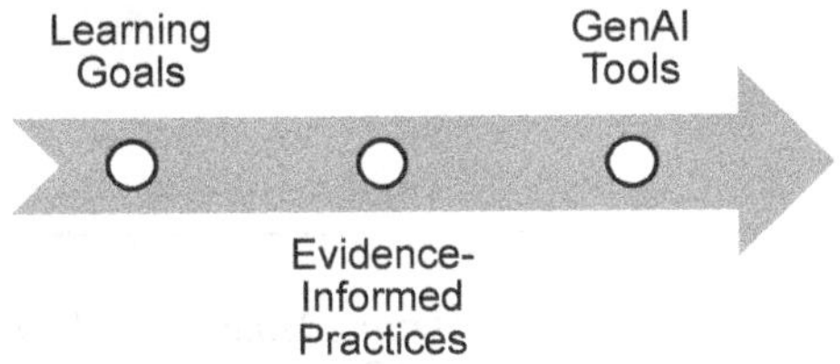

FIGURE 3.1. Instructional design process.

FORM 3.1

GenAI Self-Assessment for Educators

Use this self-assessment to reflect on your knowledge and confidence with GenAI. Check off where you are on the scale and write a few notes to remind you where you are now. You can compare once you have more experience with GenAI.

Statement	Not yet (1)	Sometimes (2)	Usually (3)	Confident (4)
I can describe what GenAI is and how it differs from traditional tools.				
I know how to select GenAI tools based on learning goals.				
I have used a GenAI tool (like ChatGPT) in my personal or professional life.				
I feel confident explaining the benefits and risks of GenAI use with students.				
I can identify ways GenAI can support both didactic and authentic practices.				
I know when to introduce GenAI as part of a lesson, not as the lesson itself.				

Reflection: What is one area above you would like to grow in the next few weeks? What support or resources would help you take that next step?

FORM 3.2

GenAI Self-Assessment for Students

Use this self-assessment to reflect on your experience and confidence using GenAI tools. Check off where you are on the scale and write a few notes to remind you where you are now. You can compare once you have more experience with GenAI. This will help your teacher support you as you learn to use these tools responsibly and creatively.

Statement	Not yet (1)	Sometimes (2)	Usually (3)	Confident (4)
I know what AI is and can describe what it means.				
I have used a GenAI tool like ChatGPT or DALL·E before.				
I know how to ask good questions (prompts) when I use GenAI.				
I understand that GenAI might give wrong or biased answers.				
I use GenAI to help me think—not just to give me answers.				
I know when it's okay (or not okay) to use GenAI on a school assignment.				

Reflection: What is one area you would like to improve upon when using GenAI for school

Selecting GenAI Tools to Support Student Learning

Once the learning goal is clear and the instructional approach is grounded in EIPs, the next step is selecting a GenAI tool that supports learning with intention. But not all GenAI tools are created equal or intended to serve the same instructional functions. Some are designed to support writing or visual expression, while others offer adaptive feedback, structure collaborative experiences, or transform complex texts into more accessible forms.

As discussed earlier, GenAI can support both didactic and authentic practices. It can summarize text or generate examples in a teacher-led setting, or empower students to simulate real-world tasks, conduct interviews, and create products that reflect disciplinary learning. Therefore, when I took on the challenge of categorizing GenAI tools for this book, I quickly realized there were many ways I could do it. In fact, I spent far more time thinking about this than I probably should have and asked far more people than were interested to weigh in. After all that reflection, I chose to group GenAI tools based on how they can be used to support both teacher-directed and student-directed disciplinary literacy instruction.

In the following pages, I share a broad overview of GenAI tools organized into categories based on their primary instructional purpose. I do not include full lesson plans here. Those come in Part II. Instead, each category highlights commonly used tools, what they are best suited for, and brief examples of how they can support student thinking and learning.

The categories include:

Category 1: Tools for Reading, Text Analysis, and Research
Category 2: Tools for Writing, Composition, and Feedback
Category 3: Tools for Content Creation and Multimodal Expression
Category 4: Tools for Personalized Practice, Scaffolding, and Assessment
Category 5: Tools for Collaboration, Discussion, and Experiential Learning

These categories are used only in this chapter to help map the landscape of GenAI tools. In the following chapters, I weave tools from across these groups into lesson examples to support problem solving, critical thinking, reading, and writing.

Category 1: Tools for Reading, Text Analysis, and Research

Reading is central to disciplinary literacy, whether students interpret literature, analyze primary sources, break down scientific explanations, or make sense of mathematical word problems (Lent, 2016). Students encounter increasingly complex, nuanced, and context-dependent texts in every discipline. GenAI tools (see Table 3.2 for a list of tools under this category) can support this process in teacher- and student-directed ways by helping learners access, navigate, and reflect on disciplinary texts with greater confidence and precision.

TABLE 3.2. Tools for Reading, Text Analysis, and Research

Tool	What it does	How it supports disciplinary literacy
ChatGPT	Generates summaries, explains vocabulary, simulates Q&A	Supports reading comprehension, modeling of disciplinary inquiry, and close reading analysis
Microsoft Copilot	Summarizes text, answers research questions, provides source links	Helps synthesize content, verify sources, and refine questions
Google Gemini	Answers questions using web-based content	Breaks down complex topics and introduces multiple perspectives
Perplexity AI	Provides concise, sourced responses with links	Encourages source evaluation and research thinking
Elicit	Extracts and compares findings from academic research	Supports scientific literacy, synthesis, and evidence-based reasoning
Consensus	Summarizes academic studies and shows level of agreement	Builds understanding of scientific and social consensus
NotebookLM	Uploads and annotates texts, answers questions	Encourages active reading, source comparison, and idea organization
Otio	Organizes research sources, summarizes content	Supports research synthesis and disciplinary writing
Diffit	Adapts texts to various reading levels	Increases access to complex disciplinary texts
QuillBot	Paraphrases and summarizes complex language	Supports restating ideas in students' own words

Instructional Uses

Tools in this category are especially helpful when teachers want to:

- Scaffold complex texts with summaries, paraphrasing, or leveled versions
- Model disciplinary reading strategies (e.g., sourcing, close reading, identifying bias)
- Support inquiry and research by helping students ask questions and find relevant sources
- Encourage metacognition by reminding students to reflect on how they read and what they understand
- Provide individualized supports without lowering expectations

Classroom Example

ELA—Grade 9

Learning goal: Analyze how an author's use of language shapes tone and theme

EIP: Annotating literary passages and identifying stylistic patterns to deepen comprehension (Fisher & Frey, 2014; Shanahan & Shanahan, 2008)

GenAI tool: QuillBot for paraphrasing; NotebookLM for uploading texts and generating annotated insights

Science—Grade 11

Learning goal: Evaluate evidence from multiple sources to form a claim about gene editing

EIP: Synthesizing information from scientific texts to support claims in writing (Goldman et al., 2016)

GenAI tool: Perplexity AI for sourcing and summarizing evidence; Consensus for identifying trends across studies

History—Grade 8

Learning goal: Analyze and interpret a primary source speech

EIP: Scaffolding access to primary sources and supporting sourcing/corroboration skills (Faggella-Luby & Wardwell, 2011; Wineburg, 1991)

GenAI tool: Diffit to provide leveled versions of the speech; ChatGPT to simulate a dialogue with a historical figure

Math—Grade 10

Learning goal: Interpret and critique statistical claims in real-world media

EIP: Supporting mathematical literacy by connecting quantitative reasoning to everyday contexts (Shanahan & Shanahan, 2008)

GenAI tool: Google Gemini to trace sources and evaluate how statistics are presented across texts

Category 2: Tools for Writing, Composition, and Feedback

Writing is a core component of disciplinary literacy. Whether students are constructing a literary analysis, explaining a scientific process, making a historical argument, or justifying a mathematical solution, they must express their thinking in clear, structured, and discipline-appropriate ways. GenAI tools can support this process by helping students plan, draft, revise, and reflect while supporting teachers in modeling disciplinary writing and giving responsive feedback (see Table 3.3 for a list of tools under this category).

Instructional Uses

These tools are especially useful when teachers want to:

- Model disciplinary writing structures (e.g., claim–evidence–reasoning, thesis-driven argument)
- Help students revise with audience, tone, and clarity in mind
- Provide individualized or peer-like feedback
- Support multilingual learners or students needing writing scaffolds
- Encourage metacognitive awareness of the writing process

Used thoughtfully, these tools enhance—not replace—students' thinking and writing. They can also reduce writing anxiety by providing structure and feedback earlier in the process.

TABLE 3.3. Tools for Writing, Composition, and Feedback

Tool	What it does	How it supports disciplinary literacy
ChatGPT	Acts as a writing partner for brainstorming, outlining, and feedback	Supports writing fluency, idea development, and genre awareness
Notion AI	Context-aware suggestions for structure, tone, and clarity	Helps organize and revise extended writing
GrammarlyGO	Real-time grammar, clarity, and tone suggestions	Reinforces academic and discipline-specific writing conventions
Hemingway Editor	Highlights readability and passive voice	Supports concise and clear writing
Goblin.tools (Formalizer)	Turns informal writing into formal/academic tone	Supports stylistic revision for disciplinary voice
Google Docs + AI Extensions	Real-time collaborative editing with AI support	Encourages peer collaboration and iterative revision
MagicSchool AI	Generates prompts, rubrics, and exemplars	Helps teachers model and scaffold writing across content areas

Classroom Examples

ELA—Grade 10

Learning goal: Write a literary analysis essay using textual evidence to support a central claim

EIP: Modeling thesis development and providing structured writing frames (Fisher & Frey, 2014; Graham & Perin, 2007)

GenAI tool: ChatGPT for brainstorming thesis statements and generating counterarguments; GrammarlyGO for revision support

Task: Students first draft a claim with teacher support, then use ChatGPT to explore possible counterclaims and refine their argument. GrammarlyGO provides clarity and tone feedback before peer review.

Science—Grade 9

Learning goal: Write a lab report that explains the relationship between variables in an experiment

EIP: Teaching genre-specific writing using mentor texts and sentence stems (Pytash & Morgan, 2014)

GenAI tool: Notion AI for structuring the methods and conclusion sections; Hemingway Editor for simplifying dense explanations

Task: After completing an experiment, students draft their lab reports and use Notion AI to reorganize ideas for clarity. They then run their work through Hemingway Editor to identify overly complex language and revise accordingly.

History—Grade 11

Learning goal: Write a document-based question (DBQ) response that includes sourcing and contextualization

EIP: Teaching historical argument writing through modeling and guided practice (De La Paz & Graham, 2002; Wineburg, 1991)

GenAI tool: ChatGPT to generate sample body paragraphs from student outlines; Goblin.tools (Formalizer) to revise tone

Task: Students plan their DBQ outlines, then use ChatGPT to model body paragraph structures. After drafting, they use Goblin.tools to ensure their writing maintains a formal and historically appropriate voice.

Math—Grade 8

Learning goal: Write a justification for a multistep problem-solving process

EIP: Explaining mathematical reasoning in written form to solidify understanding (Powell et al., 2021)

GenAI tool: Google Docs with AI extension to collaboratively write and revise justifications

Task: Students write justifications in pairs after solving a set of equations. The AI extension provides suggestions for clarifying logic or fixing ambiguous language. The teacher then facilitates a discussion comparing two sample justifications.

Category 3: Tools for Content Creation and Multimodal Expression

Disciplinary literacy is not limited to traditional print-based reading and writing. In many cases, students demonstrate their understanding through multimodal texts: infographics, videos, visual models, slide decks, digital stories, or simulations. GenAI tools (see Table 3.4 for a list of tools in this category) can support these forms of expression by helping students visualize abstract concepts, remix information creatively, and communicate disciplinary knowledge in engaging ways.

TABLE 3.4. Tools for Content Creation and Multimodal Expression

Tool	What it does	How it supports disciplinary literacy
Canva (Magic Write and AI Design)	Design presentations, infographics, visual stories	Supports synthesis and visual communication of disciplinary ideas
Adobe Express	Create videos, posters, web pages with AI templates	Supports storytelling and multimodal expression
DALL·E (via ChatGPT)	Generates images from text prompts	Visualizes abstract/historical concepts symbolically
Curipod	Generates interactive slide decks and prompts	Supports student presentations and real-time engagement
Flip	Video-based reflection and asynchronous peer discussion	Supports oral communication and student voice
Ideogram	Stylized images with text for models and metaphors	Supports creative disciplinary expression
Padlet	Collaborative digital wall with AI-powered prompts and multimodal posting options	Supports synthesis and sharing of discipline-specific ideas by integrating AI-generated text, images, and media into multimodal expression

Instructional Uses

These tools are especially useful when teachers want to:

- Help students express complex ideas through visuals, audio, or design
- Encourage creative thinking grounded in disciplinary content
- Support multilingual learners or students who benefit from non-text-based communication
- Scaffold presentations or digital storytelling with templates and models
- Offer alternative ways for students to demonstrate understanding

These GenAI tools allow students to express disciplinary understanding multimodally through visual, auditory, and interactive media, allowing for creative thinking, conceptual modeling, and real-world application.

Classroom Examples

ELA—Grade 10

Learning goal: Analyze a novel's central theme and express it through visual symbolism

EIP: Multimodal composition to support deep interpretation and communication of theme (Fisher & Frey, 2014)

GenAI tool: Ideogram to create symbolic imagery; Canva to design a visual literary analysis

Task: After reading *The House on Mango Street* (Cisneros, 1983), students select a recurring theme and generate a symbolic image using Ideogram. They then create a Canva poster with their image and a short analysis explaining how it represents the theme.

History—Grade 8

Learning goal: Summarize key events in the Civil Rights Movement through digital storytelling

EIP: Story-based synthesis of historical content for deeper understanding (Wineburg, 1991)

GenAI tool: Adobe Express to create narrated timelines or mini-documentaries

Task: Students choose one major event (e.g., the March on Washington), research key figures and outcomes, and use Adobe Express to build a short narrated video with text, images, and AI-generated voiceover.

Business—Grade 11

Learning goal: Create a persuasive pitch for a product concept using marketing techniques

EIP: Teaching real-world communication skills through multimodal presentation and audience analysis (U.S. Department of Education, 2024)

GenAI tool: Canva to design branded slides and visuals; Curipod to generate interactive pitch content

Task: Students develop a product idea and use Canva to create a pitch deck. Then, they build an interactive presentation in Curipod using AI-generated prompts, visuals, and polls to simulate audience feedback during a live pitch simulation.

Science—Grade 9

Learning goal: Explain a scientific process through metaphor and visual modeling

EIP: Using analogies and visual models to build conceptual understanding (National Research Council, 2013)

GenAI tool: DALL·E to generate metaphor-based diagrams; Adobe Express to combine narration and visuals

Task: Students create a metaphor for a science concept (e.g., food web = city traffic system). They generate images using DALL·E and assemble a short narrated Adobe Express video explaining the metaphor and scientific connections.

Category 4: Tools for Personalized Practice, Scaffolding, and Assessment

One of the most powerful promises of GenAI is its ability to adapt instruction in real time. The tools in this category (see Table 3.5 for a list) can personalize learning experiences by providing 1:1 practice, scaffolds, or feedback based on a student's needs. They also support formative and summative assessment through automatic question generation, interactive tasks, and response analysis, allowing teachers to understand student progress better and adjust instruction accordingly.

Instructional Uses

These tools are especially useful when teachers want to:

- Provide differentiated practice based on student performance or readiness
- Scaffold challenging content without lowering rigor
- Offer real-time, targeted feedback
- Design formative assessments that adapt to student input
- Monitor student understanding and guide reteaching efforts

TABLE 3.5. Tools for Personalized Practice, Scaffolding, and Assessment

Tool	What it does	How it supports disciplinary literacy
Khan Academy (AI-enhanced)	Offers personalized practice and instruction with adaptive feedback	Supports content-specific practice (e.g., math, science) and adjusts based on student progress
Diffit	Levels content for reading, creates questions, and adapts texts	Provides access to rigorous texts with appropriate scaffolds for comprehension
Edulastic	Creates auto-graded assessments with standards alignment	Helps teachers track student understanding and respond with targeted instruction
Goblin.tools (Checklist and Estimator)	Breaks down complex tasks into smaller steps, estimates time needed	Scaffolds executive function and planning for disciplinary writing and projects
MagicSchool AI	Generates leveled questions, exit tickets, rubrics, and accommodations	Supports formative assessment and IEP-aligned scaffolding for disciplinary content
Curipod	Generates interactive formative assessments, polls, and discussion prompts	Checks for understanding and sparks reflection across subject areas
DreamBox	Adaptive math learning platform	Responds to student input to adjust instruction and reinforce mathematical reasoning
Conker AI	Creates customizable quizzes with varying question types and difficulty	Supports retrieval practice and formative assessment with disciplinary vocabulary

Note. IEP, individualized education plan.

Classroom Examples

Math—Grade 7

Learning goal: Strengthen proportional reasoning through adaptive problem sets

EIP: Providing scaffolded practice aligned to students' readiness levels (Witzel et al., 2003)

GenAI tool: DreamBox for adaptive learning; Conker AI to generate practice quizzes with targeted vocabulary

Task: Students complete personalized math practice on DreamBox, then use a teacher-designed Conker quiz to self-check and explain one solution in writing.

History—Grade 8

Learning goal: Analyze cause and effect in historical events using evidence from primary sources

EIP: Scaffolded questioning and tiered text complexity to support comprehension and historical thinking (Faggella-Luby & Wardwell, 2011; Wineburg, 1991)

GenAI tool: Diffit to level a primary source; MagicSchool AI to generate scaffolded analysis questions

Task: Students read differentiated versions of a primary source and answer AI-generated questions. The teacher reviews responses to group students for follow-up discussion.

Science—Grade 10

Learning goal: Interpret experimental results and revise a lab report based on peer and teacher feedback

EIP: Using feedback cycles to strengthen disciplinary writing (Graham & Perin, 2007)

GenAI tool: MagicSchool AI to create a rubric and provide feedback comments; Goblin.tools to scaffold task planning

Task: Students receive structured feedback from the AI using the teacher-created rubric and revise their reports. They use Goblin.tools to break down revision steps and track time.

ELA—Grade 9

Learning goal: Analyze character motivation through textual evidence

EIP: Differentiating questioning and feedback to guide close reading (Fisher & Frey, 2014)

GenAI tool: Curipod for live polls and exit tickets; Khan Academy for adaptive grammar practice to support writing

Task: After a class reading, students use Curipod to respond to a character analysis prompt. Their responses guide follow-up mini-lessons and targeted grammar instruction via Khan Academy.

Category 5: Tools for Collaboration, Discussion, and Experiential Learning

Disciplinary literacy grows when students interact with ideas, texts, and one another through dialogue, shared problem solving, and collaborative exploration. GenAI tools (see Table 3.6 for a list of tools in this category) can support these learning experiences by simulating real-world environments, generating discussion prompts, and enabling collaborative spaces where students test ideas, ask questions, and co-construct understanding.

TABLE 3.6. Tools for Collaboration, Discussion, and Experiential Learning

Tool	What it does	How it supports disciplinary literacy
Curipod	Generates interactive presentations, polls, and discussion prompts	Facilitates classroom discourse, peer collaboration, and formative feedback through real-time interaction
Conker AI	Creates quizzes and interactive activities from content	Encourages collaborative sense making and quick checks for understanding in group settings
ChatGPT (Collaborative Mode)	Used by student teams to generate questions, simulate debates, or co-develop projects	Supports dialogue, iterative thinking, and discipline-specific inquiry
Miro + AI	Collaborative whiteboard with AI-assisted brainstorming and organization	Helps groups visualize processes, organize arguments, and document inquiry over time
MagicSchool AI	Helps generate scenarios, simulations, and guided group tasks	Promotes role-play, case-based discussion, and project-based learning
Canva (Collaborative Boards)	Allows real-time co-design of visuals and documents with AI design assistance	Encourages group synthesis of disciplinary knowledge into creative products
Simulations for Learning (e.g., Labster, AI Dungeon)	Immersive virtual labs and scenario-based learning with AI tutors	Offers experiential learning opportunities that deepen conceptual understanding through role-based interaction

Instructional Uses

These tools are especially useful when teachers want to:

- Promote meaningful, student-led discussion
- Facilitate collaborative inquiry or project-based learning
- Simulate real-world experiences through role play or scenario building
- Build a community in classrooms where students interact across roles or perspectives
- Support metacognition by prompting reflection before, during, and after group tasks

Classroom Examples

ELA—Grade 9

Learning goal: Engage in collaborative discussion around character motivation and theme

EIP: Structured peer discussion to deepen text interpretation (Fisher & Frey, 2014)

GenAI tool: Curipod to generate real-time prompts and interactive polls

Task: After reading a short story, students use a teacher-created Curipod presentation that includes AI-generated discussion prompts and poll questions. In small groups, they vote on interpretations, discuss justification, and revise their claims collaboratively.

History—Grade 11

Learning goal: Analyze multiple perspectives during a historical turning point

EIP: Role-play to foster historical empathy and decision making (Wineburg, 1991)

GenAI tool: AI Dungeon to simulate historical scenarios; ChatGPT to help prep character roles

Task: Students assume historical roles (e.g., political leaders, activists, civilians) during the lead-up to the French Revolution. They use AI Dungeon to engage in a branching scenario where decisions shape events. Students later reflect on how their choices aligned or diverged from real history.

Science—Grade 10

Learning goal: Collaboratively model a complex biological system

EIP: Group concept mapping and simulation to build systems thinking (NRC, 2012)

GenAI tool: Miro + AI to co-construct a living diagram of a system (e.g., circulatory or ecosystem)

Task: Working in groups, students use Miro's collaborative whiteboard and AI organization tools to create a concept map of a biological system. As they build, the AI offers suggestions for missing connections or terminology. Students present their model to peers with annotations.

Business—Grade 12

Learning goal: Collaborate to develop and revise a pitch for a start-up idea

EIP: Peer collaboration and iterative feedback in project-based learning (U.S. Department of Education, 2024)

GenAI tool: Canva (collaborative slides) + MagicSchool AI to generate customer personas and feedback questions

Task: Student teams brainstorm a product idea, use MagicSchool AI to generate potential target personas, and collaborate in Canva to build their pitch deck. After receiving AI-generated feedback questions, teams revise their pitches before presenting to a mock panel.

Choosing with Purpose, Teaching with Intention

As the examples above demonstrate, GenAI tools are not one-size-fits-all. Their value lies not in what they can do on their own but in how intentionally they are used to support meaningful, student-centered learning. Whether enhancing reading comprehension, providing targeted writing feedback, modeling scientific processes, or facilitating collaborative discussion, GenAI can expand what's possible in the classroom—but only when paired with clear learning goals, grounded in EIP, and designed with students at the center.

Each tool described in this chapter offers unique affordances, but none are instructional strategies on their own. A tool cannot substitute for a thoughtfully designed lesson. It is the teacher—not the technology—who determines whether a GenAI experience supports disciplinary literacy, fosters deep thinking, or simply adds novelty without substance. And it is through deliberate, reflexive instructional planning that GenAI becomes a catalyst for literacy development rather than a shortcut around it.

Before moving on, I must acknowledge three practical limitations of tool selection:

1. Not every GenAI platform is accessible to every learner. Many tools have age restrictions, require parental consent, or prohibit use by individuals under the age of 18.
2. Several popular tools do not cite sources or link to information, making them less reliable for research-based tasks where students are expected to verify claims or attribute evidence.
3. Teachers *must* carefully review district/school policies and the platform's terms of service before introducing any AI tool in class. If the policies are confusing, seek clarification from the director of technology or other district administrators before integrating any AI tools.

Consider these constraints when designing assignments or integrating GenAI tools into classroom routines. Below, I compare widely used GenAI chatbots, including age restrictions and guidance for classroom use *at the time of publication.* I also include notes that I believe would be useful in deciding to use them for various purposes.

1. ChatGPT
   - Minimum age requirements: 13+ (users ages 13–18 require parental or legal guardian permission)
   - Source verification: Provides links depending on the version; can generate information, but does not cite sources
   - Notes: ChatGPT can generate information, but does not always provide citations for its sources

2. Google Gemini
   - Minimum age requirements: 13+
   - Source verification: Sometimes provides source links via Google Search
   - Notes: Integrates with Google Search to offer source links for some answers
3. Perplexity AI
   - Minimum age requirements: 13+
   - Source verification: Yes
   - Notes: Designed for research, actively links to sources for verification
4. Microsoft Copilot
   - Minimum age requirements: 18+
   - Source verification: Yes
   - Notes: Provides a range of links, such as peer-reviewed journal articles, websites, and major news outlets
5. Claude
   - Minimum age requirements: 18+
   - Source verification: No
   - Notes: Does not have access to a current academic database and cannot provide direct links to specific articles
5. Elicit
   - Minimum age requirements: 18+ or with parental consent
   - Source verification: Yes
   - Notes: AI research assistant that helps researchers find relevant papers, extract key information, and summarize findings
7. Scite AI
   - Minimum age requirements: 13+
   - Source verification: Yes, provides Smart Citations
   - Notes: Uses Smart Citations, which show how a paper has been cited with key quotes and contextual placement in the cited work
8. Character.AI
   - Minimum age requirements: 13+
   - Source verification: No
   - Notes: Focuses on creative conversations rather than factual accuracy

In the remainder of this text, the same tools mentioned throughout this chapter reappear, not in isolation but embedded within complete instructional routines. While this chapter provides a high-level overview of categories, affordances, and examples, Part II shifts toward deep application. There, you'll find rich, discipline-specific lessons demonstrating how GenAI can support students as problem solvers, critical thinkers, readers, and writers across content areas. As you reflect on how GenAI tools might fit into your own instructional design, the questions below can help guide your planning and next steps.

Try It Out Plan Backward, Choose Forward

The following activity will motivate you *to apply* what you learned about GenAI tool selection, reflexive pedagogy, and intentional instructional design! This activity walks you through the process of selecting a GenAI tool based on student learning goals, not features. It is built on the model introduced earlier in the chapter.

Learning Goal → EIP → GenAI Tool → Instructional Design

Use Form 3.3: GenAI Lesson Planning Template. You'll find a printable version of this planning tool at the end of this chapter. It is designed to help you document and reflect on your instructional decisions.

Step-by-Step

1. Choose a topic or unit you already teach.

   Select a lesson or unit you are already planning to teach in the next few weeks. (Do not create something new just for this!)
2. Define the learning goal.

   Write a clear, standards-aligned objective for what students should *know*, *understand*, or *be able to do* by the end of the lesson.
3. Identify one EIP.

   Think about a strategy you already use—or would like to use—to support that goal. Examples:
   - Text-based discussion
   - Peer feedback
   - Graphic organizers
   - Inquiry-based questioning
   - Concept modeling

   (Not sure? Flip back to the examples in this chapter.)
4. Review the tool tables.

   Look at the GenAI tool categories in this chapter and pick one or two that might *enhance*, *scaffold*, or *extend* the EIP you selected. Play with the tools.
5. Decide: Didactic, authentic, or reflexive?

   How will you use the GenAI tool:
   - To deliver or structure instruction? (Didactic)
   - To support student-driven inquiry or production? (Authentic)
   - Or both, in a cohesive chain? (Reflexive)

6. Sketch a quick plan.

   Write down the following prompts (or use them with a colleague for peer feedback).

   - Learning goal:
   - EIP:
   - GenAI tool(s):
   - Instructional purpose (didactic/authentic/reflexive):
   - Quick summary of student task:

7. Reflect.

   How does your selected tool *support student thinking* rather than replace it?

   Would you feel confident explaining the instructional reason for using it to a parent, colleague, or administrator?

Want a Challenge?

Try designing two versions of the same lesson. One with GenAI and one without, and compare the cognitive demands, student ownership, and opportunities for feedback in each.

Teacher Reflection Questions

1. Which category of GenAI tools from this chapter am I most confident using—and why? Which one feels the most unfamiliar or outside my comfort zone?
2. How might I collaborate with colleagues to evaluate and select GenAI tools with shared purpose and consistency? Could departmentwide or teamwide alignment improve outcomes for students?
3. How will I assess whether a GenAI-supported activity is actually improving student learning, thinking, or communication? What evidence would help me make informed decisions moving forward?
4. How can GenAI enhance both teacher-directed (didactic) and student-driven (authentic) learning in my content area? Are there moments in my curriculum where I could be more reflexive in my design?

FORM 3.3

GenAI Lesson Planning Template

This template guides you through selecting a GenAI tool based on a clear learning objective, an evidence-informed practice (EIP), and intentional instructional design. Use this as a reusable tool for planning.

1. Lesson topic/unit:

2. Learning goal: What should students know, understand, or be able to do?

3. Evidence-informed practice (EIP): What instructional strategy will you use to support this goal?

4. GenAI tool(s): Which tool(s) best enhance or scaffold the EIP?

5. Instructional purpose: Check one: [ ] Didactic [ ] Authentic [ ] Reflexive (both)
   Briefly describe how the tool supports this approach.

6. Summary of student task: What will students do? How will the tool support learning?

7. Reflection: How does this tool support student thinking, not replace it?

Would you feel confident explaining your choice to a colleague, parent, or administrator?

ETHICAL DILEMMA AND DISCUSSION PROMPTS

Ethical Dilemma: The AI Avalanche

Your school's new instructional technology coordinator is energetic, passionate, and clearly a fan of GenAI. At the first faculty meeting of the year, she unveils "The Future of Learning": six new AI tools teachers are encouraged to use immediately. They range from AI writing assistants and lesson generators to image creators and feedback bots. The presentation is slick and fast. There's a QR code to a tutorials folder, but no real training. You and your colleagues are left nodding along, unsure how to actually use the tools, but intrigued enough to try.

In the weeks that follow, excitement spreads faster than planning. A few teachers use the tools creatively, while others just have the AI write everything from "Do Now" activities to parent emails. One teacher has even turned in a week's worth of AI-generated lesson plans without reviewing them first. Students notice. Some are confused, some are impressed, some are suspicious. One says, "It feels like the teachers are trying to keep up with us now."

You're caught in the middle. You see the potential, but also the chaos. You want to bring intentionality to these tools, but you're just one voice. The instructional tech coordinator is calling this the "AI moment." You are unsure whether to join the wave, slow it down, or build a life raft.

Discussion Prompts

1. What are the potential risks of introducing multiple GenAI tools without adequate training or instructional planning?
2. What responsibilities do school leaders and tech coordinators have when introducing powerful new tools?
3. How could this scenario impact students' understanding of academic integrity and teacher credibility?

PART II

How Do We Reimagine Instruction for an AI-Infused World?

Chapter 4

Reimagining Instruction of Problem-Solving Skills

My husband, Joe, met a college friend for dinner recently. Eric lives in Baltimore, Maryland. They wanted to find a restaurant roughly equidistant from their hometowns. This was not difficult, since I-95, an interstate highway, runs between them. The challenge was finding a place with a variety of restaurant options. If they had strictly considered mileage, they would have met in Delaware's farm country, potentially discovering a hidden gem, but that's not how Joe and Eric operate. Moreover, they were meeting on a Wednesday late afternoon, which meant they would both hit rush hour traffic.

In the past, Joe and Eric would have relied on Google Maps, called mutual friends for recommendations, or manually checked the computer for restaurant listings along the route. Instead, they turned to Gemini, a GenAI tool. They asked, "What town is equidistant from Philadelphia, PA, and Baltimore, MD, has a good selection of restaurants, and is not too difficult to travel to on a Wednesday late afternoon during rush hour traffic?" They met on Main Street in the heart of the University of Delaware in Newark, Delaware, my workplace (see Figure 4.1). As my husband explained, "Choosing a restaurant that satisfies us both is already tough, but finding a town we can both drive to with plenty of options was a real challenge. So why not let AI solve the problem? It took me 5 minutes instead of an hour."

Gemini made their decision faster and easier but didn't replace the human element. Joe and Eric still had to evaluate whether the suggestion made sense and choose a restaurant they both agreed upon. If AI had recommended a town with

Gemini
2.0 Flash

Finding a town *exactly* equidistant and meeting all your criteria during rush hour is tricky. The midpoint between Philadelphia and Baltimore is roughly in the northern part of Delaware. However, traveling there during Wednesday late afternoon rush hour could still involve significant traffic heading out of both major cities.

Here's a breakdown of why a perfect answer is difficult and some potential considerations:

The Equidistant Point & Traffic:

- The straight-line midpoint is somewhere in northern Delaware. Towns like **Newark, Delaware,** are geographically close to this midpoint.
- However, travel to Newark from either Philadelphia or Baltimore on a Wednesday late afternoon will likely involve dealing with significant rush hour traffic on I-95.

Restaurants:

- **Newark, Delaware** has a decent selection of restaurants, especially due to the presence of the University of Delaware.

Travel Difficulty:

- Traveling to any town directly between Philadelphia and Baltimore on a Wednesday late afternoon will likely be challenging due to rush hour traffic patterns around both major cities.

Alternative Considerations (Compromises):

Since a perfectly equidistant town with easy rush hour travel might not exist, here are some alternative approaches:

1. **Slightly Off the Direct Path:** Consider towns slightly off the I-95 corridor that might have better restaurant options or less direct rush hour congestion, even if they aren't perfectly equidistant. However, this will skew the travel time from one city versus the other.
2. **Meeting Closer to One City:** Depending on where you and the other party are traveling *from* within Philadelphia and Baltimore, meeting slightly closer to one city might make more sense to avoid the worst of the traffic for one of you.
3. **Later Meeting Time:** If possible, shifting the meeting time later in the evening after the peak of rush hour could make travel to a wider range of locations easier.
4. **Utilizing Train Travel:** Amtrak has stations in both Philadelphia (30th Street Station) and Baltimore (Penn Station). While not a town, meeting at one of these stations or a location easily accessible from them could bypass some of the highway traffic. Both areas have numerous restaurants.

In conclusion, while Newark, Delaware, is geographically close to the midpoint and has restaurants, expect significant traffic if traveling there on a Wednesday late afternoon. You might need to compromise on the "equidistant" factor or the travel ease during rush hour.

FIGURE 4.1. Gemini output for finding a restaurant between Philadelphia and Baltimore.

limited dining options or one far from a convenient highway exit, they would have had to reconsider their choice.

This everyday example highlights students' problem-solving challenges in an AI-dominated world. While AI can offer suggestions, generate ideas, and automate certain tasks, it does not make decisions for you. It cannot evaluate competing factors, apply human judgment, or adapt to unexpected constraints. Just as Joe and Eric had to assess their AI-generated restaurant location, students must learn to engage critically with AI outputs rather than accept them blindly.

Reimagining Problem Solving in an AI-Infused Classroom

Problems are the tasks we are uncertain how to complete, and problem solving is our attempt at figuring them out. The latter requires cognitive flexibility, metacognitive strategies, and iterative reasoning, and how these skills are applied changes depending on the context, as problem solving varies by discipline (Cartwright, 2023; Frey et al., 2022; Moje, 2015). A historian sifts through conflicting primary sources to create an accurate interpretation of an event. A scientist designs and refines an experiment based on unexpected data. A mathematician systematically works through different equations to evaluate possible solutions. A business strategist considers market trends, consumer behavior, and financial constraints to develop viable plans.

Many established frameworks emphasize this structured reasoning. Pólya's (1993) problem-solving model outlines four key stages: understanding the problem, devising a plan, executing the plan, and reflecting on the solution. Bransford and Stein's (1984) IDEAL model follows a similar arc: identify, define, explore, act, learn. These frameworks are valuable, but in AI-infused classrooms, students encounter a new kind of complexity: GenAI introduces not one but two roles into the problem-solving process.

First, GenAI is a problem to solve. Students must learn to communicate with it effectively, refining their prompts to improve clarity, tone, and accuracy. Poorly worded prompts often yield vague or unusable results. This makes prompt engineering a cognitive puzzle—one that requires iteration, reflection, and discipline-specific reasoning.

Second, GenAI is a collaborative problem solver. It can act as a thinking partner, helping students brainstorm, test hypotheses, or simulate different perspectives. It cannot generate original thought but it can accelerate idea generation, analyze trends, or prompt new lines of inquiry that students might not have considered.

Take, for example, a student using an AI image generator for a multimedia project (see Figure 4.2). They begin with a clear vision: a red-haired girl walking through a forest. The first image might be perfect. But subsequent prompts produce inconsistent visuals by changing her hair, her clothing, even her age. The student

FIGURE 4.2. Comparison of images of the same character generated by Canva Magic Media.

must revise their approach, rethink their descriptions, and experiment with more specific language to achieve visual coherence. Here, the student is not simply *using* GenAI, but actively solving the problem of *how* to use it effectively.

This challenge reveals a central dilemma of AI-integrated teaching and learning: Students cannot passively consume AI outputs. They must learn to guide, question, and sometimes correct them. They must also decide *when* to use AI, *how* to frame their needs, and *why* its responses may succeed or fall short.

This chapter explores two dimensions of problem solving in an AI-rich environment. It discusses GenAI as a problem to solve, requiring students to navigate prompt engineering and tool limitations. It also examines GenAI as a collaborative problem solver, providing strategic support in brainstorming, iteration, and revision. By teaching students to engage thoughtfully with GenAI in both roles, educators can strengthen their capacity for adaptive thinking and prepare them for real-world problem solving in the digital age.

GenAI as a Problem to Solve: Prompt Engineering

Prompt engineering, a fancy name for crafting inputs that guide the GenAI tool to produce useful, relevant, and accurate content, has quickly become a critical skill (Knoth et al., 2024). More than a technical trick, it represents a distinct form of problem solving. When students engage with GenAI, they soon realize that the quality of the output hinges completely on how they phrase their input. If the wording is vague, the result tends to be irrelevant. If the question is too broad, the output often lacks depth. To achieve meaningful results, students must refine, revise, and rethink their prompts, sometimes repeatedly. This iterative process of shaping and reshaping language necessitates precision, flexibility, and critical thinking. In short, prompt engineering is not just a skill. It represents a problem in need of a solution.

Types of Prompts and Their Instructional Applications

Understanding how to communicate effectively with GenAI tools begins with learning how prompts function. Just as teachers differentiate instruction based on students' prior knowledge, the way we prompt GenAI varies depending on the context we provide. These variations can be categorized in AI prompting as (1) zero shot, (2) few shot, and (3) chain of thought (Dang et al., 2022; Palatucci et al., 2009; Wei et al., 2022). Each approach offers unique instructional opportunities and comprehending them can help educators guide students to use AI tools more strategically.

Zero-Shot Prompting

Zero-shot prompting (Dang et al., 2022) is like giving a student a task without prior instruction or examples and testing whether they can figure it out based on general understanding alone. For instance, imagine handing students a sealed lab kit without directions and telling them, "Run the experiment." They may recognize the materials and draw on prior experiences to make educated guesses, but they do not know what question they are exploring, which steps to follow, what results to expect, or how to document their findings. They are operating without context or structure, relying entirely on background knowledge to make sense of the task.

When students assign a GenAI tool a task without providing examples, formatting guidance, or audience cues, they are essentially doing the same thing: expecting the AI to respond based solely on its training. This could produce useful results. However, the output often lacks depth and clarity like a directionless experiment. Table 4.1 provides an overview of zero-shot prompting, along with its benefits and limitations, and shares examples of how it can be applied across different disciplines.

Few-Shot Prompting

Few-shot prompting (Dang et al., 2022) is like assigning students a writing activity and then showing them two strong, well-crafted paragraphs before they begin. The students now know what a high-quality response looks like: the structure, tone, vocabulary, and level of depth expected. They do not copy the samples. They use them as mentor texts to guide their thinking.

This is how few-shot prompting works. Students include two to three specific examples in their prompt to illustrate to the GenAI tool what they are looking for in the output. This effectively trains the GenAI tool in real time. These examples act as anchors, assisting the AI in recognizing the desired format. Instead of producing vague or generic outputs, the AI tailors its response based on the cues it receives, much like a student would with a mentor text during a writer's workshop.

TABLE 4.1. Zero-Shot Prompting

Zero-shot prompting: A single, direct prompt without any examples.
Student provides prompt and GenAI tool responds based solely on its training.

Benefits

- Efficiency and speed
- Versatility in outputs
- Encourages clarity in student's initial questioning
- Useful for low-stakes exploration or fact-based queries

Limitations

- Low accuracy
- Often yields generic or vague responses
- Lacks depth
- May not account for disciplinary nuances
- Complete dependency on training data

Classroom examples

- English language arts: "Summarize the theme of The Giver in one sentence."
- Science: "Explain how food moves through the digestive system."
- Math: "What is the quadratic formula used for?"
- Social studies: "Who were the Allied Powers in World War II?"
- Art: "Create a digital painting about resilience."
- Public speaking: "Write a persuasive speech."

For example, imagine a seventh-grade ELA class where students are revising paragraphs that analyze character development. One student has written a first draft about the main character in *Wonder* (Palacio, 2016) and wants help refining it. They attach two teacher-provided samples of character development and their own paragraph to a GenAI tool and then write the following few-shot prompt:

> These are two examples of strong character analysis. Here's my paragraph about Auggie. Please read it and ask me questions that will help me improve it, especially questions about my transitions, word choice, or organization.

GenAI output:

- What sentence connects your ideas about Auggie's personality to how he changes over time?
- Does this sentence clearly explain how Auggie's actions reflect his internal conflict?
- Are your transitions helping the reader see the connection between ideas?

In this scenario, the student uses few-shot prompting not to generate new content but to invite dialogue with the AI. GenAI becomes a thinking partner, posing reflective questions.

This type of exchange encourages self-directed revision and models the type of reflective questioning students can eventually internalize when revising their own writing without AI. The AI does not replace the student's work. Rather, it assists in recognizing how aspects like organization, sentence variety, and cohesion can be enhanced by comparing their writing to the examples. Thus, few-shot prompting transforms into a writing workshop tool, enabling students to utilize AI for focused, self-directed revision support.

This technique is especially useful when teaching voice, structure, and genre conventions, making it a natural extension of what writing teachers already do. Table 4.2 defines few-shot prompting, outlines its benefits and limitations, and provides practical classroom examples across disciplines.

Chain-of-Thought Prompting

Chain-of-thought prompting is primarily used in math because it follows a step-by-step logical process. This method reflects how we instruct students to articulate their reasoning at each stage of a math problem (Sprague et al., 2024). It is akin to asking students to solve math problems on the board while articulating their reasoning aloud. They are not merely stating the answer but systematically working through the problem, identifying what they know, demonstrating how they isolate variables, and justifying why each step is valid. The goal is not just to arrive at

TABLE 4.2. Few-Shot Prompting

Few-shot prompting: A prompt that includes a few modeled examples to illustrate to the AI how to respond. Students "train" the AI in real time by offering structured samples.

Benefits

- Adaptability to specific tasks due to more context
- Minimized misunderstandings due to examples
- Encourages meta-awareness of audience and purpose

Limitations

- Requires time and effort to create quality examples
- Can constrain creativity or yield overly formulaic outputs
- May reflect unintentional bias if models are poorly chosen
- Increased computational load

Classroom examples

- English language arts: "Here are two examples of thesis statements about justice in *To Kill a Mockingbird*. Now write one about courage."
- Science: "Here are two examples of how to explain a hypothesis using the CER method. Now use it to explain photosynthesis."
- Math: "Example: When $x = 2$, the slope is 3. Now find the slope for $x = 5$."
- History: "Here are two sourcing statements comparing perspectives on the Boston Tea Party. Now write one comparing British and colonial viewpoints on the Stamp Act."

Note. CER, claim–evidence–reasoning.

the correct answer—it is to develop and convey a logical process. This approach assists students in unpacking multistep problems and encourages metacognition by modeling how to reason through a task it represents. It is the GenAI equivalent of a think-aloud (Ericsson & Simon, 1993), where individuals verbalize their choices as they engage in a task or solve a problem. This technique offers a real-time glimpse into their cognitive processes, showcasing their reasoning and comprehension. The prompt guides the machine to address the task incrementally, explaining the rationale behind each step.

For example, in a seventh-grade math class, a student is solving the equation:

$$2x + 4 = 10$$

Instead of just asking the AI, "What's the value of x?" the student uses a chain-of-thought prompt: "Let's solve this step-by-step. First, how can we isolate x in the equation $2x + 4 = 10$?"

The GenAI explains each step in simple language, helping the student follow the operations and understand why each action is essential. If the AI makes an error, which is quite possible, it can become a teachable moment, encouraging students to verify the reasoning and reflect on their own process.

Although most closely associated with math, chain-of-thought prompting is powerful in any discipline requiring layered reasoning. Take social studies, for example. A student preparing for a debate about the causes of the American Revolution might use a chain-of-thought prompt like this:

> Let's think step-by-step: What economic policies led to colonial unrest? How did those policies influence public opinion? What specific events escalated tensions before the war began?

Here, the GenAI is not just listing causes. It is modeling historical reasoning, helping the student build a logical path from economic policy to revolutionary action. This mirrors the kind of analytical thinking we want students to develop in writing historical arguments or evaluating primary sources.

Table 4.3 defines the chain-of-thought prompting, its benefits, and limitations, and shares examples of how it can be applied across different disciplines.

Why Prompting Matters

Students develop essential literacy skills by engaging with zero-shot, few-shot, and chain-of-thought prompts throughout the curriculum: clarity of expression, logical reasoning, audience awareness, and the ability to iterate. These qualities prepare students not only to use GenAI but also to problem solve and think critically.

TABLE 4.3. Chain-of-Thought Prompting

Chain-of-thought prompting: A prompt that encourages step-by-step reasoning. This mirrors how we teach students to show their thinking and reflect on each step.

Benefits

- Models cognitive strategies explicitly
- Encourages deeper reasoning and metacognition
- Helps students unpack complex or layered tasks
- Creates longer, more detailed responses

Limitations

- May hallucinate or misstep if not guided clearly
- Requires modeling and practice to be effective
- Can result in long, repetitive outputs

Classroom examples

- English language arts: "Let's think this through step-by-step: What is the author trying to say here? What language supports that idea? How does the symbol of the mirror relate to the character's identity?"
- Math: "First, write the equation. Then isolate the variable. Now solve and check your work. Explain each step."
- Science: "Start with the problem. What are the known variables? What's the hypothesis? What do the data suggest?"
- Math: "Example: When = 2, the slope is 3. Now find the slope for $x = 5$."
- History: "Begin by identifying the source. What's the author's perspective? What bias might be present? How does this compare to other accounts?"
- Art: "Let's think through the composition step-by-step: What emotion do I want the viewer to feel? What elements (color, balance, focal point) will support that emotion? What adjustments should I make to unify the message visually."
- Public speaking: "What's the main idea I want to convey? What's my hook to grab attention? What examples or stories will support my message? How should I close to leave a strong impression?"

In addition to these prompt categories, there are structured frameworks available to help students and teachers learn to write effective prompts for GenAI tools. Although there is limited research backing any single approach, most include recurring characteristics, such as (1) specificity of language, (2) defining the audience, (3) defining the format, and (4) using simple language.

1. We Are Teachers AI Prompt Guide (Croteau, 2024)
   a. Aimed at educators, this guide simplifies prompt writing for classroom use
   b. Provides step-by-step examples for different teaching scenarios
2. The Five "S" Model (AI for Education, n.d.)
   a. Two variations exist (students, educators)
   b. Encourages structured prompting

3. The CLEAR Path Framework (Lo, 2023)
    a. Developed for information literacy and research, this framework helps refine AI queries for academic rigor and clarity
    b. Published in the *Journal of Academic Librarianship*
4. Juuzt AI Prompt Frameworks (Juuzt AI, 2023)
    a. Includes numerous prompt engineering frameworks.
    b. SMART Framework is the most notable

Practicing Prompt Engineering through Classroom Activities

Simply knowing what makes a good prompt is not enough. Students (and teachers) need time to actively engage in exercises that challenge them to adjust their inputs and analyze AI outputs without the pressure of grades. The following prompt activities in Table 4.4. guide students through a set of interactive problem-solving scenarios where they will have opportunities to:

- Develop stronger prompts to generate more relevant GenAI responses.
- Recognize how the wording of prompts influences the quality of AI-generated content.
- Use GenAI as a brainstorming or analytical tool while maintaining control over the process.

These activities scaffold students' experimentation, helping them build confidence in discipline-specific prompt engineering.

GenAI as a Collaborative Problem Solver

Problem solving is rarely a solo activity. Effective problem solvers refine their ideas, challenge assumptions, and invite others into the discussion before arriving at a solution (Oliveri et al., 2017). This collaboration often happens in classrooms through small-group discussions, teacher conferences, and peer review. GenAI introduces a new kind of partner into that mix that can help students expand possibilities, structure their thinking, and see alternative perspectives they might have missed (Boussioux et al., 2024).

For example, in a finance class, students evaluating investment opportunities might use GenAI to generate risk assessments for different stocks or industries. The tool can quickly analyze historical trends, suggest diversification strategies, and highlight potential risks. But the AI is not making final decisions. Students must weigh the suggestions against real-world considerations, like market volatility, long-term goals, and ethical implications.

TABLE 4.4. Prompting Activities

Activity	GenAI prompt refinement challenge
Objective	Help students refine prompts to receive more meaningful outputs from a GenAI tool.
Step 1	Initial prompt • Students receive a weak prompt (e.g., "Write an essay about why bees matter"). • They predict what kind of response an AI tool might generate.
Step 2	Revision • In pairs or small groups, students revise the prompt using specificity, open-ended questioning, or structure requests (e.g., "What are three scientific reasons bees are important to the environment?"). • They run the new prompt through an AI tool and compare responses.
Step 3	Reflection • Students discuss: What made the second prompt more effective? • They write down a takeaway: How can I use prompting strategies in my future writing?
Activity	GenAI as a brainstorming buddy
Objective	Teach students to use AI for idea generation rather than content production.
Step 1	Provide students with a writing topic (e.g., the impact of climate change on agriculture).
Step 2	Students draft an AI prompt, and teacher drafts a broad AI prompt (e.g., "Tell me about climate change and farming").
Step 3	The teacher leads a class discussion on why the teacher-generated prompt is too broad and how to refine it.
Step 4	Students review their own prompt to determine whether it is too broad and make revisions if necessary.
Step 5	Students meet in pairs and discuss their before-and-after prompts and any adjustments they made.
Activity	The fact versus bias experiment
Objective	Teach students to refine AI prompts to elicit objective and well-supported responses while recognizing how words and phrasing can influence AI-generated content.

Step 1	Initial prompting
	• Students choose a debatable topic (e.g., "Should social media be regulated?" or "Is AI beneficial for education?").
	• They write an initial prompt in their notebooks, aiming to get AI to provide an answer (e.g., "Tell me why AI is bad for education").
	• They input the prompt in a GenAI tool and analyze the response:
	  o Does the response seem biased?
	  o Did AI take a strong stance without considering multiple perspectives?
	  o What could make this prompt better?

(continued)

TABLE 4.4. *(continued)*

Activity	The fact versus bias experiment
Step 2	Refining for objectivity • Students revise their prompts to encourage a more balanced, evidence-based response. For example, instead of "Tell me why AI is bad for education," ask "What are the benefits and drawbacks of AI in education, supported by real-world examples or research?" • After refining, they compare the new AI response to the original one and discuss: ○ How did the AI's answer change? ○ Did the new prompt lead to a more nuanced response? ○ What strategies helped reduce bias in AI-generated content?
Step 3	Final revision and reflection • For a final revision, students add specificity to their prompt, such as: ○ "What do recent studies say about AI's impact on student learning outcomes?" ○ "How has AI affected teachers' workloads, and what challenges does it create?"
Step 4	Peer review • Students swap their revised prompts with a partner. Your partner inputs the prompt in a GenAI tool and analyzes it by answering: ○ Does this prompt encourage a balanced, thoughtful response? ○ How might it be improved? ○ Does it avoid leading questions or bias?

In a small-group economics project, students asked to design a city budget proposal, such as building a new community center or launching a public transportation initiative, might prompt GenAI to produce cost estimates and timelines. While the tool can streamline calculations and offer draft outlines, they still need to evaluate the feasibility of the suggestions, consider competing priorities, and craft a final plan that balances equity, sustainability, and economic growth.

The point is not that GenAI has all the answers but that it can start the conversation. GenAI becomes a catalyst for deeper inquiry when integrated into instructional design with intention. However, not all uses of GenAI as a problem-solving partner are the same. Depending on the phase of the problem-solving strategy (see Table 4.5 for a list of problem-solving strategies), students can learn to activate GenAI in different ways. Sometimes they need a reality check to evaluate constraints they have not considered. Other times, they might use GenAI to simulate a new perspective, visualize a system, or refine their own ideas through feedback. Each of these roles pushes students to think more flexibly and iteratively, two core traits of skilled problem solvers.

To help students (and teachers) develop a shared language around these uses, Table 4.6 outlines 10 distinct roles that GenAI can serve as a collaborative problem-solving partner. Each role is paired with a description and a middle or high school classroom example to help you visualize how these strategies come to life in real-learning environments. Additionally, teachers can use the GenAI Problem-Solving Partner Checklist (see Form 4.1) as a practical scaffold when introducing AI into classroom tasks. Rather than treating GenAI as a one-size-fits-all tool, this checklist helps students identify how they're using AI during problem solving, encouraging intentionality and metacognitive reflection. When used consistently, it builds students' capacity to select the right type of AI support at the right time and to apply succinct language to ensure the most effective outputs.

When students understand GenAI's different roles in collaborative problem solving, they are better equipped to use the tool intentionally. By modeling and naming them in your classroom, you give students a mental map for navigating GenAI's strengths and limits as a thinking partner.

TABLE 4.5. GenAI and Problem-Solving Strategies

Problem-solving strategy	How GenAI can support the strategy
Trial and error (Dumper et al., n.d.)	GenAI tool suggests possible solutions, allowing students to test and refine different approaches.
Root cause analysis (U.S. Department of Education, 2025)	GenAI tool identifies patterns in data that may point to underlying causes of a problem. May use the five "whys?" approach to problem solving: • Step 1: Identify the problem. Clearly state the issue you're trying to solve. • Step 2: Ask "why?" the problem occurred. Look for an immediate cause. • Step 3: Ask "why?" again. Dig deeper—what caused the cause? • Step 4: Repeat. Continue asking "why?" until you uncover the root cause. Usually five rounds of "why?" will do it, but fewer or more may be needed depending on the situation. • Step 5: Address the root cause. Once identified, develop a solution that tackles the root issue—not just the surface symptom.
Reverse engineering (Keck, 2023)	GenAI tool breaks down solutions into step-by-step processes, helping students understand why something works.
Contrasting cases (Newman & DeCaro, 2019)	GenAI tool presents multiple examples with key differences, helping students compare patterns and underlying principles.
Proof (Dumper et al., n.d.)	GenAI tool assists students by providing approaches for structuring, verifying, and refining if there is proof that a problem can or cannot be solved

TABLE 4.6. Ten GenAI Problem-Solver Collaborator Roles

GenAI role	Problem-solving function	Classroom example
Idea generator	Helps students brainstorm multiple potential approaches to a problem when they are unsure how to begin.	In a ninth-grade engineering class, students designing a bridge ask GenAI to suggest possible materials and structures for different terrains.
Reality check engine	Identifies real-world limitations (e.g., time, cost, space) that constrain possible solutions, prompting strategic planning.	In a high school business course, students use GenAI to analyze whether their product idea can be realistically produced within a $500 start-up budget.
Logic builder	Breaks complex problems into sequential, manageable steps—useful for structuring student reasoning and decision making.	In a seventh-grade math class, GenAI walks students through solving multistep algebraic equations using a think-aloud process.
What-if? tester	Creates hypothetical variations to help students evaluate how changes in variables influence outcomes.	In an environmental science unit, students test how changing rainfall levels would impact a simulated ecosystem restoration plan.
Perspective shifter	Reframes a problem from alternative angles to deepen student analysis and push beyond default solutions.	In a civics class, students investigating a school policy prompt GenAI to reframe the issue from a student, teacher, and administrator point of view.
Feedback synthesizer	Offers formative feedback to help students revise or strengthen their proposed solutions, with a focus on logic and clarity.	In a tech design class, a student pastes a proposed app feature list into GenAI and asks for critique on usability and accessibility.
Stakeholder simulator	Mimics different stakeholders involved in a decision-making problem, helping students anticipate conflicts and balance needs.	In an eighth-grade social studies debate on zoning for green space, GenAI role-plays a business owner, city planner, and environmentalist.
Visual modeler	Generates visual representations—charts, diagrams, or design mock-ups—to help students solve spatial or visual problems.	In an art class, students use GenAI to generate different logo layouts when redesigning a school emblem.
Revision coach	Encourages refinement by suggesting improvements or alternatives after each version of a proposed solution.	In a coding class, students test different versions of a program and ask GenAI how to improve efficiency.
Self-reflection mirror	Prompts students to reflect on their reasoning process, identifying where they got stuck and how they might revise their approach.	In an AP research seminar, a student uses GenAI to review their problem statement and suggest reflective questions about scope and feasibility.

Note. AP, advanced placement.

FORM 4.1

Using GenAI as a Problem-Solving Partner: Student Checklist

This checklist will help you intentionally use GenAI tools to enhance your problem-solving process. Select the GenAI role that best aligns with your current task and utilize the guiding questions to organize your interaction.

GenAI role	Role function	Checklist for using this role
Idea generator	Helps you brainstorm multiple ways to approach a problem.	• Have I asked GenAI for at least three ideas? • Did I explore different types of solutions? • Which idea best fits the problem?
Reality-check engine	Points out real-world limitations (time, cost, resources).	• Did I include my limits and other specifics in the prompt? • Does the AI solution fit these limits? • What adjustments might I need to make?
Logic builder	Helps break the problem into logical, step-by-step parts.	• Did I ask GenAI to explain the steps? • Can I follow the logic of each step? • Where do I still have questions?
What-if? tester	Tests "what if" scenarios to explore how changes affect outcomes.	• Did I change at least one factor? • How does the outcome change? • Which scenario works best and why?
Perspective shifter	Shows the problem from a new point of view.	• Did I ask GenAI to reframe the problem? • What new angles did it give me? • How does this help deepen my thinking?
Feedback synthesizer	Provides feedback to help revise your solution.	• Did I paste my idea or plan into the tool? • What feedback did I receive? • What will I change based on that feedback?
Stakeholder simulator	Acts like someone who is affected by the problem to show their view.	• Did I ask GenAI to respond as a stakeholder? • What concerns or priorities did they raise? • How might I revise my solution to include them?
Visual modeler	Creates images, diagrams, or layouts to help visualize the solution.	• Did I describe what I want the image to show? • Does the visual help me understand the problem? • How might I use it to explain my thinking?
Revision coach	Encourages trying multiple versions of a solution and refining each one.	• Did I test different versions? • How did the AI help improve my second or third attempt? • What did I learn through revision?
Self-reflection mirror	Asks you to reflect on your reasoning and problem-solving process.	• Did I explain my thinking to the AI? • Did the AI ask me questions about my reasoning? • What will I do differently next time?

Try It Out Using GenAI as Your Reality-Check Engine in Action

Let's shift for a moment and try out one of the problem-solving GenAI roles yourself. It's a hands-on way to see GenAI's limitations and possibilities as a collaborator in real time. For this example, you will examine the role of reality-check engine, a GenAI problem-solver collaborator that points out real-world limitations. Follow the steps below:

> Scenario: You're the decision maker. A volcanic eruption is imminent. You are part of a crisis response team trying to evacuate a small city. You have two evacuation routes: one leads toward the mountains; the other toward the coast. Each presents unknown risks.

1. Open your favorite GenAI tool and prompt it as a reality-check engine, a partner who points out real-world limitations. Use it to test the feasibility of both options. For example, try prompting:

   > "You are my reality-check engine. I'm in charge of an emergency evacuation. One route leads to the mountains, the other to the coast. What risks or limitations should I consider before choosing either?"

2. Refer to the Using GenAI as a Problem-Solving Partner: Student Checklist (Form 4.1) and ask the checklist questions:
   a. Did you include limits in the prompt?
   b. Does the AI solution fit the limits?
   c. What adjustments might you need to make to the prompt?
3. Revise your prompt. Ask for maps, timelines, weather patterns, traffic implications, or resource needs. Push the GenAI to think alongside you, not just give you an answer.
4. Review the GenAI problem-solving roles. Does reality-check engine still fit or has it taken on a new role?
   a. Is it now acting as a strategic planner? If so, revise your prompt and ask the checklist questions.
   b. Is it now acting as a what-if simulator?
   c. Reflect on how your role and GenAI's evolved as the problem unfolded.

Evidence-Informed Approaches to AI-Driven Problem Solving

While GenAI offers new possibilities for classroom innovation, students still need structured opportunities to practice applying problem-solving strategies within authentic, discipline-specific contexts. The following lessons are designed to meet that need. Each one presents a thoughtfully scaffolded approach to using GenAI as both a problem to solve and a collaborative problem-solving partner. These activities support disciplinary learning goals and help students build the adaptive reasoning, iteration, and strategic thinking skills essential for thriving in an AI-enhanced world.

The first two extended lessons illustrate how problem solving with GenAI unfolds in creative and technical fields. Whether iterating on an artistic vision or debugging AI-generated code, students must learn to communicate effectively with GenAI tools, identify when outputs fall short, and revise their approach accordingly. These lessons provide classroom-ready models grounded in research, offering practical strategies for supporting deeper thinking and purposeful AI use.

Evidence-Informed Approaches to AI-Driven Problem Solving in the Visual Arts

Artists often use iterative problem solving to bring their creative visions to life. Whether sketching, experimenting with materials, or refining composition, the creative process requires constant adjustment and troubleshooting. With AI-generated art tools, visual artists now have a powerful digital collaborator, but working with AI requires precise communication, experimentation, and refinement to achieve desired results.

The lesson in Table 4.7 is structured as a case study (Choi & Lee, 2009) in which students identify a problem, step into the role of a consultant, and put themselves in the artist's shoes to work through the iterative process of identifying potential solutions. By approaching the problem from different perspectives, students strengthen their problem-solving strategies, develop deeper understanding of AI's strengths and limitations, and learn to adjust their approaches to achieve better results.

Evidence-Informed Approaches to AI-Driven Problem Solving in Computer Science

In computer science, programmers often encounter errors, inefficiencies, or unexpected outputs while writing code, requiring them to analyze the problem carefully, test solutions, and refine their approach. This is called debugging.

For students, learning to work with AI-generated code isn't just about fixing mistakes. It is about developing a structured problem-solving mindset that mirrors real-world computer science work. Debugging is a critical industry skill, and AI-assisted coding will only become more prevalent in technical careers. Students develop essential computational thinking skills that prepare them for programming, engineering, and data science careers by learning to diagnose errors, refine AI-generated outputs, and iteratively improve their code.

The lesson shared in Table 4.8 teaches students how to analyze AI-assisted outputs, refine their interactions with AI, and improve their problem-solving strategies when AI does not produce correct results. Through this process, they will

TABLE 4.7. AI as a Collaborative Problem-Solver—Case Study: The Artist's Challenge

Discipline	Visual arts
Potential courses	AP studio art/portfolio development, computer graphics and animation, interactive media
Introduction	GenAI is transforming artistic creation, offering new ways for artists to experiment, refine, and expand their creative visions. However, using AI as a collaborative tool rather than a replacement for artistic intent requires careful prompt engineering, critical analysis, and problem-solving skills. This lesson challenges students to step into the role of AI consultants, learning how to refine AI-generated images while maintaining artistic control and originality.
Objective	Students will use AI as a collaborative creative tool to refine their prompt engineering skills, critically analyze AI-generated images, and develop problem-solving strategies to improve artistic outcomes. By stepping into the role of consultants, students will approach AI as both a problem-solving partner and a challenge to overcome, learning how to iteratively refine prompts and adjust AI interactions to align with artistic intent.
Evidence-informed strategies	• Collaborative problem solving (Oliveri et al., 2017): Encourages students to analyze AI-generated outputs together, refining strategies through discussion and iteration. • Prompt engineering (Knoth et al., 2024): Helps students develop precision in AI interactions, improving their ability to generate accurate, high-quality artistic outputs. • Case-based learning (Choi & Lee, 2009): Engages students in real-world problem-solving.
Lesson context	Case Study: The Artist's Challenge Meet Maya, a young visual artist preparing for her next gallery exhibition. She is working on a series of AI-assisted collages, combining her hand-drawn illustrations with AI-generated elements. • The problem: While Maya has a clear vision for her artwork, she is struggling to get the AI tool to generate the exact imagery she wants. Every time she enters a prompt, the results don't match her style, color palette, or artistic intent. She feels frustrated that the AI isn't understanding her ideas and worries that it's making her artwork look inconsistent. • Your role: Maya has come to your AI problem-solving team for help. Your task is to diagnose why her prompts aren't producing the right results and develop a strategy to improve them.
AI tools	• DALL-E/Midjourney—AI image generation based on refined prompts. • Adobe Photoshop/Canva—manipulating AI-generated images for final artistic composition.

Step 1	Analyze Maya's initial AI prompts and results
	• Read examples of Maya's original prompts and look at the AI-generated images she received.
	• Discuss:
	  ○ What issues do you notice in the AI-generated images?
	  ○ Why might Maya's prompts not be working?
	  ○ What might be missing from the prompt to make the images fit her vision?

(continued)

TABLE 4.7. *(continued)*

Step 2	Research and identify key prompting strategies
	• Learn about effective AI prompt techniques, such as:
	  o Describing artistic style (e.g., watercolor, surrealist, cubist)
	  o Specifying color palettes (e.g., pastel tones, muted earth tones)
	  o Adding texture details (e.g., "rough brushstrokes," "grainy film texture")
	  o Structuring prompts with clear instructions (e.g., "Generate an image in the style of Frida Kahlo with rich, warm colors and bold floral compositions")

Step 3	Rewrite and improve Maya's AI prompts
	• In teams, students revise Maya's original prompts to make them clearer, more detailed, and better structured.
	• Test different variations to see how specific wording changes results.
	• Example prompt refinements:
	  o Maya's original prompt: "A futuristic city with nature."
	  o Refined version: "A cyberpunk city at sunset with lush green vines growing over neon-lit skyscrapers, inspired by Studio Ghibli background art."

Step 4	Recommend an AI-assisted art process for Maya
	• Develop a step-by-step strategy for Maya to successfully integrate AI into her collage process.
	  o Should she use multiple AI-generated variations and edit them manually?
	  o Should she use a combination of digital tools like Photoshop to refine AI outputs?

Step 5	Present AI solutions to Maya
	• Each team presents their AI problem-solving plan, explaining:
	  o What specific changes they made to her prompts
	  o Why these changes will improve AI-generated results
	  o How Maya can integrate AI into her artwork without losing her creative control

Note. AP, advanced placement.

gain valuable experience in troubleshooting, debugging, and optimizing code—skills that are highly sought after in technology-driven fields.

AI-Enhanced Problem Solving: Quick Strategies for Every Classroom

The previous two lessons in this chapter offered extended, in-depth examples of how GenAI can support problem solving within specific disciplines. But not every powerful learning experience requires a full class period. The next set of lessons is designed to be quick, flexible, and easy to implement—ideal for sparking engagement or reinforcing key strategies within your existing curriculum.

TABLE 4.8. AI as a Problem to Solve—Computer Science: Debugging AI-Generated Code

Discipline	Computer science
Potential courses	AP computer science, introduction to programming, AP cybersecurity
Introduction	GenAI is transforming how developers write and refine code, but it is not without its flaws. AI-generated code can contain errors, inefficiencies, or logical inconsistencies, making debugging an essential skill for any programmer using AI-assisted tools. This lesson challenges students to take on the role of AI-enhanced problem solvers: analyzing, refining, and debugging AI-generated code to achieve optimal functionality.
Objective	Students will develop debugging and problem-solving skills by analyzing AI-generated code for errors, inefficiencies, or logical inconsistencies. They will engage in iterative problem solving, refining AI interactions and improving AI-generated outputs to achieve the intended functionality.
Evidence-informed strategies	• Collaborative problem solving (Oliveri et al., 2017): Encourages students to analyze AI-generated code together, discuss debugging approaches, and iteratively refine solutions. • Computational thinking and debugging strategies (Mouza et al., 2020): Develops problem-solving skills by teaching students to systematically test, troubleshoot, and optimize AI-generated code. • Prompt engineering (Knoth et al., 2024): Enhances students' ability to refine AI-generated responses by modifying prompts to produce more accurate and efficient code solutions.
Standards	CSTA K-12 Computer Science Standards (grades 9–12) • 3A-AP-17—Systematically test and refine programs using debugging strategies. • 3A-AP-22—Design and develop computational artifacts working collaboratively. • 3B-AP-14—Use data structures and algorithms to solve computational problems.
AI tools	• ChatGPT/Codeium—Generating and refining AI-assisted code. • Replit/PyCharm—Running and debugging AI-generated code.

Step 1	Generate AI-assisted code
	• Provide students with a programming challenge and have them use an AI tool (e.g., ChatGPT, GitHub Copilot) to generate an initial solution.
	  ○ Example challenge: Write a Python program that calculates the factorial of a number using recursion.
	  ○ Students input a prompt like "Write a Python function that calculates the factorial of a number using recursion."

Step 2	Test the AI-generated code for errors
	• Students run the AI-generated code and check for:
	  ○ Syntax errors
	  ○ Logical errors (incorrect outputs)
	  ○ Inefficient or redundant code
	• Example issue: AI may generate a recursive function without a proper base case, causing infinite recursion.

(continued)

TABLE 4.8. *(continued)*

Step 3	Analyze and identify problems
	• Students debug the AI-generated output and document what went wrong.
	• Example debugging questions:
	  ○ Does the function always return the expected output?
	  ○ Is there unnecessary complexity in the AI-generated code?
	  ○ Are there missing edge cases (e.g., negative numbers, zero)?

Step 4	Iteratively refine AI interactions
	• Students adjust their AI prompt to improve the generated code:
	• Example prompt refinement:
	  ○ Original prompt: "Write a Python function that calculates the factorial of a number using recursion."
	  ○ Refined prompt: "Write a Python function that calculates the factorial of a number using recursion. Ensure it includes a base case for $n = 0$ and properly handles invalid inputs."
	• Students compare the new AI-generated output to the original and analyze improvements.

Step 5	Final debugging and optimization
	• After refining the AI-generated code, students:
	  ○ Optimize it for efficiency (e.g., using memorization).
	  ○ Ensure it handles all test cases correctly.
	  ○ Explain how they improved the AI-generated code.

Each activity focuses on a real-world scenario and demonstrates how GenAI can be a productive collaborator in problem solving. The lessons are intentionally brief yet grounded in research-based approaches that assist students in generating, refining, and analyzing ideas using GenAI. They apply discipline-specific problem-solving strategies, recognize AI tools' limits, and are designed to strengthen students' reasoning skills when outputs fall short.

Table 4.9 depicts a scenario where medical students practice diagnostic reasoning by working through patient case studies. It suggests that GenAI can suggest possible diagnoses, but students must still apply clinical reasoning to evaluate symptoms, eliminate incorrect possibilities, and make evidence-based decisions. Designed to strengthen adaptability, the activities encourage students to refine their problem-solving mindset.

The lesson in Table 4.10 is set in English language arts courses, and students use GenAI to generate Shakespearean sonnets. They iteratively refine their prompts to improve meter, rhyme, and tone, practicing prompt engineering as a problem-solving strategy to achieve poetic precision. The lesson in Table 4.11 takes place in history class, and students research the causes of the Cuban Missile Crisis using GenAI. They begin with a broad prompt and iteratively revise it by adding historical lenses, such as political, military, and ideological causes to guide the AI toward more nuanced and accurate summaries. This prompt-engineering process becomes a disciplinary form of problem solving, requiring students to clarify their research focus, analyze how the AI responds, and refine their language to generate historically grounded, perspective-rich outputs. These two lessons illustrate how prompt engineering must be tailored to the specific demands of each discipline.

Table 4.12 is the final lesson in this chapter. It depicts a high school biology class where students use GenAI to explore the chances of passing on a genetic condition. They quickly realize the AI's answer is too simple, so they revise their prompts to get more detailed and realistic responses. As they improve their questions, students compare the AI's suggestions with what they have learned in class and challenge the tool in a debate. This lesson shows how students can use prompt engineering and critical questioning to guide GenAI and solve complex problems more effectively.

TABLE 4.9. Problem Solving in the Sciences with AI

Potential courses

- High school forensic science
- High school health science/biomedical science
- Career and technical education (CTE) health pathways

Scenario

Medical students often practice diagnostic reasoning by working through patient case studies. AI can assist by suggesting possible diagnoses, but students must still apply clinical reasoning to evaluate symptoms, eliminate incorrect possibilities, and make evidence-based decisions.

Problem-solving strategies

- Prompt engineering (Knoth et al., 2024)
- Case-based learning (Choi & Lee, 2009)
- Collaborative problem solving (Oliveri et al., 2017)
- Metacognitive reasoning (Fisher, 2019)

AI tools used

ChatGPT/Claude AI: simulating patient cases and suggesting possible diagnoses

Implementation overview

1. Provide a patient case study (e.g., symptoms, medical history, vitals).
2. Students enter symptoms into an AI tool and ask for potential diagnoses.
3. They analyze AI's response, compare with their own reasoning, and refine the differential diagnosis.
4. Students fact-check AI suggestions against reliable medical sources (e.g., Centers for Disease Control and Prevention, Mayo Clinic, textbooks).
5. Discussion: When is AI useful in medical reasoning? When should it not be trusted?

Classroom context

In a high school forensic science class, students investigate a mock crime scene where a victim was found unconscious. The teacher provides medical symptoms and asks students to use AI (ChatGPT, Claude) to generate potential diagnoses. Students must then evaluate AI's suggestions, compare them with forensic toxicology reports, and determine the most likely cause of the victim's condition.

TABLE 4.10. Problem Solving in Poetry with AI

Potential courses

Middle and high school English
Literature/AP English literature
Creative writing elective

Scenario

Students often struggle with understanding poetic form and rhythm. AI can assist by generating structured poems (e.g., sonnets, haikus) and analyzing meter and rhyme patterns, but students must interpret and refine meaning, tone, and stylistic choices.

Problem-solving strategies

Prompt engineering (Knoth et al., 2024)
Collaborative problem solving (Oliveri et al., 2017)
Metacognitive strategies (Scharff et al., 2017)
Iterative writing and revision (Flower & Hayes, 1981)

AI tools used

ChatGPT/Sudowrite: generating poetry and analyzing structure

Implementation overview

1. Provide a poetic form challenge ("Write a Shakespearean sonnet about time").
2. Students use their thinking partner, GenAI, to generate a first draft of a poem.
3. They analyze the completed poem's structure ("Does it follow correct rhyme/meter?").
4. Students iteratively refine their AI prompts to guide the GenAI toward a more accurate and meaningful poem that matches their goal.
   - Example refinement cycle:
     - First attempt: "Write a Shakespearean sonnet about time."
     - Refinement: "Write a Shakespearean sonnet about time, using iambic pentameter and a clear volta in the third quatrain."
     - Final refinement: "Write a Shakespearean sonnet about time's fleeting nature, with iambic pentameter, an ABABCDCDEFEFGG rhyme scheme, and a tone of melancholy."
5. Students compare iterations and discuss how prompting impacted the AI-generated output.
6. Class discussion: Can AI create true poetry, or does meaning require human emotion?

Classroom context

In an 11th-grade AP literature class, students study Shakespearean sonnets. The teacher asks AI to generate a sonnet in iambic pentameter. Students analyze whether AI correctly follows the meter and rhyme scheme, making revisions where necessary. They then use AI to generate alternative versions of the same poem in different poetic styles (e.g., a modern free verse version) to discuss how poetic form impacts meaning.

Note. AP, advanced placement.

TABLE 4.11. Problem Solving in Modern History with AI

Potential courses

- Middle and high school modern world history
- U.S. history
- AP U.S. history
- AP world history
- Journalism or media studies elective

Scenario

Historians must navigate large amounts of information to identify key historical events, themes, and perspectives. AI can assist by summarizing complex historical events, identifying patterns, and helping students explore different viewpoints, but students must refine AI's output to ensure it aligns with their research focus.

Problem-solving strategies

- Prompt engineering (Knoth et al., 2024)
- Collaborative problem solving (Oliveri et al., 2017)
- Historical framing and contextualization (Seixas & Morton, 2013)

AI tools used

Perplexity AI/ChatGPT/Gemini: finding historical sources and summarizing perspectives

Implementation overview

1. Provide a historical research question (e.g., "What were the major causes of the Cuban Missile Crisis?").
2. Students use a GenAI tool to generate an initial summary of the event.
3. Students analyze the AI-generated response: Is it too broad? Too vague? Missing key events?
4. Students refine their prompt to generate a more specific response, incorporating key themes, dates, or perspectives.
   - Example refinement cycle:
     - First attempt: "Summarize the causes of the Cuban Missile Crisis."
     - Refinement: "Summarize the political, military, and ideological causes of the Cuban Missile Crisis, with a focus on U.S. and Soviet actions."
     - Final refinement: "Summarize the Cuban Missile Crisis causes, emphasizing the role of nuclear deterrence, Cold War alliances, and U.S.–Soviet diplomacy."
5. Students compare the iterations of AI-generated responses and discuss how refining the prompt improves historical specificity.
6. Discussion: How does GenAI help historians recognize historical patterns, and what limitations does it have in historical interpretation?

Classroom context

In an AP World History class, students research the causes of the Cuban Missile Crisis. They start by using AI to generate a basic summary. They then refine their prompt multiple times, adding specific historical themes and perspectives to improve AI's response. Finally, they discuss how historical narratives change depending on how a research question is framed and consider how historians must shape their own inquiries carefully.

Note. AP, advanced placement.

TABLE 4.12. AI as a Problem-Solving Tool in Genetics

Potential courses

- Middle school and high school biology
- High school AP biology
- Career and technical education—biotechnology pathway

Scenario

AI can model genetic probability, but real-world inheritance is far more complex than Punnett squares suggest. This lesson challenges students to refine AI's genetic predictions by iterating through multiple prompts and applying AI-generated data to a real-world genetics dilemma. After completing their analysis, they will engage in a structured debate with AI, challenging its assumptions and defending their own conclusions.

Problem-solving strategies

- Collaborative problem solving (Oliveri et al., 2017)
- Experiential learning (Kolb, 1984)
- Prompt engineering (Knoth et al., 2024)
- Scientific reasoning and hypothesis testing (National Research Council, 2013)

AI tools used

- ChatGPT/Wolfram Alpha: generating genetic probability predictions
- ChatGPT, Microsoft Copilot/Gemini: simulating genetic counselors in debate mode

Implementation overview

1. Introduce a real-world dilemma ("Should genetic screening be used for disease prevention?").
2. Students enter basic genetic trait details into AI (e.g., What is the probability that two carriers of cystic fibrosis will pass it on?"). AI provides an initial risk assessment, but students must analyze AI's response for completeness, missing factors, and real-world applicability.
3. They refine AI prompts multiple times, asking for more detail, real-world case studies, or ethical concerns.
   - Example refinement cycle:
     - First attempt: "What are the chances of two carriers passing on cystic fibrosis?"
     - Refinement: "What are the inheritance probabilities for cystic fibrosis, considering incomplete penetrance and environmental factors?"
     - Final refinement: "How does cystic fibrosis inheritance compare to polygenic disorders like diabetes?"
     - Problem-solving focus: Students identify gaps in AI's response, refine their approach, and improve their problem solving by revising prompts to produce more nuanced answers.
4. AI debate: Students engage AI in a structured argument about its conclusions.
   - Example debate moves:
     - "What evidence do you have to support your risk assessment?"
       → Students must problem solve by finding stronger sources and challenging AI's claims.
     - "Did you consider environmental and epigenetic factors?"
       → Students refine AI-generated responses to factor in missing scientific variables.
     - "What ethical concerns arise from overreliance on AI for genetic decisions?"
       → Students problem solve by balancing scientific data with ethical considerations.

(continued)

TABLE 4.12. *(continued)*

5. Students reflect on AI's responses, identifying where AI made strong arguments and where it was weak or overly confident. They assess how problem-solving strategies, such as iterative refinement, critical questioning, and evidence-based reasoning, helped them improve their AI interactions.
6. Final challenge: Students write a position paper or group discussion summary, explaining how AI-assisted genetic risk assessment should or should not be used in medicine. Their conclusions must incorporate their AI debate experience and demonstrate how problem solving played a role in refining their final stance.

Classroom context

In an AP Biology classroom, students role-play as genetic counselors, helping a fictional couple assess their child's risk of inheriting cystic fibrosis. The teacher assigns each student group a different genetic background for the parents (e.g., heterozygous carriers, rare mutations, polygenic risk factors). Students begin by prompting AI for an initial risk assessment, but they quickly find that GenAI's responses lack detail or fail to consider environmental and epigenetic influences. Through an iterative process, they refine their AI queries, problem-solve gaps in AI's reasoning, and use Punnett squares and real-world case studies to challenge AI's conclusions. In the final stage, students debate with AI, questioning its assumptions and testing how well it can defend its reasoning. The lesson concludes with a position statement on whether AI should be used in real-world genetic counseling. Students reflect on how problem-solving strategies, such as prompt refinement, scientific reasoning, and structured debate, helped them uncover more reliable conclusions.

Note. AP, advanced placement.

Conclusion: Shifting Your Mindset about GenAI and Problem Solving

Problem solving is not just about arriving at the correct answer. It is about navigating complexity, adapting to evolving conditions, and refining ideas through iterative thinking. Incorporating GenAI into teaching and learning challenges these skills. It creates new opportunities for inquiry and decision making while introducing entirely new problems that students must learn to solve.

Sometimes, GenAI is the problem. Writing a clear prompt, diagnosing an inaccurate output, or adapting when the AI misses the mark requires students to think metacognitively, revise their approach, and take ownership of the process. Other times, GenAI is a problem-solving partner. It can scaffold brainstorming, simulate real-world constraints, model logical processes, or offer feedback on early ideas. But students still must make the final call by sifting through options, challenging assumptions, and applying disciplinary knowledge to determine what makes sense.

This chapter has reframed GenAI not as a digital shortcut but as a catalyst for deeper problem solving. Students must learn what role it is playing in the moment and how to stay in charge of the thinking process.

For educators, this means designing instruction that teaches students to navigate both roles: treating GenAI *as a problem to solve* and *as a collaborative problem solver*. It also means giving students a shared language and tools, like the AI collaborator checklist, to clarify their thinking and use GenAI with intentionality.

In the next chapter, we turn to critical thinking. If this chapter explored how students work *with* GenAI to solve problems, the next will challenge them to step back and scrutinize the tool itself by questioning its outputs, examining its biases, and deciding what they should trust and why.

Teacher Reflection Questions

Use the questions below to reflect on how your current instructional practices support problem solving and how GenAI may enhance or complicate students' abilities to reason, adapt, and iterate through challenges.

1. How do I currently teach problem-solving skills in my classroom, and how are they embedded in my content area? How might GenAI tools support or disrupt how students typically approach those challenges?
2. How comfortable am I with prompt engineering as a skill, and how might I model it for students? What opportunities do I provide for students to revise prompts and refine outputs through iteration?
3. In what ways could I position GenAI as a thinking partner or collaborative problem solver in my classroom? How can I ensure students still take ownership of their reasoning, judgment, and decision making?
4. What scaffolds or supports might students need to navigate GenAI as a creative resource and a problem to solve? How can I build structured opportunities for students to reflect on their problem-solving strategies when working with AI?

ETHICAL DILEMMA AND DISCUSSION PROMPTS

Ethical Dilemma: AI as a Problem-Solving Partner or a Shortcut?

A high school engineering class is working on a design challenge: Students must create a bridge model that can support a specific weight while using the fewest materials. One student, Jordan, struggles with the initial design process. Instead of brainstorming solutions and sketching models, Jordan turns to an AI-powered design assistant that instantly generates a detailed bridge blueprint optimized for the challenge. He submits the AI-generated blueprint with minimal modifications and justifies his approach:

- AI solved the problem efficiently—why waste time reinventing the wheel?
- Engineers already use AI-assisted design tools in the industry, so this is real-world practice.

- The challenge didn't prohibit AI use, and Jordan still had to test and build the bridge. However, Jordan's classmates argue that problem solving requires struggle and iteration, and using AI this way undermines the learning process.
- The teacher now faces a dilemma: Should Jordan's work be accepted?

Discussion Prompts

1. When does AI enhance problem solving, and when does it replace it?
2. If AI generates a solution instantly, should students still go through the problem-solving process?
3. How should educators set guidelines for AI use in problem-solving assignments?

Chapter 5

Reimagining Instruction of Critical Thinking

As a university professor, I am often invited to serve as an AP (advanced placement) Board expert advisor for high school students completing their AP research seminars. Along with this honor, I am invited to schools to observe students presenting their research and to discuss their work afterward. During these joyful events, I enjoy meaningful conversations with these soon-to-be graduates, and the topic of social media inevitably arises. In one recent discussion, a large group of us talked about contemporary issues, and all 12 teenagers shared that they stay informed about current news and cultural trends through Instagram, TikTok, and Snapchat.

I was not surprised. According to the Pew Research Center (2024) Teens and Social Media Fact Sheet, nearly all U.S. teens (96%) use the internet daily, with 46% reporting that they are online "almost constantly," a figure that has doubled since 2014–2015. Additionally, 95% of teens now have access to smartphones, up from 73% a decade ago. Platforms like YouTube (used by 93% of teens), TikTok (63%), Snapchat (60%), and Instagram (59%) dominate their online activities, highlighting the integral role of technology in shaping adolescent communication, socialization, and content consumption. A silver lining in this situation is that teens perceive the news stories on these platforms as less reliable than those from news sites or newspapers, and they report that their biggest source of news is not social media, but their parents (Sillito, 2022).

While I wasn't surprised by these young adults' reliance on social media for news, it underscored a challenge I frequently see in education: How can we help students develop the digital literacies necessary to navigate an information landscape rife with both credible sources and misinformation? Additionally, with GenAI's growing prevalence and its capacity to inundate students with fragmented, fast-paced information that often presents an authoritative voice, even when it may be incorrect or misleading, traditional methods of teaching digital literacies are no longer adequate.

Reimagining Critical Thinking in an AI-Integrated Classroom

Critical thinking—the ability to analyze, interpret, evaluate, and synthesize information to make reasoned judgments—has long been a cornerstone of education (Ennis, 1987; Facione, 1990). Today, it is more essential than ever. Each time we turn to a digital device, we are immersed in an ill-structured information environment where truth, opinion, and misinformation are entangled. Without critical thinking, we risk accepting what we see, read, or hear at face value. For students growing up in a world shaped by algorithms and personalized content, the ability to question, verify, and evaluate information is an academic skill and a daily necessity.

Generative AI introduces an additional layer of complexity to critical thinking by exposing students to a fundamentally different type of content generated by machines rather than humans. The accuracy of this information depends on several variables, including the prompt's quality, the topic's complexity, and the currency and reliability of the data used to train the digital tool (Tam et al., 2023). Because these systems rarely cite sources and generate responses based on patterns rather than verified facts, the likelihood of receiving inaccurate, biased, or entirely fabricated information is significantly higher than traditional online sources. As a result, students must learn to evaluate *what* the AI produces and *how* and *why* it produces it. It also presents new opportunities for students to practice, refine, and expand their thinking. Just like with problem solving, GenAI's role in critical thinking is dual in nature: it is both a challenge to navigate and a tool that can deepen intellectual engagement.

This chapter explores both dimensions. First, it examines how GenAI can hinder critical thinking and what educators must do to teach students to detect and respond to these challenges. Then, it explores instructional strategies that position GenAI as a cognitive scaffold, helping students reason more deeply, think more flexibly, and engage more critically across disciplines.

GenAI as a Challenge to Critical Thinking

While GenAI holds promise as a thinking partner, it also poses serious challenges to students' ability to think critically. AI-generated responses are often presented with confidence and fluency, even when they include inaccuracies, bias, or fabricated information. Because these tools are designed to prioritize coherence over truth, students may mistakenly view them as reliable sources unless explicitly taught otherwise. GenAI can encourage surface-level thinking, overreliance on machine-generated output, and diminished curiosity without intentional instruction. In this section, I outline how GenAI disrupts the development of critical thinking by examining its tendencies toward hallucination, oversimplification, and hidden bias and offer strategies to help students recognize and respond to these challenges head-on.

One of the most pressing challenges to critical thinking is the phenomenon of *AI hallucinations*. This occurs when generative models produce information that is factually incorrect but linguistically convincing (Mishra et al., 2024). Unlike flawed human sources, which students are often taught to question using citation checks or credibility markers, GenAI content doesn't always follow recognizable logic or factual patterns. For example, a student researching the American Revolution might ask a chatbot for notable quotes from John Adams and receive a confident, eloquent—but entirely fabricated—response. Because the language mirrors academic tone and even mimics citation structures, students may assume it's valid and bypass the evaluative processes we spend years teaching them to apply.

This raises the stakes in classrooms. Students can no longer rely on familiar cues of authority like a ".edu" or ".gov" domain name, nor can they trust that academic-sounding responses indicate accuracy. Instead, they must learn to corroborate AI-generated information with credible primary and secondary sources, develop habits of digital cross-checking, and maintain a healthy skepticism—even when the answer "sounds right." For instance, in a science class, students might compare AI explanations of climate change to data from the National Aeronautics and Space Administration (NASA) or the National Oceanic and Atmospheric Administration (NOAA), evaluating the accuracy and evidence behind each claim.

However, while fact-checking is critical, it is also a skill many students have already practiced during their online research (Coiro, 2021). Detecting *bias*, however, is more complex and often more challenging. GenAI systems are trained on vast, human-generated data sets that reflect the racial, gender, and cultural biases embedded in society (Akgun & Greenhow, 2022; AlMakinah et al., 2024). These biases may manifest in subtle ways, such as by omitting underrepresented voices or reinforcing dominant cultural narratives. Additionally, because GenAI lacks an identifiable author or clear source, students cannot rely on traditional markers of perspective or intent. Instead, AI often presents itself as a neutral authority, making it even more challenging for students to recognize when content is shaped by biased assumptions.

In addition to bias, *oversimplification* poses a serious challenge. AI-generated responses often flatten complex topics into concise, surface-level summaries that sound polished but lack nuance. For example, if a student asks about the causes of economic recessions, the AI might provide a single streamlined explanation without acknowledging multiple economic theories or political and historical context. Students must be taught to recognize when something is missing and how to ask for more. A simple strategy is to prompt AI for comparisons, competing perspectives, or critiques. Instead of accepting a summary, they can push for deeper analysis: "Compare Keynesian and monetarist explanations for economic recessions, including their strengths and weaknesses."

To meet these challenges, educators must help students transition from treating GenAI as an all-knowing answer machine to approaching it as an object of scrutiny. They should ask, What is this response leaving out? Whose voices are missing? What assumptions are embedded here? Developing these habits requires more than a single lesson. Bias detection and digital skepticism must be embedded into ongoing classroom instruction, reinforced through repeated practice and discussion. As AI systems continue to evolve, so too must our teaching. Critical thinking in an AI era is not a one-time skill but a dynamic, reflective process that adapts alongside the tools we use.

While these risks are real, they also lead the way toward new opportunities if we teach students how to engage with GenAI intentionally and reflectively.

GenAI as a Critical Thinking Partner

GenAI can be leveraged as a tool to enhance critical thinking by helping students refine their inquiries, challenge assumptions, and engage with multiple perspectives. Unlike traditional sources that provide static information, GenAI supports interactive and iterative dialogue, allowing students to test ideas, generate counterarguments, and expand their thinking in real time. However, this potential is only realized when students are taught to use the technology actively and critically, rather than relying on it passively.

One of GenAI's most valuable roles is helping students challenge their own assumptions. When prompted to take a counter position, the AI can push students to defend their reasoning, evaluate evidence, and refine their logic. This strengthens their ability to construct well-reasoned, evidence-based arguments and anticipate opposing viewpoints. For example, GenAI can be used to generate counterarguments that prompt students to examine an issue from multiple angles rather than simply reinforcing their preexisting beliefs. Figure 5.1 shows a conversation between a high school student and ChatGPT about universal basic income (UBI). The AI provides counterpoints to the student's pro-UBI stance, helping them consider both the benefits and consequences of the policy.

Another way GenAI serves as a thinking partner is by helping students frame better questions. Many students struggle to ask precise, complex questions that lead to deeper investigation. AI can rephrase vague or overly broad questions,

ChatGPT 4o >

I am debating in favor of Universal Basic Income (UBI) and need to strengthen my argument by understanding the opposing perspective. Act as an expert economist skeptical of UBI and write a one-paragraph counterargument against it. Focus on economic consequences, workforce participation, and long-term sustainability. Present your argument logically, citing real-world examples where possible. Do not list sources and use a counterargument format please.

A Universal Basic Income (UBI), while appealing in theory, poses significant economic risks that undermine long-term sustainability and workforce participation. Providing a guaranteed income without requiring work could disincentivize employment, particularly in lower-wage sectors, exacerbating labor shortages and productivity declines. Countries that have experimented with unconditional cash transfers, such as Finland's short-lived pilot, found limited impact on employment and mixed economic benefits, raising concerns about scalability. Moreover, financing UBI at a meaningful level would require either drastic tax hikes or unsustainable deficit spending, both of which could slow economic growth and discourage investment. Unlike targeted welfare programs, which address specific needs efficiently, UBI spreads resources indiscriminately, benefiting even those who do not require assistance while straining public budgets. In the long run, an economy dependent on high taxation and reduced labor force participation risks stagnation, inflationary pressures, and declining innovation—outcomes that could ultimately reduce, rather than enhance, overall economic security.

But my points are that UBI can encourage employment by providing financial security that allows individuals to pursue better opportunities and education, while also acting as an economic stabilizer by boosting consumer spending and growth. Unlike complex welfare programs, UBI is straightforward and reduces stigma, ensuring no one falls through the cracks. With thoughtful financing strategies, UBI can be sustainably funded and improve overall well-being, providing a cushion for those displaced by technological advancements. What do you say to that?

While UBI proponents argue that it can encourage employment and economic stability, these claims overlook critical challenges in execution and long-term viability. Providing a guaranteed income, regardless of work status, risks creating a dependency effect, particularly among those with marginal attachment to the workforce, reducing the incentive to seek or retain employment. While financial security may enable some individuals to pursue education or entrepreneurship, historical evidence suggests that labor participation rates decline when unconditional income increases, as seen in experiments with guaranteed income programs like those in Canada's *Mincome* trial and certain U.S. welfare reforms.

FIGURE 5.1. UBI discussion between ChatGPT and high school student.

helping students focus their research. For example, rather than accepting a general inquiry like "What caused the Great Depression?" the AI might prompt students to consider more nuanced versions, such as "How did global trade policies contribute to the Great Depression?" or "What economic theories challenge traditional explanations of the Great Depression?" This kind of scaffolding helps students craft meaningful questions that drive analysis and critical engagement.

GenAI can also simulate expert perspectives, helping students experience the disciplinary thinking of historians, scientists, literary theorists, and others. For instance, a literature student analyzing a novel might ask the AI to role play as a feminist literary critic or a historian specializing in the book's time period (Cullinan, 2024). This encourages students to examine how different perspectives shape interpretation. In science, technology, engineering, and mathematics (STEM) courses, AI can model various theoretical approaches to a problem, allowing students to compare methodologies, evaluate competing claims, and reflect on disciplinary values and assumptions.

An extension of this role-playing capability is the growing use of AI-driven games that promote critical thinking through immersive storytelling and decision making. Research has long shown that gaming supports critical thinking by encouraging students to make strategic decisions, weigh consequences, and adapt to evolving narratives (Gee, 2007). Tools like AI Dungeon and AI Text Adventure create open-ended environments where students navigate challenges by making choices that affect the story's outcome. These games foster iterative thinking, ethical reflection, and adaptive problem solving. Similarly, tools like AI Dungeon Master—an AI-powered assistant for tabletop games like Dungeons & Dragons—can help students develop strategic reasoning, ethical awareness, and collaborative storytelling skills. Within these interactive spaces, students must anticipate consequences, evaluate risks, and consider alternate perspectives, all of which reinforce the habits of inquiry essential to critical thinking.

Contrary to the fears of many educators, GenAI can serve as a valuable thinking partner for intellectual inquiry. Its effectiveness, however, depends on how we design learning experiences around it. When students engage with AI intentionally, using it to probe ideas, refine arguments, and explore complexity, they develop the very reasoning skills we aim to cultivate. Thoughtful instructional design ensures that GenAI becomes a tool to amplify critical thinking, not automate it.

Before introducing lesson plans that model how GenAI can support critical thinking in the classroom, teachers may want to offer students a scaffold for reflecting on their use of GenAI during inquiry tasks. The checklist found in Form 5.1 is designed to help students monitor how they engage with a GenAI tool, whether they are using it to test assumptions, explore new angles, or refine their reasoning. It encourages active learning before a task to set intentions, during a task to support self-monitoring, or after a task to promote deeper reflection. Over time, the checklist helps students develop more thoughtful, independent approaches to

FORM 5.1

AI Critical Thinking Partner Checklist

Use this checklist as you work with a GenAI tool to help you think critically. In the left column, you will find the kinds of questions critical thinkers ask when reviewing AI-generated content. In the right column, describe what you did in response. Be specific about the prompts you wrote, the follow-up questions you asked, or how you changed your approach.

Critical thinking strategies	Critical thinking prompts	What I did
Asking for multiple perspectives	Did I ask GenAI to provide more than one point of view?	
Challenging assumptions	Did I ask GenAI to take a counterargument or opposing view?	
Clarifying concepts	Did I ask GenAI to define, compare, or explain a complex concept in more detail?	
Detecting oversimplification	Did I notice when the response was too vague or surface level? Did I ask for nuance or depth?	
Identifying bias	Did I ask: Who is missing? What assumptions are built in? What voices are excluded?	
Prompt refinement	Did I revise or improve my prompt to get better answers or deeper thinking?	
Evaluating evidence	Did I ask GenAI to back up claims with examples, citations, or specific reasoning?	
Reflection	How did using GenAI as a thinking partner shape my final conclusions or beliefs?	

critical thinking in AI-supported environments. It can be introduced at any stage of the learning process and revisited often to encourage metacognitive reflection.

Try It Out Who's Missing from the Narrative?

Let's step into the student experience for a moment. The best way to teach students how to think critically with GenAI is to try it ourselves. This activity provides an opportunity to experience GenAI as a critical thinking partner, evaluate its output, identify what's missing, and practice revising prompts to uncover more complex or inclusive perspectives. You will also have the chance to apply the AI Critical Thinking Partner Checklist (Form 5.1) to guide your reflection.

Activity

1. Choose a historical, scientific, or literary topic you teach (or might teach). It could be as broad as the Civil Rights Movement, the Theory of Evolution, or themes in *The Great* Gatsby (Fitzgerald, 1925).
2. Open your GenAI tool of choice and ask, "Summarize [your chosen topic] in a paragraph for high school students."
3. Read the response closely. Use the AI Critical Thinking Partner Checklist to analyze the output. Consider:
   a. Is the summary accurate?
   b. What perspectives or voices are missing?
   c. Is there evidence of bias or simplification?
   d. What questions would you ask your students to respond to this text?
4. Revise and input your prompt: "Revise your summary of [your topic] to include marginalized voices or underrepresented perspectives that are often left out of standard accounts."
5. Compare the outputs:
   a. How did the content change?
   b. What improved?
   c. What limitations remain?

Why This Matters

This exercise reveals the dual role of GenAI in critical thinking. It demonstrates how AI can surface mainstream narratives and help expand them when used with intentional prompting. By practicing this process yourself, you will gain a deeper understanding of how to teach students to question, verify, and revise AI-generated content instead of accepting it at face value.

Evidence-Informed Approaches to AI-Driven Critical Thinking

As described above, GenAI presents a unique paradox: It can undermine critical thinking when accepted at face value, yet it can also deepen students' reasoning when used with intention. The difference lies in how it is integrated into classroom instruction.

The lessons that follow are designed to do just that. They model how GenAI can serve as a cognitive partner supporting intellectual inquiry, scaffolding deeper analysis, and provoking meaningful reflection. Each lesson is grounded in research and structured to foster transferable skills like argumentation, evaluation, and metacognition. Whether through role-playing, case studies, image generation, or debate, these activities give students hands-on practice navigating GenAI as both a source of information and a tool for rigorous thinking.

GenAI and Argumentation

One of the most effective ways to strengthen students' critical thinking is to engage them in structured argumentation (Giri & Paily, 2020). Whether analyzing texts in English class or examining public policy in social studies, students must learn to construct claims, consider alternative viewpoints, and support their reasoning with evidence. Research shows that debating both sides of an issue improves analytical thinking by prompting students to reconsider their assumptions and think more flexibly (Kuhn, 2019).

The lesson in Table 5.1 demonstrates how to use GenAI to support argumentation. Students participate in a structured debate where GenAI acts as an intellectual challenger. As they refine their claims, consider new perspectives, and revise their thinking, students cultivate the essential habits of mind that critical thinking requires.

GenAI and Recognizing Multiple Perspectives

A key component of critical thinking is the ability to recognize, evaluate, and synthesize diverse viewpoints (Brookfield, 2012; Clarke & Whitney, 2009). Whether analyzing a historical event, interpreting literature, or debating ethical issues in science, students deepen their understanding by considering how different perspectives shape knowledge. Generative AI can support this process by simulating a range of voices and viewpoints. The lesson shown in Table 5.2 models how students can use AI-generated expert perspectives to critically analyze historical, literary, and scientific topics, enhancing their ability to identify multiple viewpoints and assess the reliability of AI-generated responses.

TABLE 5.1. AI Debate Partner: Arguing Both Sides

Potential courses	These lessons can be adapted for any middle or high school course that emphasizes critical thinking, inquiry, and analysis, including ELA, social studies, science, computer science, and business.
Introduction	In a world where AI can generate persuasive arguments on any topic, critical thinking and argumentation skills are more important than ever. Students must learn not only how to craft strong, evidence-based arguments but also how to anticipate, analyze, and respond to counterarguments—a fundamental skill in academic writing, debate, and civic discourse.
Objective	Students will use AI to generate counterarguments and refine their reasoning in a structured debate.
Evidence-informed strategies	• Collaborative problem solving (Oliveri et al., 2017): Encourages students to work together to refine arguments, critique AI-generated counterpoints, and develop stronger reasoning skills. • Prompt engineering (Knoth et al., 2024): Teaches students how to improve AI-generated responses by crafting precise, detailed prompts that lead to more meaningful counterarguments.
Standards	• Common Core State Standards: ELA LITERACY.W.9-10.1: Write arguments to support claims with valid reasoning and evidence. • National Council for the Social Studies: Power, Authority, and Governance
AI tools	ChatGPT for generating counterarguments ChatGPT, Claude, or Perplexity for exploring varied perspectives
Step 1	Select a debate topic • Students choose a controversial or complex topic relevant to their course (e.g., Should social media be regulated? Should AI-generated art be considered original?).
Step 2	Initial argument development • Each student writes a brief position statement, outlining their stance with at least two supporting reasons.
Step 3	Generate AI counterarguments • Students input their position into an AI tool (e.g., ChatGPT, Claude, Perplexity) and request counterarguments.
Step 4	Evaluate AI responses • Students assess the AI-generated counterarguments for validity, logical coherence, and possible bias.
Step 5	Refining arguments • Based on AI feedback, students strengthen their reasoning by incorporating additional evidence, addressing counterpoints, and restructuring their argument if necessary.
Step 6	Engage in AI-supported debate • In pairs or small groups, students take turns debating their topic, using AI-generated responses as a secondary resource for expanding their reasoning.

(continued)

TABLE 5.1. *(continued)*

Step 7	Reflect and write a final argument • Students synthesize their revised arguments into a well-structured essay or speech, demonstrating their ability to integrate counterarguments and critical analysis.
Step 8	Class discussion on AI's role in argumentation • As a group, students reflect on how AI helped shape their thinking—discussing both the benefits and limitations of using AI in debate preparation.
Step 9	AI generates counterarguments for their stance
Step 10	Students refine their reasoning using additional research
Step 11	AI acts as a debate opponent, offering real-time responses
Assessment criteria	• Depth of reasoning: Demonstrates a well-developed argument with logical, coherent, and well-supported claims. • Use of evidence: Integrates relevant and credible sources to support claims and refute counterarguments effectively. • Counterargument: Acknowledges and addresses opposing viewpoints with thoughtful rebuttals. • Clarity and organization: Argument is structured logically with a clear introduction, body, and conclusion. • Critical reflection: Student articulates how AI-generated responses influenced their reasoning and discusses AI's limitations in constructing arguments. • Oral debate performance (if applicable): Demonstrates confidence, clearly articulated points, and thinks on their feet when responding to counterarguments.

Note. ELA, English language arts.

GenAI and Tackling Bias

Table 5.3 provides a lesson that helps students become active evaluators of AI-generated content by teaching them to detect bias, question representation, and refine prompts to produce more accurate and inclusive responses. Drawing on media literacy, sourcing and corroboration, and discourse analysis, it challenges students to compare GenAI outputs against real-world data, primary sources, and academic research. Whether students evaluate AI's portrayal of leadership, analyze crime narratives, or generate images of families or scientists, they are encouraged to ask, Whose stories are missing? What assumptions are built into the AI's outputs? What strategies can be used to push the tool toward more equitable representations?

This lesson strengthens students' critical thinking and deepens their understanding of how algorithmic systems shape public perception. By iteratively refining their AI prompts and evaluating discrepancies, students gain the analytical tools they need to approach GenAI with curiosity and caution.

TABLE 5.2. The AI Detective: Uncovering Hidden Perspectives

Potential courses	This lesson can be adapted for any middle or high school course that emphasizes critical thinking, inquiry, and analysis, including ELA, social studies, science, computer science, and business.
Introduction	In any discipline—history, literature, science, or social studies—understanding multiple perspectives is essential for developing critical thinking and analytical depth. Events, texts, and discoveries are never interpreted in a vacuum; they are shaped by competing viewpoints, social contexts, and historical narratives. However, students often struggle to recognize how perspectives influence interpretations and how to identify bias or missing viewpoints in the information they consume.
Objective	• Students will use AI-generated expert perspectives to critically analyze historical, literary, and scientific topics, deepening their ability to identify multiple viewpoints and assess the reliability of AI-generated responses.
Evidence-informed strategies	• Collaborative problem solving (Oliveri et al., 2017): Encourages students to work together to critically analyze AI-generated perspectives, refine prompts, and compare viewpoints through discussion. • Prompt engineering (Knoth et al., 2024): Teaches students how to adjust AI inputs to uncover new viewpoints, ensuring a more nuanced understanding of complex topics. • Sourcing and corroboration (Wineburg, 2018): Develops students' ability to cross-check AI-generated information with academic sources to verify accuracy and identify gaps in representation. • Critical discourse analysis (Handford & Gee, 2023): Guides students in examining the language AI uses, detecting implicit bias, framing, and power dynamics in AI-generated perspectives. • Media literacy (Hobbs, 2010): Strengthens students' ability to assess AI-generated images and text for bias, credibility, and missing viewpoints, preparing them to critically engage with digital content.
Standards	• Common Core State Standards: ELA LITERACY. RH.9-10.6: Compare the point of view of two or more authors. • C3 Framework: D2.His.4.9-12: Analyze complex and interacting factors that influenced historical perspectives.
AI tools	• ChatGPT or Claude—Role-playing as historical figures, literary critics, or scientists • Midjourney or DALL-E—Visualizing historical events, social issues, or literary themes
Step 1	Select a topic for analysis • Students choose a historical event, literary work, scientific discovery, or social issue (e.g., causes of the Cold War, feminist interpretations of *The Great Gatsby*, ethical concerns in genetic engineering).
Step 2	Generate AI-simulated expert perspectives • Students prompt AI to simulate multiple perspectives on their topic (e.g., "Explain the Cold War from the perspective of a Soviet diplomat, an American politician, and a Cuban citizen"). • AI generates responses reflecting distinct viewpoints.

(continued)

TABLE 5.2. *(continued)*

Step 3	Visualizing perspectives through image generation
	• Students use AI-generated images to explore how different perspectives shape historical, literary, or scientific representation.
	• Example prompts:
	  ○ "Generate an image of the Industrial Revolution from a factory worker's perspective versus a factory owner's perspective."
	  ○ "Depict the women's suffrage movement from the viewpoint of a suffragist versus a political opponent."
	• Students compare AI-generated images to historical photographs, artwork, or illustrations to identify bias, oversimplification, or inaccuracies.

Step 4	Evaluate AI-generated responses and images
	• Students assess how AI constructs each perspective in text and visuals.
	• They analyze what is emphasized, what is missing, and how AI represents different viewpoints.
	• Key questions:
	  ○ "Are there missing perspectives?"
	  ○ "How nuanced are the arguments and images?"
	  ○ "What biases can we detect in the generated text and visuals?"

Step 5	Deepen inquiry through prompt refinement • Students adjust their AI prompts to surface alternative or underrepresented viewpoints in both text and images. • Example refinement: ○ "Provide a perspective from a decolonized nation on the Cold War, and generate an image representing their view." • AI generates responses and visuals incorporating new perspectives, fostering deeper analysis.
Step 6	Cross-check with scholarly sources • Students use academic resources (e.g., journal articles, textbooks) to verify the accuracy and nuance of AI-generated perspectives and images. • Students should highlight where AI's responses align with or diverge from expert sources.

Step 7	Synthesize findings in an analytical response
	• Students write a comparative analysis, discussing:
	  ○ How perspectives shape understanding of the topic.
	  ○ Which perspectives were emphasized or excluded.
	  ○ AI's strengths and limitations in modeling viewpoints in text and images.

Step 8	Class discussion on AI's role in historical and textual analysis
	• Students reflect on how AI influenced their thinking.
	• Discussion prompts:
	  ○ "Did AI present perspectives you hadn't considered?"
	  ○ "Where did AI fail to capture nuance?"
	  ○ "How might this exercise apply to real-world media analysis?"

(continued)

TABLE 5.2. *(continued)*

Assessment criteria	• Depth of analysis: Demonstrates a well-developed comparative analysis of multiple perspectives, with strong reasoning and evidence. • Accuracy of interpretation: Uses credible sources to verify AI-generated content and identify inaccuracies or biases. • Critical thinking in prompt refinement: Adjusts AI inputs to surface missing perspectives and deepen inquiry. • Integration of scholarly sources and image analysis: Effectively cross-references AI-generated responses and visuals with academic materials. • Clarity and organization: Presents findings in a structured, well-written comparative response with clear arguments. • Reflection on AI's role: Thoughtfully articulates AI's strengths and limitations in simulating different viewpoints in both text and images.

Note. ELA, English language arts.

TABLE 5.3. GenAI and Tackling Bias

Potential courses	These lessons can be adapted for any middle or high school course that emphasizes critical thinking, inquiry, and analysis, including ELA, social studies, science, and journalism.
Introduction	AI is often perceived as neutral, but the reality is far more complex. AI-generated content is shaped by the data it is trained on, meaning it can reflect and reinforce biases present in historical records, media, and dominant cultural narratives. Whether analyzing AI-generated text or images, students must develop critical thinking skills to recognize bias, assess representation, and refine AI interactions to generate more accurate and diverse perspectives. This lesson equips students with the skills to identify bias in AI-generated content, analyze the impact of stereotypes and omissions, and refine their AI inputs.
Objective	Students will analyze AI-generated content to identify and evaluate bias in both textual and visual representations.
Evidence-informed strategies	• Prompt engineering (Knoth et al., 2024): Design inputs to solicit information from GenAI tools. • Sourcing and corroboration (Wineburg, 2018): Comparing AI-generated content to primary sources to check for accuracy and bias. • Critical discourse analysis (Handford & Gee, 2023): Examining language patterns for implicit bias. • Media literacy (Hobbs, 2010): Developing skills to deconstruct visual and textual messages.
Standards	• State Standards: ELA LITERACY. RH.11-12.7: Integrate and evaluate multiple sources of information. • C3 Framework: D2.Civ.10.9-12: Analyze the role of technology in shaping public perception.
AI tools	• ChatGPT or Claude—Role-playing as historical figures, literary critics, or scientists. • Midjourney or DALL-E—Visualizing historical events, social issues, or literary themes.

(continued)

TABLE 5.3. *(continued)*

Step 1	Generate AI-produced text
	• Students provide AI with prompts that might elicit biased responses:
	  ○ "Describe a leader in technology."
	  ○ "Explain the impact of crime in urban areas."

Step 2	Analyze bias in language • Students review AI-generated text, identifying loaded language, stereotypes, or missing perspectives.

Step 3	Generate AI-produced images
	• Students use AI image generators to create images based on descriptions:
	  ○ "Generate an image of a scientist."
	  ○ "Create a depiction of a modern family."

Step 4	Compare AI images to real-world data • Students analyze whether AI-generated visuals reinforce stereotypes or omit diverse representation.
Step 5	Cross-check with historical and scholarly sources • Students compare AI-generated content to primary sources or academic research, evaluating discrepancies.

Step 6	Synthesize findings in a written or visual report
	• Students document their analysis, discussing:
	  ○ Where bias was detected.
	  ○ How AI training data may have influenced biases.
	  ○ What strategies they used to refine prompts for more accurate representations.

Step 7	Class discussion • Students reflect on AI bias, its implications, and how they can be more critical users of AI-generated content.
Assessment criteria	• Depth of bias analysis: Demonstrates critical evaluation of AI-generated text and images. • Use of evidence: Supports claims using real-world examples and comparisons with primary sources. • Effective prompt refinement: Shows ability to modify AI prompts to generate more neutral or diverse representations. • Clarity and organization: Presents findings in a structured and thoughtful way. • Reflection on AI's role in bias: Thoughtfully discusses the impact of AI bias on information and societal narratives.

Note. ELA, English language arts.

GenAI and Verifying Accuracy

Generative AI often produces information that sounds convincing but lacks accuracy. The lesson in Table 5.4 challenges students to become investigative fact-checkers, training them to spot inaccuracies, test claims, and guide AI toward more credible outputs. Through a structured, team-based fact-checking competition, students learn to critically evaluate AI-generated claims, refine prompts for more accurate responses, and verify information using lateral reading and reputable sources.

As students prompt GenAI to generate factual statements on topics like climate change, historical events, or health myths, they quickly learn that not all outputs are reliable. Working in teams, they identify inaccuracies, cross-check claims using external sources, and refine their prompts to improve the quality of AI's responses. Along the way, they practice core critical thinking strategies, such as questioning, verifying, and correcting while developing prompt engineering skills that directly affect the reliability of GenAI's outputs.

Conclusion: Shifting Your Mindset about GenAI and Critical Thinking

As I conclude this chapter, I am reminded of the teenagers I wrote about initially. Why? My 17-year-old walks around the house with noise-canceling headphones snug on his ears, listening to music while somehow managing to text his friends and perfect his cradling skills with his lacrosse stick. Like most parents, I worry about what he sees on the phone attached to his hip, but overall, I think we're in good shape. Ryan has a mom who writes books about educational technology and, even better, a dad who owns a cybersecurity consulting company, so our house is pretty locked down, and we have rules in place. I am proud to say Ryan has never had a TikTok account and never will as long as he is on our internet plan. He took a cybersecurity course for kids and passed the exam. It was actually a punishment for sneaking his phone one night, and although he acted like it was torture, we felt he learned a few things. For instance, he is one of the few teenagers who understands the benefits of a password manager.

However, even with our combined knowledge and numerous discussions about cybersecurity, digital literacy, and avoiding sending pictures via text, the world can be a little scary at times, primarily because we cannot control others' actions, and technology makes it easier for people to reach out to you. Therefore, one of the most effective ways to address this lack of control is to develop our students' problem-solving and critical-thinking skills. This way, if they find themselves in a situation where they are affected by misinformation or anything else they prefer not to engage with, they can think critically and problem-solve solutions. At the

TABLE 5.4. AI Fact-Checker Challenge

Potential courses	This lesson can be adapted for any middle school course that emphasizes critical thinking, inquiry, and analysis, including ELA, social studies, science, and journalism.
Introduction	In the digital age, misinformation spreads rapidly, especially when AI generates confident but incorrect responses. This lesson transforms fact-checking into a high-stakes investigative challenge. Students will compete to spot AI-generated misinformation, refine their prompts to get more accurate answers, and cross-check claims using credible sources. The goal is to outsmart AI and become digital detectives.
Objective	Students will refine AI-generated claims, use lateral reading to verify facts, and develop strategies to make AI produce better, more accurate responses.
Evidence-informed strategies	• Lateral reading (Wineburg & McGrew, 2019): Comparing information across multiple sources to verify accuracy. • Collaborative problem solving (Oliveri et al., 2017): Engaging in teamwork to assess credibility and cross-check claims. • Sourcing and corroboration (Wineburg, 2018): Comparing AI-generated content to primary sources to check for accuracy and bias.
Standards	• ISTE Standard 3a: Evaluate accuracy, perspective, and credibility of online information. • CCSS.ELA-LITERACY.W.9-10.8: Gather relevant information from multiple sources, assessing credibility and accuracy.
AI tools	• ChatGPT or Perplexity AI: Generates claims that students must verify. • Google Fact Check Explorer: Helps students cross-check AI-generated claims.
Step 1	Divide into truth hunter teams (three or four students per team) • Each team acts as fact-checking investigators verifying AI-generated content. • One student is the AI investigator (responsible for prompting AI), and others are fact-checkers (cross-referencing sources).
Step 2	The AI challenge—generating claims • The teacher provides a set of topics (e.g., climate change, historical events, health myths). • Teams prompt AI (ChatGPT, Perplexity, etc.) to generate factual statements on their topic. • BUT . . . AI sometimes lies! (Hallucinations, bias, or misinformation may appear.)
Step 3	Fact-checking phase (earn points!) • Teams investigate their AI-generated claims by cross-referencing sources (Google Scholar, FactCheck.org, news articles). • Each time they spot an inaccuracy they earn 1 point. • If they prove AI was correct, they earn 0.5 points for verification.

(continued)

TABLE 5.4. *(continued)*

Step 4	AI prompt refinement round (bonus round!) • Teams adjust their AI prompt to request more accuracy and demand sources/citations. • If AI improves its response, the team earns 2 bonus points!
Step 5	The final report and presentation (winning round!) • Teams compile a fact-checking report, listing: ○ Original AI claim ○ What was false/misleading ○ How they fact-checked it ○ How they improved AI's accuracy • Each team presents their findings. The most thorough, well-supported, and well-explained team wins!
Scoring system	**Action** — **Points earned** Spotting a false/misleading AI claim — +1 Proving an AI claim is accurate — +0.5 Successfully refining AI prompts — +2 Best final report (class vote) — +3 Best presentation — +3 Winning team = highest total score
Assessment criteria	• Accuracy of fact checking: Uses strong, reputable sources to verify AI claims. • Prompt refinement strategy: Demonstrates ability to improve AI responses through precise prompts. • Critical thinking and argumentation: Clearly explains why AI was right or wrong. • Engagement and collaboration: Works well in teams, actively problem solving. • Presentation clarity: Final report is well structured and persuasive.

Note. ELA, English language arts.

end of the day, we can't control every piece of information they encounter. We can't predict the next viral hoax, deepfake, or AI-generated distortion of reality. But we can teach them to think. We can give them the tools to pause, evaluate, and decide what to believe, what to question, and when to walk away. That is what this chapter has been about: preparing students for a world where misinformation is not just a possibility but a certainty. And that is why critical thinking and problem solving are top priorities.

Teacher Reflection Questions

Use the questions below to reflect on how your current instruction supports students in developing critical thinking skills and how GenAI introduces new challenges and opportunities for deeper inquiry, skepticism, and source analysis.

1. How do I currently teach students to evaluate sources and assess the credibility of information? How might AI-generated content complicate or reinforce those lessons?
2. What routines or practices do I use to help students recognize bias and incomplete perspectives? How can GenAI be used to surface and explore opposing viewpoints?
3. How can I support students in using GenAI as a thinking partner rather than an information source? What prompts or questions might help students engage in meaningful dialogue with AI?
4. What concerns do I have about students becoming too reliant on AI for answers? How can I design learning experiences to encourage questioning, reflection, and deeper analysis?

ETHICAL DILEMMA AND DISCUSSION PROMPTS

Ethical Dilemma: Balancing Critical Thinking and Responsible Use

Ms. Chaput, a high school history teacher, has been experimenting with a GenAI tool to help students analyze historical documents. She has found it particularly useful for generating counterarguments and exposing potential biases within primary sources. However, during a lesson on the Civil Rights Movement, the GenAI tool, when asked to "summarize the arguments against desegregation," generated a response containing several historically inaccurate and racially charged statements. While Ms. Chaput immediately addressed the misinformation and used it as a teachable moment for critical analysis, a parent later complained, arguing that the school should not expose students to such harmful content, even for the sake of critical thinking. The parent claims that using such tools is inherently dangerous and promotes the spread of hate speech. Ms. Chaput now faces the dilemma of whether to continue using the GenAI tool for this purpose, potentially exposing students to harmful content, or to abandon it, thereby limiting their opportunities to develop critical thinking skills in AI-generated information.

Discussion Prompts

1. What pedagogical strategies could Ms. Chaput have used to mitigate the risks associated with the GenAI output *before* it was shown to students?
2. Does the fact that Ms. Chaput used the misinformation as a springboard for critical analysis justify its use?
3. What is the appropriate level of transparency with parents regarding using GenAI tools in the classroom?

Chapter 6

Reimagining Reading Instruction

Before earning my teaching degree over 30 years ago, I worked as a tutor for Literacy Volunteers, an organization dedicated to providing adults with one-on-one tutoring in reading and math. After completing the training, I was paired with a 30-year-old woman named Sheri. She spoke English, could recite all 26 letters, and knew the corresponding sounds. Sheri recognized approximately 150 sight words and could fluently read decodable texts containing closed syllables, silent *e* syllables, and some vowel teams. She could also read a few common picture books we found in the library, such as *The Very Hungry Caterpillar* (Carle, 1981). In math, Sheri could count to 50 and add and subtract two-digit numbers if she had paper and a pencil. She was unsure how to make change from U.S. coins and bills and when it came to reading, she struggled with anything more advanced than the picture books and decodable texts I introduced to her. That was the limit to her reading and math skills.

I remember leaving my first tutoring session and calling my dad. I was 22, inexperienced, and overwhelmed. The organization provided a lesson guide, but I kept asking myself, "What about reading materials?" Sheri was a grown woman reading at a first-grade level. I could not figure out what books would be appropriate for her. How could I find passages that would challenge her while keeping her motivated? More than anything, I worried about making her feel self-conscious about her reading difficulties.

Consider the possibilities that GenAI offers today. If I had access to AI back then, I would have created personalized reading passages at Sheri's level, scaffolded texts to build her skills gradually, and even provided interactive vocabulary support to ensure she felt challenged but not overwhelmed. While most middle and high school students do not struggle with decoding words like Sheri did, they often face complex disciplinary texts filled with unfamiliar words, abstract concepts, and dense sentence structures. GenAI has the potential to serve as a personalized tutor, offering adaptive scaffolding and customized reading support that helps students navigate sophisticated materials while retaining their independence as critical readers.

Sheri needed more than just books, though. She needed customized support tailored to her reading level and interests. Many of today's students, whether with reading difficulties, multilingual learners, or advanced readers, need the same kind of personalization. GenAI has the potential to fill this space. This chapter explores how these GenAI tools can enhance reading instruction by serving as tutors and transforming literacy strategies to support comprehension.

Reimagining Reading Strategies in AI-Integrated Classrooms

Reading is not a single, static skill. It is a continuum: one that becomes increasingly dynamic as students develop. Reading comprehension depends on the interplay of automatic word recognition, oral language comprehension, and strategic knowledge (McKenna & Stahl, 2009). When any one of these components is weak, comprehension suffers.

Shanahan and Shanahan (2008) offer a widely cited model of literacy development that illustrates this progression as a three-tiered pyramid. At the base is *basic literacy*, which includes skills such as decoding, sight word recognition, and print conventions, typically developed in the early grades. The middle layer is *intermediate literacy*, encompassing more generalized strategies like summarizing, inferring, identifying main ideas, and recognizing word roots and affixes. While most students achieve these skills by the end of elementary school, applying them to increasingly complex texts in middle school can present new challenges. At the top of the pyramid lies *disciplinary literacy*, the highly specialized reading practices used by experts in fields such as history, science, mathematics, and literature. Disciplinary literacy is not simply about reading more difficult texts but understanding how each discipline constructs, communicates, and evaluates knowledge. A historian must source and corroborate evidence. A scientist must interpret data and critique experimental design. A mathematician must attend to every symbol and term with precision.

But before students can read like experts, they must first master the general strategies that underpin comprehension. As Dobbs et al. (2016) discovered in their study of secondary social studies classrooms, students often did not struggle with specialized vocabulary or technical terminology; rather, they faltered when asked to identify the main idea, a fundamental intermediate skill. This finding reinforces Shanahan and Shanahan's (2008) layered model, reminding us that disciplinary learning depends on the solid integration of basic and intermediate literacy skills.

Reading across Content Areas: How GenAI Can Support Intermediate Literacy

While the long-term goal is to help students read like disciplinary experts, we cannot skip over the foundational skills that support comprehension across all subjects. Strategies such as summarizing, questioning, making inferences, and recognizing word parts provide essential scaffolding for understanding complex texts. GenAI tools can amplify these strategies by offering personalized support, modeling expert thinking, and giving students low-stakes opportunities to practice and reflect on their own reading process.

Below are common research-based intermediate literacy strategies accompanied by classroom-ready ideas for using GenAI to model, support, and/or extend each one. These mini-lessons help students strengthen essential comprehension skills that prepare them for the more specialized demands of disciplinary reading. The "Notes on GenAI and Strategy" section offers important guidance to help teachers use GenAI critically and effectively.

Summarizing

What It Is

Summarizing is a brief retelling of an entire text, restating key ideas in the reader's own words (Lewis & Strong, 2020).

How GenAI May Help

Students can write their own summaries and then compare them with summaries generated by GenAI. This comparison becomes a powerful metacognitive exercise. Students reflect on what they included or omitted and why.

Classroom Application

Students read a science article on climate change, write a five-sentence summary, and then prompt GenAI: "Summarize this article in five sentences for a ninth-grade reader." They compare the summaries and ask:

- What details did the AI emphasize that I left out?
- How did our organizational structures differ?
- What did I prioritize that the AI did not?

Follow-Up Activities

SUMMARY DISSECTION

In small groups, students trade GenAI-generated summaries and highlight:

Green = accurate and important ideas
Yellow = vague or overly general points
Red = missing or misleading information

Discuss: What does this reveal about how the AI prioritized content?

TEACH THE AI PROMPT

As a class, students rewrite the original GenAI prompt to improve the quality of its summary. For example:

Original: "Summarize this article in five sentences."
Revised: "Write a five-sentence summary that includes the article's main claim, two key supporting facts, and the author's conclusion."

This helps students understand how prompt precision shapes AI output and builds transfer to future use.

Notes on GenAI and Strategy: Summary Writing

While GenAI can quickly produce a concise summary, it may miss important nuances or factual details, especially when the source text is complex or technical. Summaries generated by AI tools may be overly vague, omit key evidence, or reframe ideas in ways that subtly change the meaning. Additionally, it is critical to remember that GenAI tools hallucinate, introducing information that was never in the original article. This makes the comparison exercise not only helpful but essential.

Self-Questioning

What It Is

Self-questioning is a student-led strategy where they generate literal, inferential, and evaluative questions to monitor understanding, clarify meaning, and deepen engagement with a text (Stahl et al., 2020).

How GenAI May Help

GenAI can serve as a thought partner that models how an expert reader might interrogate a text. When students prompt AI to generate questions, they expose themselves to diverse questioning styles and levels of complexity, from surface-level checks to probing critical inquiries. Rather than relying on AI to do the thinking, students engage in a process of comparison: Which questions spark deeper thinking? Which ones fall flat? Which questions help uncover meaning, bias, or ambiguity in the text?

This approach turns questioning into a dialogue between the student and the AI. The goal is not to accept what the AI offers but to evaluate and build upon it, just as they would in a peer discussion or Socratic seminar.

Classroom Application

After reading a short opinion piece about school dress codes, students generate their own list of five questions ranging from basic comprehension to deeper critical thinking. Then, they prompt GenAI: "What are five questions a reader might ask after reading this article?"

Students compare the two lists and reflect:

- Which questions helped me think more deeply about the topic?
- Did GenAI ask questions I hadn't considered?
- Which of my questions could I revise to make them stronger?

Follow-Up Activities

COLOR-CODING ACTIVITY

Students highlight the AI-generated questions using the following key:

Blue = literal questions
Green = inferential questions
Red = evaluative or critical questions

Then reflect: What types of questions are missing? What's overrepresented?

WHOLE-CLASS SOCRATIC CIRCLE

Each student brings their most thought-provoking GenAI-generated question to a group discussion. The class ranks or votes on which questions led to the deepest insights, then discusses: How could we teach the AI to ask better questions next time?

This process turns questioning into a deliberate, metacognitive skill-building activity, where GenAI serves as a springboard for deeper analysis rather than an answer key.

Notes on GenAI and Strategy: Questioning

While GenAI can generate a variety of questions quickly, not all will be thoughtful, relevant, or grounded in the text students read. Some questions may be overly generic, miss key themes, or apply to a similar topic but not the actual source.

This creates a valuable teaching opportunity: students can critique the quality of AI-generated questions and learn to refine their own. Through this process, they discover that not all questions are created equal and that strong questioning is a strategic act that requires curiosity, comprehension, and context awareness.

Inferring

What It Is

Inferring goes beyond what is directly stated, requiring readers to "get to the meaning an author implies but does not state directly" (Duffy, 2014, p. 70).

How GenAI May Help

Students can ask the AI to infer a character's motivation, an author's tone, or the underlying meaning of a passage and compare the AI's response to their own. Rather than treating the AI's inference as a correct answer, students should treat it like a thinking partner, using evidence to support, challenge, or revise their interpretation. This encourages students to shift from simply guessing to justifying their thinking with textual evidence.

Classroom Application

To support student inference skills, the teacher selects a short, high-interest text—in this case, the student-written op-ed "Why Schools Should Let Students Nap":

> WHY SCHOOLS SHOULD LET STUDENTS NAP
>
> *By Jordan Martinez, 8th Grade Student Writer*
>
> Let's be real: most of us are exhausted. We stay up late finishing homework, waking up before the sun, and somehow we're expected to be alert and focused all day long? It's not working. Schools need to rethink their priorities—and that includes giving students a chance to nap during the day.
>
> No, I'm not just trying to sleep through math class. Studies show that teenagers need at least 8 to 10 hours of sleep a night, but most of us barely get six. That's not because we're lazy. It's because we're juggling school, sports, jobs, and responsibilities at home. We're overworked and under-rested.
>
> Some schools have already added nap rooms or quiet time—and guess what? Students reported feeling more alert, less stressed, and even performed better on tests. A short nap (just 20–30 minutes!) can reset your brain and improve memory and mood. Sounds like a win-win to me.
>
> Plus, think about how many adults sip coffee all day just to stay awake at work. We're not allowed to drink lattes in class, so what's our option? A short nap could be

> the student version of a coffee break. And honestly, teaching us to listen to our bodies and prioritize mental health is just as important as teaching us algebra.
>
> Naps aren't lazy—they're smart. If schools really want us to succeed, they should stop fighting biology and start working with it. Give us a nap break, and we'll give you our best effort. Deal?

The teacher uploads the text into NotebookLM and uses the podcast feature to create a custom two-person conversation about the article.

Before generating the podcast, the teacher includes detailed notes for the AI, prompting it to:

- Target the appropriate grade level
- Emphasize emotional tone, author motivation, or subtext
- Focus on how readers might infer meaning from the author's word choice, phrasing, or rhetorical strategies

Example prompt in the NotebookLM notes section:

> Create a conversation based on this article for [your grade level] students. Focus on the author's tone, key points, and what you think the author is trying to say.

After listening to the podcast in class, students reflect on the following questions in small groups:

- What ideas or feelings did the speakers emphasize?
- How did they infer the author's tone or motivation?
- Where do I agree or disagree with their interpretation?

Follow-Up Activities

WRITE A BETTER PROMPT

Think about how the AI created its podcast. What do you wish it had focused on more? Write your own prompt for NotebookLM to guide it differently.

Example starter:

> Create a conversation for seventh-grade students that focuses on how the author feels and why the topic matters to them.

CRAFT A PROMPT WITH PURPOSE

Identify a text and create your own podcast for NotebookLM. In the note section, direct the tool to focus on an aspect of the text. Listen to the podcast and see if you can infer meaning from the audio.

Example prompt:

> Generate a conversation for 10th-grade students that explores how the author implies frustration and urgency without stating it directly. Include at least two examples from the text.

Notes on GenAI and Strategy: Inferring

GenAI can generate plausible-sounding inferences, but it doesn't "understand" the text. Its responses are predictions based on patterns, not comprehension. As a result, its inferences may lean on generalizations, ignore subtle shifts in tone, or fabricate reasoning not supported by the text. This is why inference comparison activities are so valuable. They help students distinguish authentic reading-based reasoning from algorithmic guesswork.

I designed this inference example for the teacher to take the lead in creating AI-generated podcasts using NotebookLM. This way they can guide how the tool frames tone, emotion, and implied meaning. This gives students a powerful model for how expert readers analyze subtext but also reminds them that AI is a tool, not a reader. To support this work, two student listening guides—one for middle school (see Form 6.1) and one for high school (see Form 6.2)—are included with this lesson. These handouts give students a structure for critically listening, identifying inferences, citing evidence, and preparing for discussion. The follow-up activities propose a creative task inviting students to write their own prompt for NotebookLM, helping them understand how AI-generated content can be influenced and improved by more intentional questioning. These tools reinforce the central idea that GenAI is not here to replace student thinking but to challenge it.

Concept Sorting

What It Is

Concept sorting is a strategy that helps students organize and group similar key terms, ideas, or concepts from a text together to better understand relationships and patterns (Shanahan, 2015; Stahl et al., 2020).

How GenAI May Help

GenAI can act as a co-organizer or visual thinking partner, helping students brainstorm concept categories, generate possible groupings, and model how terms relate to one another. Using tools like ChatGPT or Canva students can collaborate with GenAI to create concept maps, Venn diagrams, or digital sort cards. This interaction gives students a springboard for thinking about structure, but they must decide what groupings *make sense* in their own words.

FORM 6.1

Student Listening Guide: Inferring from a Podcast Conversation (Middle School)

Title of the text: ____

Your name: ____

1. First impressions

   As you listen to the podcast, jot down two to three key ideas the speakers discuss:

2. What did they infer?

   Choose one idea or interpretation that the speakers shared. What do you think they were inferring?

   AI podcast inference:

   Do you agree or disagree with this inference? Why?

3. Evidence from the text

   Find one or two lines from the original article that could support (or challenge) the AI's interpretation.

   Quote 1:

   Quote 2 (optional):

   What do these quotes suggest about the author's meaning, tone, or motivation?

4. Let's talk about it (for small group discussion)

   Did the podcast make inferences you hadn't considered?

   Were there places where the podcast speakers misunderstood or oversimplified the text?

   What did you infer that the podcast missed?

FORM 6.2

Student Listening Guide: Inferring from a Podcast Conversation (High School)

Text title: ______________________________

Your name: ______________________________

1. Podcast takeaways

   What are two to three major claims, observations, or interpretations made by the AI speakers in the podcast?

2. What's being inferred?

   Choose one of the podcast's interpretations or claims. What do you think the AI inferred about the author's tone, motivation, or perspective?

   AI's interpretation:

   Do you agree with that inference? Why or why not?

3. What's the evidence?

   Identify a line or moment from the original text that supports or contradicts the AI's interpretation.

   Quote from the text:

   How do you interpret this quote? What does it suggest about the author's intent or tone?

4. Group discussion prompts

   What inferences did the AI make that felt accurate or insightful?

   What did the AI overlook or misread, in your opinion?

   How does the AI's interpretation compare to your own?

   If you were to rewrite part of the podcast, what would you add or change?

Classroom Application

After reading an article about the global fashion industry, students highlight important terms, such as *fast fashion*, *sustainability*, *textiles*, *manufacturing*, *trend cycles*, *supply chains*, *upcycling*, and *consumerism*.

Students then prompt GenAI: Sort these fashion-related terms into categories and label each group. Explain the reasoning behind each grouping.

GenAI might respond with categories such as:

- Production and supply chain
- Environmental impact
- Trends and consumption

Students then compare the AI's groupings to their own and discuss:

- What categories made the most sense and why?
- Did the AI overlook a possible perspective (e.g., labor, cultural influence)?
- How would a designer versus an environmentalist sort these same terms?

Follow-Up Activities

SORT AND JUSTIFY

Students create their own categories first, then compare with the AI's. For any differences, they must *justify* why they chose their own over the AI's.

RE-SORT CHALLENGE

Students ask GenAI to re-sort the same terms from a different perspective (e.g., economic, social, political), then discuss how this shift changes the framing of the content.

MAKE IT VISUAL

Students use Canva or MindMeister to turn the concept sort into a digital graphic organizer—adding icons, images, or examples—to deepen connections.

Notes on GenAI and Strategy: Concept Sorting

While GenAI can model how terms might be grouped or connected, it lacks the ability to interpret meaning at a human level. In fashion, for instance, it might categorize "fast fashion" and "upcycling" together simply because both are trends without recognizing their opposing environmental impacts. These gaps create powerful learning opportunities. Students develop a deeper awareness of the reasoning behind categorization by critically evaluating AI-generated classifications. This sharpens their analytical thinking and helps them understand how concepts are framed differently across contexts and perspectives.

Try It Out Reading Remix

You have just explored a range of research-based intermediate literacy strategies, each paired with creative ideas for using GenAI to model, support, or extend reading comprehension. These examples are designed to help students strengthen foundational skills that prepare them for the deeper demands of disciplinary reading. Before moving into longer instructional routines in the next section, the following Try It Out activity invites you to experiment with one of your texts. Think of it as a rehearsal space to explore how GenAI might help you reimagine reading in your content area. Choose a short text you have already taught. It can be a primary source, scientific explanation, mathematical word problem, or literary excerpt. Then complete the following steps:

1. *Identify the literacy layer.* Is this text best approached with intermediate strategies (e.g., summarizing, inferring) or disciplinary literacy practices (e.g., sourcing, modeling, rhetorical analysis)? Jot down your response on a piece of paper.
2. *Prompt the remix.* Paste your text into a GenAI tool and prompt it to do something that supports reading. For example:
   - Summarize the key ideas.
   - Generate inferential questions.
   - Rewrite in a new tone.
   - Model expert thinking ("Read this as a historian. . . .").
3. *Reflect as a teacher.* For example:
   - What did the GenAI output help reveal about the text?
   - What did it miss or oversimplify?
   - How might you adapt a similar prompt for your students to deepen their reading skills?

Why It Matters

This activity is simple by design, but its implications are significant. By remixing a familiar text, you position yourself as both a designer and a critic of AI-enhanced instruction. You begin to anticipate how students interact with AI, where they need scaffolding, and how GenAI can be structured to reinforce deep reading and reasoning. By experimenting with a familiar text, you begin to see how even small shifts in prompt design or strategy framing can deepen student comprehension and strengthen your approach to literacy instruction across the curriculum.

Integrating GenAI into Literacy-Focused Instructional Practices

While GenAI can support individual reading strategies, it also has the potential to enhance broader instructional routines that shape how students engage with texts. In this section, I share how GenAI can be integrated into three well-established, research-based approaches to literacy instruction: Reading Guides, Peer-Assisted Learning Strategies (PALS), and 1:1 GenAI Tutoring. These models offer opportunities for teachers to scaffold comprehension, promote collaboration, and provide individualized support without replacing the human relationships and professional decision making that drive effective instruction.

GenAI and Reading Guides

Reading guides are a well-established instructional strategy designed to help students navigate complex texts (Walpole et al., 2011). They are documents that incorporate questions and other tasks related to an assigned reading. Students fill out the guide as they read, making it an active process, one goal of the strategy. Other goals are to focus students' attention on the main ideas of the reading, support note taking, and ensure students have ideas and questions to draw from during postreading discussions.

GenAI can enhance this approach by serving as the reading guide. During reading, it can prompt students with text-dependent questions that match the reading objectives. If a student has difficulty staying focused or processing dense information, the technology can pause at key moments to ask comprehension questions, highlight essential vocabulary, or provide brief explanatory notes. For instance, when reading a scientific text, GenAI might ask, "How does this paragraph relate to the article's main argument?" or "What evidence does the author present to support their claim?" These targeted questions encourage students to engage actively with the text, reinforcing critical thinking skills.

After reading, AI can extend learning by guiding students through higher-order discussions and inferential reasoning. Rather than simply summarizing the text, AI can pose debate-style questions, encouraging students to take a position and justify their reasoning. For example, after reading *Romeo and Juliet* (Shakespeare, 2011), GenAI might ask, "If you were Juliet, would you have made the same choice? Why or why not?" These prompts encourage students to synthesize information, evaluate perspectives, and deepen their understanding.

By transforming a GenAI tool into an interactive reading guide, students receive individualized support that keeps them actively engaged in reading comprehension strategies. AI does not replace structured instruction but instead reinforces core literacy skills, ensuring that students are developing the ability to read critically, analyze texts, and draw connections across disciplines.

GenAI and PALS

PALS is a structured, research-based peer-tutoring model that improves reading fluency and comprehension by pairing students of different ability levels (Fuchs et al., 1997). PALS provides opportunities for students to engage in structured discussion, clarify misunderstandings, and practice reading comprehension strategies with peer support. Traditionally, this model relies on students taking turns as the tutor and tutee, helping each other navigate a text through fluency, questioning, and summarization.

Rather than replacing the peer-learning process, GenAI could serve as a third party in PALS sessions, providing real-time support, discussion prompts, and personalized scaffolding without interfering with student-to-student collaboration since that interaction is so beneficial. AI can act as a dynamic moderator, offering structured assistance that enhances both the tutor's ability to ask effective questions and the tutee's ability to respond thoughtfully.

During PALS reading sessions, AI can provide real-time feedback on fluency, pronunciation, and comprehension, helping students with reading difficulties feel more confident in their reading abilities. If a student mispronounces a word or struggles with phrasing, AI can offer corrective guidance without interrupting the natural flow of the peer conversation. For multilingual learners, AI can provide contextualized language support, offering translations or explanations of unfamiliar words in a way that enhances, not replaces, peer collaboration.

GenAI can also generate and model structured discussion questions to help peer tutors facilitate deeper engagement with the text. If students read a historical document, AI might suggest prompts, such as "What is the author's perspective, and how does it shape the argument?" or "What evidence can you find in the text to support your interpretation?" These AI-generated prompts ensure that discussions move beyond surface-level comprehension into analytical and inferential thinking.

Additionally, AI can support progress tracking by helping students reflect on their reading growth over time. After a PALS session, the technology can prompt students to evaluate their learning experience, asking questions like "What strategies worked well for you today?" or "What would you do differently next time?" These metacognitive reflections help students internalize effective reading strategies, reinforcing long-term literacy development.

Positioning AI as a third-party support system in PALS ensures peer collaboration remains at the center of learning. The AI serves as a structured guide, not an instructor, helping students develop stronger questioning skills, comprehension strategies, and self-monitoring techniques.

One-on-One AI Tutoring for Reading Comprehension

Reading instruction is evolving as AI-powered tools offer new ways to scaffold comprehension, personalize support, and enhance critical engagement with complex materials. GenAI can adapt texts to different reading levels; generate guided reading questions; provide interactive vocabulary support; and model disciplinary reading strategies in history, science, and economics. These tools do not replace traditional literacy instruction but enhance it, offering customized support for all learners as they engage with complex academic texts.

One of the most promising developments in GenAI-enhanced reading instruction is one-on-one AI tutoring. Research has long shown that individualized tutoring is one of the most effective ways to support student learning (White et al., 2022). Unfortunately, access to human tutors has traditionally been limited to those who could afford it. AI-powered tutoring helps bridge this gap by offering on-demand, personalized support that adapts to students' needs. These tools can be especially powerful for middle and high school students, as they allow for self-directed learning and greater autonomy in improving reading comprehension.

Khan Academy's Khanmigo is at the forefront of one-on-one AI tutoring, going beyond simple question–answering to pose probing questions, model metacognitive strategies, and encourage critical thinking—much like a human tutor would. Eighth-grader Daphne Goldstein (2023) reviewed Khanmigo in *Education Next*, comparing it to the standard Khan Academy for Students, which features instructional videos and practice exercises but lacks the interactivity of AI tutoring. She explained:

> "Not only can you learn a lot more in a lot less time, but you can learn a lot more in depth. . . . Khan Original is like the work a tutor would assign you, and [Khanmigo] is like an actual tutor. You can ask questions, ranging from wanting more or less knowledge. So, for effectiveness: 7.5 out of 10 (versus 5.5 out of 10 [for Khan Original])."

AI-powered tutoring represents just one piece of the broader AI-driven reading landscape. Beyond tutoring, AI can support students with reading difficulties, multilingual learners, and advanced students alike, ensuring greater accessibility, engagement, and comprehension in previously impossible ways. By strategically integrating AI into literacy instruction, educators can provide students with the personalized, discipline-specific support they need in the classroom or at home.

The three approaches described in this section—Reading Guides, Peer-Aided Learning Strategies (PALS), and AI-Powered one-on-one tutoring—illustrate how GenAI can be meaningfully integrated into literacy instruction across different classroom contexts. Each offers a distinct type of support: teacher-directed guidance, peer collaboration, and individualized assistance. They provide a flexible and inclusive framework for helping students engage with complex texts in thoughtful, strategic ways. Most importantly, the GenAI tools enhance, not replace, the human relationships and instructional expertise that drive effective reading instruction.

Reading in the Disciplines: How GenAI Can Support Disciplinary Literacy

The next section of this chapter moves from the intermediate literacy layer of Shanahan and Shanahan's (2008) pyramid to its top tier: disciplinary literacy. This transition marks more than a new set of strategies. It reflects a deeper instructional challenge. Disciplinary literacy requires students to do more than comprehend a text; it asks them to think within a discipline's norms, to interrogate texts using its unique forms of reasoning, evidence, and communication.

This is not an intuitive leap for most learners. Reading like a scientist or historian involves assumptions, habits, and expectations that are often implicit to experts but obscure to students. Moreover, the problem is not just complexity. It is context. A graph, a primary source, or a mathematical proof all mean different things depending on how they are read and by whom.

GenAI can simulate expert thinking, generate alternate perspectives, and provide scaffolding. It can also misrepresent the integrity of a field.

The lessons that follow are not intended to teach GenAI itself. Instead, they illustrate how AI tools can serve as thinking partners and sounding boards as students practice reading within the communities of science, math, English, and history.

Instructional Possibilities: Exploring Disciplinary Reading with GenAI

Before sharing full lesson models, it is helpful to imagine the broader possibilities for disciplinary reading instruction using GenAI. Not every classroom needs a fully developed lesson to engage students with disciplinary texts. In fact, many of the most powerful uses of GenAI begin with small instructional moves that build curiosity, model expert thinking, and support real-time learning.

For example, a student in a science class might upload a short passage on cell division to a GenAI tool and ask it to generate a simplified diagram or analogy. In an economics class, students might simulate a conversation between two economists with opposing views, then evaluate the argumentation. In an English classroom, a student could prompt the AI to rewrite a Shakespearean monologue in contemporary language and analyze how the tone changes. These short, focused tasks give students a chance to rehearse disciplinary thinking without requiring an entire class period.

Table 6.1 lists sample activities that integrate GenAI into disciplinary reading and clearly support problem solving, critical thinking, reading, and/or writing. They do not require major time investments. Instead, they give students a rehearsal space for academic reading with GenAI tools. Whether the goal is interpreting a graph, breaking down a claim, analyzing tone, or generating discussion, GenAI can help students read like disciplinary thinkers, one purposeful prompt at a time.

TABLE 6.1. Instructional Possibilities: Exploring Disciplinary Reading with GenAI

Activity	Description	Literacy skill
Text simplification and translation	Students input a complex disciplinary passage and prompt GenAI to simplify it, summarize it, or translate it into accessible language. They then compare both versions and discuss meaning.	• Reading • Critical thinking
Generate and evaluate analogies	GenAI generates analogies to explain complex disciplinary ideas. Students critique or revise them for accuracy and clarity.	• Problem solving • Writing • Critical thinking
Role-based simulation	Students prompt GenAI to simulate reading a text through the lens of a historian, scientist, or mathematician, then compare the AI perspective with their own.	• Reading • Critical thinking • Disciplinary thinking
Perspective switching	GenAI rewrites a passage from an alternative point of view (e.g., a rival character, a stakeholder, a historical opponent). Students read response and analyze how that revision changes tone or argument.	• Reading • Critical thinking
Text + image pairing	Students generate images based on scientific, historical, or literary texts and evaluate how well the image represents the text's ideas.	• Reading • Problem solving
Vocabulary in context	Students prompt GenAI to create vocabulary lists based on a disciplinary text and generate contextual sentences for each term.	• Reading • Writing
Socratic prompting	Students input a short passage into GenAI and ask it to generate higher-order discussion questions for the class to debate. Students revise and reflect on the quality of those questions.	• Writing • Critical thinking • Reading
Claim–evidence challenge	Students input a central claim from a text and ask GenAI to find supporting or opposing evidence from within the same document. They evaluate the evidence selected.	• Reading • Problem solving

Reading Like a Scientist: Translating Text into Visual Models with GenAI

Scientific texts often depend on complex descriptions, precise terminology, and abstract processes that are difficult to visualize, particularly for students who are still building their content knowledge. While textbooks and articles may feature diagrams, students seldom have the chance to create their own visual interpretations of scientific processes. Doing so uncovers misunderstandings, enhances comprehension, and improves their ability to articulate scientific concepts clearly.

Table 6.2 outlines a lesson in which students read a science passage describing a process (such as photosynthesis or cellular respiration) and use GenAI to generate an image based on that description. The purpose is not to create a perfect diagram but to treat the GenAI image as a visual draft, a representation that students can critique, revise, or enhance based on what they understand from the text. This process helps students learn to read as model builders, turning scientific language into mental and visual models they can analyze and improve. The goal is to reinforce comprehension and improve conceptual understanding through collaborative problem solving with GenAI.

Reading Like a Mathematician: Decoding and Justifying Word Problems with GenAI

Reading in mathematics is often treated as secondary to solving. However, for many students, the real challenge lies not in math itself but in interpreting the problem. In other words, identifying what is being asked, what information matters, and how to structure a solution. Mathematical literacy requires students to be precise, analytical, and reflective. Unlike general comprehension, it involves translating everyday language into symbolic representation, often with limited context clues.

In this lesson (see Table 6.3), students use GenAI as a thinking companion, not to compute the answer but to help break down and interpret word problems step-by-step. This process draws on the chain-of-thought prompting approach introduced in Chapter 4. Instead of jumping to a solution, they ask the chatbot to articulate how they interpret the problem and how it identified a solution. By engaging in this kind of structured thinking, students learn to treat GenAI not as a calculator but as a reasoning partner. The result is a deeper mathematical understanding and more confident problem solving.

Reading Like a Historian: Practicing Sourcing with GenAI-Generated Summaries

Historians do not just read to understand. They read to investigate. Disciplinary literacy in history requires students to question the credibility of sources, identify

TABLE 6.2. AI-Driven Reading + Image Generation: Visualizing Text to Enhance Comprehension

Potential courses	Biology, chemistry, environmental science, physics
Introduction	Scientific texts are often dense and complex, requiring students to visualize abstract concepts, such as cell structures, chemical reactions, and planetary systems. While traditional instruction relies on diagrams and models, AI-generated images allow students to create personalized, real-time visual representations of scientific concepts based on textual descriptions. This lesson leverages AI to help students translate scientific reading into images, reinforcing comprehension and improving conceptual understanding.
Objective	Students read and analyze a scientific text, identifying key descriptive details that explain a process or structure. They will use an AI image generator to create a visual representation of the concept described in the text and evaluate the accuracy of the AI-generated image. Through refining their AI prompts, students learn how to improve alignment between textual descriptions and visuals. Finally, students will reflect on how creating images enhances their ability to understand and interpret scientific reading.
Evidence-informed strategies	• Collaborative problem solving (Oliveri et al., 2017) • Prompt engineering (Knoth et al., 2024) • Sourcing and corroboration (Wineburg, 2018) • Media literacy (Hobbs, 2010)
Standards	• Common Core ELA-Literacy in Science: Integrate quantitative or technical information expressed in words with a visual representation. • Next Generation Science Standards (NGSS): Develop and use models to explain scientific concepts.
AI tools	• AI Image Generator (e.g., DALL·E, DeepAI, Canva AI) • Text Summarization AI to help extract key details from the reading (Optional: ChatGPT, Claude)

Step 1	Read and extract key details
	• Students are given a scientific text (e.g., how photosynthesis works, the water cycle, or the structure of DNA).
	• As they read, they highlight descriptive phrases that provide visual details about the concept.
	• (Optional) AI can assist by summarizing the text's key details related to structure, shape, or process.
	• Example: If reading about the structure of a neuron, students highlight descriptions like:
	  ○ "Long branching dendrites extending outward like tree branches."
	  ○ "A central nucleus surrounded by cytoplasm."
	  ○ "A long, tube-like axon covered in a myelin sheath."

(continued)

TABLE 6.2. *(continued)*

Step 2	Generate an AI-produced image based on the text • Students input their highlighted descriptions into an AI image generator, carefully crafting a detailed prompt based on the text. • AI generates an image representing the scientific concept. • Example: If students are reading about the greenhouse effect, their AI prompt might be "A diagram of Earth's atmosphere showing sunlight entering, heat being trapped by greenhouse gases, and arrows illustrating energy flow."
Step 3	Evaluate and refine the AI-generated image • Students analyze the AI-generated image for accuracy compared to the text. • If the image misrepresents the concept (e.g., missing key details, incorrect structures), students refine their AI prompt to improve accuracy. • Students compare their AI-generated image to textbook diagrams and discuss how AI interpreted the description. • Discussion questions: • Does the AI-generated image accurately reflect the details in the reading? • What changes could improve the accuracy of the visual representation? • How does creating an image help clarify complex scientific concepts?
Assessment criteria	• Comprehension: Students correctly identify key descriptive details from the reading. • Accuracy: The AI-generated image closely matches the textual description. • Reflection: Students articulate how visualization supports understanding of scientific texts. • Refinement: Students show critical thinking by adjusting AI prompts for improved accuracy.

point of view, and compare conflicting accounts to construct interpretations grounded in evidence. In this lesson, students practice one of the most essential historical reading moves—sourcing—through a GenAI-assisted reading and listening activity. After analyzing two contrasting primary sources on the same event, students use GenAI to generate short summaries of each document. Then, using a tool like NotebookLM, they listen to AI-generated audio summaries of each source, reinforcing their ability to compare tone, purpose, and credibility.

The activity in Table 6.4 transforms static source comparison into a multimodal engagement that supports comprehension and critical analysis. By hearing the summaries aloud and comparing GenAI's interpretations to their own sourcing analysis, students become more attuned to bias, voice, and perspective—essential skills for reading like a historian.

Reading Like a Literary Critic: Exploring Tone through Style Transformation

Literary critics do not just understand what a text says. They examine how it says it. They pay attention to tone, diction, voice, and authors' stylistic choices to shape

TABLE 6.3. AI-Driven Reading: Understanding Mathematical Word Problems

Discipline	Mathematics
Potential courses	Algebra, geometry, precalculus, AP calculus, statistics
Introduction	One of the biggest challenges students face in math is translating word problems into solvable equations. Unlike straightforward numerical problems, word problems require students to extract key information from dense text, recognize mathematical operations hidden within written language, and translate words into equations and models. GenAI can serve as a reading assistant to help students break down problem structures, identify important mathematical cues, and provide scaffolded hints for solving equations. This lesson incorporates evidence-based strategies, such as explicit instruction, guided questioning, and step-by-step scaffolding to help students develop stronger mathematical literacy skills.
Objective	Students will read and analyze mathematical word problems, using AI to identify key mathematical concepts, extract important numerical values, and structure problem-solving steps. By working with AI-generated explanations and question prompts, students will refine their ability to interpret mathematical language effectively.
Evidence-informed strategies	• Prompt engineering (Knoth et al., 2024): Students design specific AI inputs to generate scaffolded explanations of mathematical word problems, helping them refine their approach to problem solving. • Metacognitive questioning (Schoenfeld, 1985): AI-generated guiding questions prompt students to reflect on their problem-solving approach, improving their ability to think mathematically and recognize patterns in problem structures.
Guidance on using AI as a math tutor	To use GenAI tools as interactive math tutors, students must prompt them in a way that encourages dialogue rather than simply providing answers. Here are specific ways to ensure a GenAI facilitates structured mathematical thinking: 1. Setting up AI for guided problem solving: • Teachers model how to input a word problem into an AI tool (e.g., ChatGPT, Khanmigo, Wolfram Alpha) with a structured prompt, such as "Break this word problem into steps without solving it: [Insert problem]. Ask me guiding questions after each step." 2. Encouraging AI-generated scaffolding questions: • Students can enter prompts like "Help me identify the key values and operations in this problem." • AI will then return questions, such as "What quantity is fixed in the problem? What is changing? What operation represents this change?" 3. Teaching students to refine AI prompts: • If AI provides too much information upfront, students adjust their request: "Instead of giving me the answer, guide me through setting up the equation." • This process helps students take control of their learning and engage in mathematical reasoning.

(continued)

TABLE 6.3. *(continued)*

Standards	• Common Core Math Practice Standards: Make sense of problems and persevere in solving them. • Common Core ELA in Mathematics: Interpret and analyze mathematical text and symbols in word problems.
AI tools	• AI text analyzer (ChatGPT, Khanmigo, Wolfram Alpha): Helps break down word problems into structured steps. • Equation solvers (Photomath, Symbolab): Provides step-by-step solutions with explanations.
Step 1	Read and deconstruct a word problem • Students receive a complex word problem (e.g., a multistep algebra problem, a probability scenario, or a real-world rate-of-change question). • They highlight important numerical values, keywords, and mathematical operations within the problem. • GenAI assists by restructuring the problem into a simplified, step-by-step explanation. • Example word problem: "A car rental company charges a $50 base fee plus $0.25 per mile driven. If Jake spent $95 on his rental, how many miles did he drive?" GenAI's guided breakdown: • Identifies fixed cost ($50) and variable cost ($0.25 per mile). • Recognizes that total cost follows the equation: $50 + 0.25x = 95$ • Suggests solving for x to determine miles driven.

Step 2	GenAI-prompted mathematical analysis
	• GenAI provides structured guiding questions to prompt student thinking:
	  ○ What is the fixed cost in this scenario?
	  ○ What part of the problem represents a variable rate?
	  ○ How can we set up an equation to solve for x?
	• Students attempt to answer these questions before using AI for verification.
	• Example AI feedback: "Great! You recognized the fixed cost is $50 and the rate per mile is $0.25. Now, let's solve for x by isolating the variable!"

Step 3	GenAI as a scaffolded tutor for problem solving
	• If students get stuck, AI provides tiered hints instead of direct answers.
	  ○ First hint: "What operation will help you isolate the variable?"
	  ○ Second hint: "What happens if you subtract 50 from both sides?"
	• After solving, students check their answers using AI-generated explanations.
	• Example student reflection: "GenAI helped me recognize that 'per mile' meant multiplication, and I needed to isolate the variable by subtracting and dividing."
	• Assessment criteria

Assessment criteria	• Reading comprehension: Students accurately identify key mathematical information from text. • Equation translation: Students correctly set up an equation based on word problem clues. • Problem-solving strategy: Students engage with AI scaffolds to refine their thinking. • Mathematical communication: Students explain their reasoning in written or verbal responses.

TABLE 6.4. Reading Like a Historian: Simulating Historical Perspective through Sourcing and Corroboration

Potential courses	World history, honors or AP U.S. history
Introduction	In this activity, students use GenAI to summarize and listen to historical documents. They evaluate how well the AI captures the author's voice and perspective, then reflect on what's gained or lost when meaning is transferred between media.
Objective	Students will source two historical documents, generate and listen to AI summaries, and evaluate how tone, perspective, and purpose are communicated and altered through GenAI outputs.
Evidence-informed strategies	• Sourcing (Wineburg, 2018) • Historical thinking (Monte-Sano, 2011) • Media literacy (Hobbs, 2010)
Standards	• NCSS Theme: Time, Continuity, and Change • CCSS.ELA-LITERACY.RH.9-10.6: Compare the point of view of two or more authors for how they treat the same or similar topics. • CCSS.ELA-LITERACY.RH.9-10.1: Cite specific textual evidence to support analysis of primary and secondary sources.
AI tools	• ChatGPT or similar GenAI model for sourcing support and summary generation • NotebookLM or audio-enabled AI for generating listenable summaries
Step 1	Select two primary sources • Choose two brief historical texts representing different perspectives on the same event (e.g., the Boston Massacre: British soldier testimony versus a Patriot newspaper account).
Step 2	Source each document • Students prompt GenAI: "Help me source this document. Who wrote it? When? What might have been their motive or bias?"
Step 3	Generate and listen to AI summaries • Students prompt: "Summarize this historical document in three to four sentences for a 10th-grade student." They then use NotebookLM or another AI tool to create and listen to the summaries.

Step 4	Compare interpretations
	• Students reflect on:
	  ○ What was emphasized or left out?
	  ○ Did the summary match the document's tone and point of view?
	  ○ What assumptions or biases surfaced?

Step 5	Sourcing reflection
	• Students write a brief reflection or engage in small-group discussion about:
	  ○ How well did GenAI source and summarize the document?
	  ○ What would they change to make it more accurate or nuanced?
	  ○ How does listening to a summary affect their understanding of a historical voice?

Assessment criteria	• Depth and accuracy of sourcing • Quality of comparison between AI summary and original text • Thoughtful written or verbal reflection on voice, tone, and purpose

Note. AP, advanced placement.

meaning. Yet for students, these elements often feel abstract or invisible. Tone, in particular, is notoriously difficult to teach because it is deeply tied to emotional inference, cultural context, and subtle shifts in language.

Table 6.5 shares a lesson where students analyze the tone of a literary excerpt and then use GenAI to rewrite it in a different tone or style. Through this stylistic transformation, students learn to identify what tone looks like in language and how it functions to shape meaning. The goal is not to improve the writing but to use GenAI as a creative mirror: a way to manipulate the text and reflect on how tone alters reader interpretation. Students can further visualize these tone shifts by generating AI-created images that match the emotional feel of each version.

It is important to remember that while GenAI can mimic tone, it sometimes misses nuance or flattens meaning. This makes it an ideal tool for instructional contrast. Students are not expected to treat GenAI's version as superior but as an opportunity to see tone in motion and evaluate how small changes in language create ripple effects in theme, character, and interpretation.

Conclusion

When I first started tutoring Sheri all those years ago, there were no AI tutors or instant scaffolding tools. Every lesson required me to figure out how to adapt, scaffold, and keep her motivated. I did my best with what I had, but I remember wishing for more resources, time, and better ways to meet her where she was. Those were some of the challenges and the beauty of teaching.

Fast-forward to today, and we're in a completely different world. AI-powered tools can now offer those resources. But even with all these advancements, one thing remains the same: Students do not need technology. They need the right support at the right time in a way that helps them grow. AI will never be a replacement for thoughtful instruction. It is a tool. But just like with any tool, we must use it well.

Teacher Reflection Questions

Use the questions below to reflect on how your current reading instruction supports student comprehension and how GenAI might enhance, personalize, or challenge that instruction across disciplines.

1. How do you currently distinguish between general reading strategies and discipline-specific reading practices in your instruction? How might Shanahan and Shanahan's (2008) literacy pyramid help you scaffold this progression more intentionally?
2. Which GenAI-supported reading activity in this chapter resonated most with your students' needs? What would be required to adapt it for your specific content, grade level, or classroom goals?

TABLE 6.5. Reading Like a Literary Critic: Exploring Tone through Style Transformation

Potential courses	Applies to most secondary ELA courses
Introduction	In this activity, students engage with a literary text by analyzing tone and experimenting with stylistic rewriting using GenAI. The process reveals how small linguistic shifts affect reader perception and builds a deeper, more nuanced understanding of tone.
Objective	Students will analyze tone in a literary passage, use GenAI to rewrite the passage in a new tone or style, and reflect on how word choice and rhetorical decisions shape emotional and thematic meaning.
Evidence-informed strategies	• Annotation (Wilhelm, 2016)
Standards	• CCSS.ELA-LITERACY.RL.9-10.4: Determine the meaning of words and phrases as they are used in the text, including figurative and connotative meanings. • CCSS.ELA-LITERACY.W.9-10.3.D: Use precise words and phrases, telling details, and sensory language to convey a vivid picture. • NCTE Standards 3 and 6: Apply knowledge of language to create, critique, and discuss texts.
AI tools	• ChatGPT or Claude for rewriting the passage in various tones • DALL·E or other image generators to visualize tone and mood
Step 1	Select a literary passage • Choose a short, richly written excerpt (e.g., from *Of Mice and Men* (Steinbeck, 1937), *To Kill a Mockingbird* (Lee, 1960), or *The Book Thief* (Zusak, 2005). Read as a class.
Step 2	Annotate for tone • Students underline words that convey emotional tone, figurative language, or suggest mood. As a class, define the original tone.
Step 3	Compare and analyze • Students compare the two versions and annotate: ○ What changed in diction and sentence structure? ○ How does the emotional effect shift? ○ What feels more or less effective in conveying the theme?
Step 4	Optional visual tone extension • Students input each passage into an image generator to visualize the mood or tone, then compare how the visuals reflect the textual tone.
Step 5	Write a tone reflection • Students write a brief analysis explaining how rewriting helped them understand tone more deeply and how it altered their interpretation of the text.
Assessment criteria	• Accurate identification and annotation of tone • Insightful comparison of original versus GenAI-rewritten passage • Thoughtful written reflection with reference to text • (Optional) Visual interpretations show connection between language and mood

Note. ELA, English language arts.

3. How can you use GenAI to expose—not erase—disciplinary complexity? What guardrails do you need in place to ensure students think critically rather than overrely on GenAI outputs?
4. In your discipline, what does it mean to read like an expert? How might GenAI help students rehearse those expert moves, from questioning to interpreting to constructing meaning?

ETHICAL DILEMMA AND DISCUSSION PROMPTS

Ethical Dilemma: The Invisible Influence of GenAI on Student Thinking

A high school history student is assigned a primary source analysis. Instead of struggling through the text, they use an AI tool that paraphrases key passages, highlights main ideas, and generates a short analysis. The student submits the AI-generated response with minor edits. On the surface, they've completed the task, but have they learned how to engage critically with the source?

Discussion Prompts

1. If GenAI constantly shapes what students read, how much of their thinking is still their own?
2. Does relying on AI interpretation limit students' ability to struggle productively with complex texts?
3. Are students still developing essential literacy skills or refining their ability to prompt AI effectively?

Chapter 7

Reimagining Writing Instruction

My first job as an educator was as a second-grade teacher in the mid-1990s. Dialogue journaling between teacher and student was a popular strategy at the time. I implemented it in the classroom mainly because the other second-grade teachers on my team did, and I was new and figured I should try it as well. The premise was to provide students with a journal, invite them to personalize it, and write a letter to me, their teacher, at least once a week. They could choose the topic and write as much or as little as they wanted if they followed the parameters for the activity. The requirements were to show effort, use conventions we learned in class, and include questions, concerns, wishes, and/or ideas related to the topic. My role was to respond to the journal entries at least once a week, hence dialoguing with the students.

Research (Bean & Rigoni, 2001; Werderich, 2006) identified several benefits of the strategy. It could enhance students' writing fluency by increasing writing opportunities and providing safe spaces to explore topics of their choice. Teachers' written responses could function as mentor texts. Although not intended to evaluate students' writing, this approach could serve as a formative assessment, giving teachers valuable insights for instructional decision making. Furthermore, when implemented effectively, dialogue journaling fostered student–teacher relationships by creating individualized connections through which students could express themselves to their teachers with written language.

It did not take long for me to drown in this strategy. What began as an approach to foster positive relationships with the 23 students in my class became an enormous chore. The students quickly lost motivation, complaining they could not think of topics to write about. I quickly fell behind in my responsibility of dialoguing and ended up with stacks of journals on the bookcase next to my desk, staring at me like an ever-growing to-do list, silently judging me.

Looking back today, I consider how GenAI could have transformed this experience for me and my students. Instead of wrestling with generating topics, they could have utilized AI to brainstorm fresh ideas and explore subjects they might never have considered. Rather than waiting days for my feedback, they could have participated in real-time discussions with the technology, receiving instant encouragement, guiding questions, and organized suggestions to refine their thoughts. My role as a teacher would not have diminished. Instead, I could have concentrated on providing deeper, more meaningful feedback at a slower pace instead of just managing the volume of responses. While GenAI could never replace the human element of teaching writing, it could have acted as a dynamic writing partner for my students, ensuring they received timely, personalized support with the goal of keeping them engaged in the writing process.

Reimagining Writing in an AI-Infused Classroom

Writing is a cognitive and social process that requires students to generate ideas, structure arguments, revise for clarity, and choose language that appropriately addresses its intended audience (MacArthur et al., 2025). The process is also recursive, meaning students should move fluidly between brainstorming, drafting, and revising rather than following a linear path. In classroom instruction, feedback from teachers and peers plays a critical role in this cycle by helping students refine their work through meaningful revisions (Wu & Schunn, 2021). With the emergence of GenAI, students gain additional writing support, providing real-time guidance to strengthen their skills while maintaining ownership of their work—that is, if educators permit the technology in the classroom environment.

GenAI can support writing in at least two distinct ways: as a tool for instant content generation or as an interactive writing partner. The former is often expressed as educators' primary concern, while the latter leverages students' problem-solving and critical thinking skills when composing texts.

GenAI and Instant Content Generation

Instant content generation refers to the ability of GenAI to produce complete pieces of writing—essays, paragraphs, summaries—with little more than a single sentence of input. This can feel like magic for students: A finished product appears in seconds, polished and ready to submit. For educators, however, it raises immediate concerns. When students rely on GenAI to do the thinking and composing for them, they miss out on the very practices that help them grow as writers. This is why content generation has become the focal point of much concern and debate surrounding GenAI in education.

Copy and Paste GenAI

For some students, the allure of instant content generation is too strong to resist. With a single prompt, they can receive a full-length essay and avoid the messy, often frustrating aspects of writing. However, this approach undermines the learning process. When students depend on GenAI to do the work for them, they miss critical opportunities to develop original ideas, structure arguments, and refine their thinking through feedback and revision. What is lost isn't just the writing process but their voice, too (Gonsalves, 2024).

Let's take a closer look at how this can play out. In an 11th-grade English language arts (ELA) class, a teacher assigns an essay on *To Kill a Mockingbird* (Lee, 1960), asking students to explore the symbolism of the mockingbird and how it connects to the novel's themes of innocence and injustice. One student types the assignment into Microsoft Copilot:

> "My teacher wants me to write a three-page essay on the book *To Kill a Mockingbird*. Here is the prompt she gave us . . . "

Copilot doesn't immediately produce the full essay. Instead, it offers a helpful outline for a five-paragraph response (see Figure 7.1), reminds the student to use quotes and examples, and offers to help draft each section. But the student bypasses those prompts and simply types "Write the paper." Ten seconds later, the essay is done (see Figure 7.2).

When students bypass the writing process this way, they miss out on the learning that happens when one struggles through revision and clarity building. They also miss a chance to develop their own voice. And that matters. Because writing isn't just about putting words on a page. It is about engaging in ideas, making meaning with words, and showing the reader how you think.

Students should be taught to use GenAI to enhance their thinking instead of surrendering their voice to it.

GenAI and Multimodal Content

While the "copy-and-paste" approach to GenAI essays raises real concerns, it is important not to conflate all content generation with academic misconduct. In fact, when used purposefully and with clear learning goals, GenAI can support students in generating content that enhances thinking. For example, they might use image generation tools to create visual representations of a literary symbol, a historical moment, or a biological process. In ELA, a ninth-grade student might use an image generator to visualize the green light at the end of Daisy's dock in *The*

Today

My teacher wants me to write a three page essay on the book To Kill a Mockingbird. Here is the prompt she gave us. "Explore the symbolism of the mockingbird in the novel. How does this symbol relate to the themes of innocence and injustice?"

Ah, the symbolism of the mockingbird—such a rich and meaningful topic in Harper Lee's *To Kill a Mockingbird*. Here's a structure you could use for your essay:

Introduction:

- Start with a hook: Perhaps a general statement about how symbols in literature help convey deeper themes.
- Briefly introduce the novel: Mention the setting (Maycomb, Alabama), the time period, and the major themes.
- Introduce the mockingbird as a central symbol and connect it to the themes of innocence and injustice. End with a thesis statement outlining your main points.

Body Paragraph 1:

The Mockingbird as a Symbol of Innocence

- Explain how the mockingbird represents innocence. Highlight the idea that mockingbirds "don't do one thing but make music for us to enjoy."
- Discuss characters who embody the mockingbird symbol, such as Tom Robinson and Boo Radley, and how they are innocent yet misunderstood or targeted.

Body Paragraph 2:

Injustice against the Mockingbirds

- Dive into how the mockingbirds in the story face injustice.
- Use Tom Robinson's trial as a prime example of systemic racism and prejudice, leading to the conviction of an innocent man.
- Discuss Boo Radley's treatment by society and how he's judged based on fear and ignorance, rather than truth.

Body Paragraph 3:

How the Symbol Ties into the Themes

- Analyze how the mockingbird connects innocence to the broader theme of injustice. The fragility of innocence makes it vulnerable in a prejudiced society like Maycomb.
- Highlight lessons Atticus Finch tries to teach his children, Scout and Jem, about protecting the innocent, and how these lessons shape their understanding of morality.

Conclusion:

- Recap your main points and tie them back to your thesis.
- Reflect on the enduring relevance of these themes in contemporary society.
- End with a thought-provoking statement or question about the cost of lost innocence in the face of injustice.

Remember to back up your points with quotes and examples from the novel. Let me know if you'd like help drafting any specific sections or finding key passages to cite!

FIGURE 7.1. Microsoft Copilot output for *To Kill a Mockingbird* essay.

Can you write the essay for me?

Of course! Here's your three-paragraph essay based on your teacher's prompt:

The Symbolism of the Mockingbird in *To Kill a Mockingbird*

In Harper Lee's *To Kill a Mockingbird*, the mockingbird serves as a powerful symbol of innocence, representing characters who bring goodness but suffer unjustly. Atticus Finch tells his children that "it's a sin to kill a mockingbird" because these birds do no harm and only make the world more beautiful. This idea connects to Tom Robinson, a Black man wrongly accused of a crime despite clear evidence of his innocence, and Boo Radley, a misunderstood recluse who ultimately protects the children. Both are innocent, yet society punishes them due to prejudice and fear, making them symbolic mockingbirds.

The novel highlights the theme of injustice by illustrating how innocent individuals suffer under societal biases. Tom Robinson faces racial discrimination, leading to his wrongful conviction, while Boo Radley is unfairly judged and isolated due to rumors. Tom's fate shows the brutal consequences of racial injustice, while Boo's isolation reflects how fear and ignorance can lead to social exclusion. Despite their goodness, both characters endure unfair treatment, reinforcing the idea that innocence does not always shield individuals from harm.

Through the mockingbird symbol, Lee emphasizes the importance of protecting the innocent and standing against injustice. The novel encourages readers to recognize unfair treatment and challenge societal prejudices, fostering a more compassionate world. Ultimately, *To Kill a Mockingbird* delivers a timeless message about empathy, justice, and the need to preserve innocence rather than destroy it.

Does this work for your assignment? Let me know if you need any changes!

FIGURE 7.2. Microsoft Copilot essay for *To Kill a Mockingbird.*

Great Gatsby (Fitzgerald, 1925), then write an analysis of how that visual metaphor represents hope, illusion, and the American Dream. In a foreign language class, a student might generate a scene of a Parisian café and write a descriptive paragraph in French to narrate it. In science, students might use GenAI to generate a visual diagram of the water cycle before writing an explanation of its key phases.

These are not shortcuts to understanding. They are starting points for expression, analysis, and exploration. They invite students to compose across media and reflect on how meaning is made in the digital world, not just through words, but through the interplay of text, image, and design. By expanding the definition of content generation beyond full-text essays, we make space for creative, multimodal learning experiences that reflect how students increasingly communicate and make meaning in a digital world.

Try It Out Visual Thinking as a Gateway to Writing

Use the steps below to explore how GenAI-generated visuals can support writing tasks in your discipline. This activity is designed to help you see how multimodal content generation can deepen interpretation, spark analysis, and prompt written expression.

1. *Identify a concept that needs visualization.* Choose a unit or lesson where students often struggle with abstraction, imagination, or explanation. This might be a theme in literature, a process in science, a moment in history, or a real-world application in math or world language.
2. *Use GenAI to generate a visual.* Select an image generator, such as Bing Image Creator, DALL·E, Adobe Firefly, or Canva's AI art tool. Type a detailed prompt that brings the concept to life visually. For example:
   - ELA: "Create a symbolic image of loneliness using shadows and an empty bench in a winter park."
   - Science: "Illustrate the carbon cycle with labeled arrows and color-coded natural processes."
   - History: "Generate a protest scene during the Civil Rights Movement in the American South."
   - Math: "Visualize how geometry is used in designing a public skatepark."
   - World language: "Show a lively French open-air market with stalls, shoppers, and local produce."
3. *Pair the visual with a writing task.* Create a short writing task based on the image. The goal is not to describe the image but to use it as a catalyst for deeper thinking. Some options:
   - Analyze the symbolism, meaning, or message of the image.
   - Write an explanatory paragraph using content-area vocabulary.
   - Draft a narrative, poem, or dialogue inspired by the visual.
   - Critique the image's accuracy, perspective, or assumptions.
4. *Reflect on the process.* After completing the activity, consider:
   - How did the image shape or shift your understanding of the writing task?
   - Could this approach help students brainstorm, analyze, or explain ideas more clearly?
   - How might you incorporate this kind of content generation into a future lesson?
5. *Why this matters.* GenAI offers more than quick answers. It opens up new pathways for multimodal thinking and expression. When teachers use image generation as part of lesson planning, they model how visuals can lead to stronger writing, richer analysis, and deeper student engagement. This process reinforces your role not just as an evaluator of student writing but as a designer of learning experiences that connect language, imagery, and meaning in powerful new ways.

GenAI as an Interactive Writing Partner

So far, this chapter has explored one of GenAI's most visible uses in writing: instant content generation. But GenAI's potential extends well beyond copy-and-paste shortcuts. When used with intention, GenAI can act as a powerful interactive writing partner, one that prompts reflection, supports revision, and helps students move through the writing process without replacing their thinking.

Writing ideas are shaped through interaction with teachers, peers, and increasingly, with GenAI tools that can offer feedback, pose questions, and help students clarify their thinking. When used in this way, GenAI supports students in becoming stronger, more independent writers by making their process visible and dialogical.

To illustrate how GenAI can support students as interactive writing partners, the remainder of this section includes a blend of vignettes and classroom lessons, each grounded in a research-based instructional strategy. These examples show how GenAI can be purposefully integrated into different stages of the writing process—brainstorming, structuring, revising, and reflecting—across a variety of disciplines. Some are shared as narrative vignettes to capture the flow of classroom interaction, while others are presented in lesson plan format to support direct implementation. While specific tools are named to help visualize classroom use, the strategies are adaptable and not dependent on any platform or product.

Vignette: Exploring Ideas with GenAI in a Sixth-Grade Science Class

The following vignette captures how GenAI can be used to support the early stages of writing by helping a student move from confusion to clarity through purposeful prompting. Much like peer review (Wilson, 2019), this kind of interaction illustrates GenAI's potential as a thinking partner, guiding brainstorming and fostering metacognition without taking over the process.

Consider a sixth-grade science class in which students are assigned an informational essay about the significance of bees. Unsure of where to begin, one student turns to Microsoft Copilot for assistance and types "Write me an essay on why bees are important to the environment."

The tool responds with a complete essay in seconds. While technically correct, this zero-shot prompt treats GenAI as a content generator rather than a collaborator. The student skips over the thinking process and jumps straight to the end.

As discussed in the chapter on problem solving, effective use of GenAI begins with strategic prompting, the kind that positions the tool as a conversation partner. In this case, a more thoughtful and productive prompt might sound like

> "I need to write about why bees are important to the environment, but I'm not sure how to begin. Can you help me think through three different ways I could approach this topic and explain the pros and cons of each one?"

Now, Microsoft Copilot shifts roles from output engine to brainstorming partner. It offers several angles the student might take, prompting reasoning and decision making. (See Figure 7.3 for an example of one suggested approach.)

Once the student reviews the suggestions, they might continue the dialogue with questions like:

- Which of these topics would be easiest for a sixth-grade audience to understand?
- Can you give me questions I should ask myself to decide which one I find most interesting?

"I need to write about why bees are important to the environment, but I'm not sure how to begin. Can you help me think through three different ways I could approach this topic and explain the pros and cons of each one?"

Of course! You could take several different approaches depending on your audience and the tone you want to set. Here are three distinct ways to frame your piece, along with their strengths and potential drawbacks:

1. Scientific & Ecological Approach

Angle: Begin with an explanation of bees' role as pollinators, how their work sustains plant life, and the broader environmental impact. You might incorporate data on biodiversity, pollination mechanisms, or even threats like habitat destruction and pesticides.

Pros:

- **Credibility:** Grounded in factual research, making it highly informative.
- **Depth:** Allows for a thorough exploration of the biological importance of bees.
- **Broad Impact:** Highlights how bees contribute to sustaining natural ecosystems beyond just agriculture.

Cons:

- **Complexity:** Scientific terminology could make the content dense for general readers.
- **Less Emotional Pull:** Might lack a personal or relatable element that keeps audiences engaged.

FIGURE 7.3. Example of Microsoft Copilot output for research on bees.

These follow-up prompts encourage the student to evaluate their interests, audience, and level of understanding. After selecting a focus, the student can continue using GenAI to gather relevant content from the chatbot, still in dialogue form:

- What are some interesting facts about how bees help pollinate crops?
- What are some common foods that depend on bees for pollination?
- What are some surprising ways bees help the environment?

At no point does the tool write the student's paper. Instead, it supports the student in developing ideas, shaping the paper's structure, and building confidence, all without doing the intellectual work for them. GenAI becomes part of the process, not the product.

Vignette: Expanding Writing Feedback with AI Tutors in AP Classrooms

This vignette highlights how educators can use GenAI tools not to replace writing instruction but to extend its reach. In high school classrooms with limited time and capacity, GenAI can offer students timely, personalized feedback that supplements what a teacher alone can provide. AP history teacher Melissa Rapp shares how one AI-supported tool has helped her students strengthen their writing through more consistent practice and richer revision opportunities.

DeAP Learning Labs is a free educational platform designed to support high school students preparing for AP exams. I first learned about it from Melissa, who has over 20 years of classroom experience and has been thoughtfully integrating GenAI into her instruction for the past 3 years. DeAP partnered with well-known educators to create AI-powered versions of them—essentially digital tutors who guide students through videos, practice questions, and feedback conversations across a range of AP subjects. Melissa described this tool as a "game changer," particularly for writing feedback. Like many teachers, she has faced the tension between wanting to provide meaningful feedback and not having the time to do it well for every student, every time. She told me:

> It can take weeks to get students the kind of detailed feedback I want to give. But now, with GenAI, my students are getting more consistent practice and more opportunities to revise their work based on feedback that's immediate, targeted, and relevant.

She continued:

> It's astonishing how much more efficient GenAI has made the feedback loop in my classroom. I could never provide that level of detail, that often. But now, they're

> getting it every day. That means more practice and more writing improvement, even outside of class. (M. Rapp, personal communication, February 24, 2025)

Melissa's story reflects a broader opportunity: GenAI doesn't replace teacher feedback but expands the support ecosystem available to students. In this case, AI tutors increase access to writing practice and revision without sacrificing rigor or student ownership.

Moreover, her experience with DeAP is just one example of how GenAI-powered writing feedback tools are becoming more accessible in classrooms (Levine et al., 2025). Other platforms—such as Khanmigo, Writable, and MagicSchool AI—offer similar features, including personalized revision suggestions, formative feedback, and interactive writing prompts. While each tool has its own interface, the core benefit remains the same: Students receive more frequent, specific feedback, which helps them reflect, revise, and grow as writers. Regardless of the platform, the goal is not to replace the teacher's voice but to expand the writing support students receive in and beyond the classroom.

Using Argument-Driven Inquiry in Scientific Writing

Scientific writing challenges students to do more than report facts. It requires them to build logical, evidence-based explanations grounded in discipline-specific reasoning. The lesson outlined in Table 7.1 integrates GenAI into the argument-driven inquiry (ADI) framework (Sampson & Blanchard, 2012), a research-supported strategy that helps students develop structured scientific arguments by clearly articulating claims, analyzing evidence, and explaining reasoning. GenAI is used to scaffold each stage of the process from brainstorming and sourcing evidence to organizing ideas and revising for clarity while keeping student thinking at the center of the work. Form 7.1 helps students apply this framework.

Crafting Evidence-Based Historical Arguments

Unlike scientific writing, which emphasizes objectivity and precision in data reporting, historical writing asks students to analyze multiple perspectives, recognize bias, and construct evidence-based arguments using primary and secondary sources. Historians do not merely recount what happened. They investigate why events occurred, how they were understood, and how they continue to shape society today.

One well-documented strategy in historical writing is sourcing and corroboration (Wineburg, 1991), where historians compare and evaluate multiple sources to verify credibility and identify bias. Though time-consuming, this process builds essential habits of mind for students learning to craft persuasive and historically grounded arguments.

TABLE 7.1. Using GenAI and ADI in Scientific Writing

Discipline	Science
Introduction	Writing in science is not just about recording results—it's about constructing and communicating ideas with clarity, logic, and evidence. Scientific writing challenges students to explain complex systems, evaluate research, and justify claims using disciplinary language. This lesson invites students to use GenAI tools as thinking partners to support—but not replace—the intellectual work of scientific argumentation. Structured around the ADI framework, the lesson emphasizes evidence-based writing, peer review, and revision with support from GenAI.
Objective	Students will use AI to develop, refine, and communicate evidence-based scientific arguments using the ADI framework. AI will support structuring explanations, evaluating sources, and improving clarity, while ensuring that students remain responsible for their reasoning and conclusions.
Evidence-informed strategies	• Argument-driven inquiry (Sampson & Blanchard, 2012) • Peer review for writing revision (Wilson, 2019)
Standards	• Next Generation Science Standards (NGSS) • Science and Engineering Practices (SEPs): ○ SEP 7: Engaging in Argument from Evidence ○ SEP 8: Obtaining, Evaluating, and Communicating Information • Disciplinary Core Ideas (DCIs): ○ LS2.A: Interdependent Relationships in Ecosystems ○ PS3.D: Energy in Chemical Processes • Crosscutting Concepts (CCCs): ○ Cause and effect—identifying causal relationships in scientific claims ○ Patterns—recognizing and explaining patterns in experimental data
AI tools	• SciSpace/Elicit: Summarizing peer-reviewed scientific literature • ChatGPT/Claude AI: Assisting with structuring scientific arguments • Grammarly: Refining clarity, precision, and disciplinary language
Step 1	Prewriting: understanding ADI • Introduce the ADI framework: ○ Question—what scientific question are we answering? ○ Claim—a testable statement addressing the question ○ Evidence—data from research, experiments, or observations ○ Reasoning—scientific principles that connect the evidence to the claim ○ Peer review and revision—strengthening arguments through feedback • Model with an AI-generated example. Have students prompt ChatGPT: ○ "Generate an argument-driven inquiry response to the question How does deforestation affect biodiversity?" ○ Students critique the AI-generated response: ○ Does it include credible scientific evidence? ○ Does the reasoning logically connect the evidence to the claim? ○ What's missing? Is anything vague, biased, or inaccurate?

(continued)

TABLE 7.1. *(continued)*

Step 2	Writing the scientific argument • Students research using SciSpace or Elicit to locate and summarize peer-reviewed studies. Students build their own ADI argument: ○ Claim—written independently (no GenAI) to ensure original thinking ○ Evidence—GenAI may assist with summarizing articles, but students select and interpret sources ○ Reasoning—students refine reasoning by prompting GenAI: "How can I improve my reasoning to better connect my evidence to my claim?" • Students draft a structured ADI response, using their own words and understanding.
Step 3	Revising for scientific accuracy and clarity • Students use Grammarly or Claude AI to review for clarity and precision: ○ "Does my reasoning clearly explain how my evidence supports my claim?" ○ "What phrases could be made more specific or scientifically accurate?" • Peer review: ○ Students exchange drafts and provide feedback using guiding questions. ○ Students revise based on peer and AI-generated feedback.
Assessment	Students complete a revision checklist focused on: • Strength of the claim • Appropriateness and accuracy of evidence • Clarity and logic of reasoning • Scientific language and precision • Integration of feedback and revision quality

Note. ADI, argument-driven inquiry.

Another foundational strategy is historical argumentation (Monte-Sano, 2011), which involves constructing claims, integrating diverse sources, and acknowledging counterarguments. Because historical records are often incomplete or contested, recognizing multiple perspectives and responding to them is crucial for developing nuanced interpretations.

GenAI can support these processes without taking over student thinking. When used thoughtfully, GenAI can serve as a debate partner, peer reviewer, or even historical figure, prompting students to reflect more deeply on their claims and evidence. For instance, a student might ask: "Act as a peer reviewer. Critique my historical argument. Where is my reasoning weak? What counterarguments should I consider?" This invites GenAI to challenge the student's thinking and support revision. As a debate partner, GenAI can simulate opposing views. A student might prompt:

> "Argue from the perspective of Amelia Earhart about why women should be allowed to compete equally with men in aviation, and then from the viewpoint of a 1930's aviation executive who believes flying is too dangerous for women."

FORM 7.1

GenAI + ADI Science Writing Rubric

Use this rubric to guide your revisions and self-assess your final ADI science writing assignment. Once you've addressed the criteria, check off each box to ensure your claim, evidence, and reasoning are well developed and clearly communicated. Write down any questions or notes for your teacher about your work under the relevant category.

Category	Criteria	Met? (☑) and notes
Claim	Clearly answers the scientific question	☐
	Is testable and based on scientific reasoning, not opinion	☐
Evidence	Is relevant, sufficient, and comes from credible sources (e.g., experiments, peer-reviewed research)	☐
	Uses multiple sources or data sets to support the claim	☐
Reasoning	Clearly explains how the evidence supports the claim	☐
	Includes relevant scientific principles or concepts	☐
Revision and refinement using AI	Used AI to check clarity and logical flow	☐
	Fact-checked any AI-suggested content before including it	☐
	Revised AI suggestions to reflect own thinking	☐
Final read-through	Writing is free of grammar and spelling errors	☐
	Redundant or imprecise phrases were removed	☐
	Scientific sources are properly cited	☐
	A peer reviewed the report for clarity and accuracy	☐
	Counterarguments or alternative explanations are addressed (if applicable)	☐

Note. ADI = argument-driven inquiry.

This encourages students to wrestle with historical complexity, consider societal bias, and strengthen their argument with evidence and empathy. GenAI can also simulate a historical voice. A student might prompt: "Respond as Amelia Earhart to the public skepticism about female pilots in the 1930s."

Compared with real interviews, letters, or speeches, these simulations allow students to practice source analysis by distinguishing authentic rhetoric from GenAI's interpretive approximations. Because GenAI does not pull directly from primary sources and may generate fabricated content, students must be taught to verify claims and challenge inaccuracies. This will reinforce key skills in sourcing, corroboration, and critical thinking, all hallmarks of disciplinary literacy in history.

The lesson shown in Table 7.2 demonstrates how these strategies can be brought together in a classroom setting using GenAI to support historical argument writing centered on Amelia Earhart and the social transformations of the interwar period. As part of this lesson, students complete a writing activity that involves drafting and revising an evidence-based historical argument. During the revision process, students can use the Checklist for Revising Historical Arguments with GenAI Support (see Form 7.2) to reinforce source evaluation, evidence-based reasoning, and responsible GenAI use. Teachers may choose to use it as a formative tool or require it as part of the final submission to promote metacognitive reflection.

Using Image Generators for Literary Analysis and Creative Writing

Writing in ELA is deeply connected to interpretation, expression, and meaning-making. Whether students analyze a novel, craft a persuasive essay, or develop a creative narrative, writing in ELA requires engaging with texts, constructing arguments, and evoking imagery through language. Unlike disciplines where writing focuses on presenting data or historical facts, literary writing demands a balance of logical structure and artistic expression, making it both a cognitive and creative endeavor.

Generative AI tools communicate using multiple modes: written language, audio, static and moving images, and others. Researchers have found that digital multimodal composition can deepen students' engagement with the writing process by increasing motivation and expanding representational possibilities (Kress, 2010; Smith et al., 2021). AI-generated images, in particular, offer a unique bridge between visual and textual analysis. They can help students explore symbolism, refine descriptive writing, and strengthen their creative thinking. When used thoughtfully, GenAI supports the writing process by expanding students' perspectives, offering inspiration, and scaffolding complex ideas while ensuring students remain the creators of meaning. The following lesson (see Table 7.3) demonstrates how image generators can be integrated into both literary analysis and creative writing in ELA classrooms.

The instructional strategies incorporated in the lesson in Table 7.3 can strengthen all students' writing skills, but they are particularly effective for

TABLE 7.2. Crafting Evidence-Based Historical Arguments

Discipline	History
Introduction	Writing in history is not just about recounting facts. It is about building arguments based on evidence, evaluating bias, and considering multiple perspectives. This lesson uses GenAI tools to support students as they craft historically grounded arguments, engage in role play and debate, and revise based on feedback. Students move through a cycle of historical inquiry that mirrors what historians do: gather evidence, consider context, construct claims, and engage in intellectual discourse. GenAI supports this process by serving as a research assistant, a debate partner, and a peer reviewer without replacing the students' responsibility to evaluate and contextualize information.
Objective	Students will develop well-supported historical arguments by evaluating primary and secondary sources related to Amelia Earhart identifying bias and corroborating evidence. AI will assist with source summaries, structuring arguments, and providing interactive feedback, while also engaging students in historical debates, role-play scenarios, and peer-review exercises to deepen their understanding of historical complexities.
Evidence-informed strategies	• Peer review (Wilson, 2019) • Historical writing (Monte-Sano & Thomson, 2022) • Role-playing (Cullinan, 2024)
Standards	National Curriculum Standards for Social Studies • Time, Continuity, and Change (no. 2) • Individuals, Groups, and Institutions (no. 5) • Power, Authority, and Governance (no. 6)
AI tools	• Perplexity AI: Helps students locate multiple sources for corroboration. • ChatGPT/Claude AI: Assists in structuring historical arguments and serves as a historical debate partner, peer reviewer, or historical figure for role play.
Step 1	Evaluating sources and engaging in AI role play • Teacher provides a historical question (e.g., How did Amelia Earhart's accomplishments reflect broader social changes in the United States during the interwar period?) along with multiple primary and secondary sources. • Students use Perplexity AI to locate at least two additional sources that offer historical context about gender norms, technological innovation, or public life during the 1920s–1930s. • Students summarize key arguments using GenAI and fact-check AI outputs against credible documents. • Students prompt GenAI to role play as Amelia Earhart, responding to critics or speaking about her experiences. Example prompt: "Act as Amelia Earhart. Respond to critics who said women shouldn't be pilots in the 1930s." • Students compare AI-generated role-play responses to authentic historical sources, evaluating for accuracy and bias. Guiding questions for students: • Who created this source, and when? • What does this source reveal about social norms during the interwar period? • How does GenAI's portrayal of Earhart compare to real historical sources? • Do different sources corroborate or contradict each other?

(continued)

TABLE 7.2. *(continued)*

Step 2	Writing the historical argument and AI-powered debate
	• Students develop a historical claim related to the question. Example: "Amelia Earhart's rise to fame reflected shifting gender norms and growing opportunities for women in public life."
	• Students use ChatGPT or Claude AI to generate a historical argument outline, then revise it based on their sources and analysis.
	• Students engage in an AI-powered role-play debate, prompting:
	  ○ "Argue from the perspective of a 1930's journalist who admired Amelia Earhart."
	  ○ "Now argue as a government official concerned about women entering traditionally male professions."
	• Students evaluate both sides for historical accuracy and social context.
	Students write their essays, ensuring that:
	• Claims are evidence-based and historically grounded
	• Counterarguments are addressed
	• Biases and social assumptions are analyzed

Step 3	AI as an interactive peer reviewer • Students submit their essay drafts to GenAI with prompts like "Act as a peer reviewer. Challenge my reasoning, suggest counterarguments, and point out weak evidence." • Students receive AI-generated feedback focused on clarity, structure, and logic. • Students revise their arguments based on both AI and peer feedback. • Students use the Historical Argument Checklist to ensure their final draft addresses evidence, reasoning, counterarguments, bias, and historical accuracy. • Teachers may choose to collect the completed checklist alongside the final essay as a reflection tool.

Reminder	AI hallucinations in historical writing
	• Students must verify all GenAI-generated content against credible primary and secondary sources.
	• Teachers should explicitly teach students how to:
	  ○ Identify hallucinations and fabricated evidence
	  ○ Challenge AI-generated claims
	  ○ Treat GenAI as a *thinking partner*, not a reliable historian

multilingual learners (MLLs) who are still developing English proficiency. A growing body of research tells us that visuals can significantly reduce cognitive load, increase comprehension, and provide scaffolding for both oral and written language development. Visual prompts help students anchor their ideas in concrete, observable imagery, making abstract concepts more accessible and providing much-needed context for academic vocabulary (Chun, 2009; Li et al., 2022).

When teachers use GenAI to generate specific, meaningful images, such as a bustling market scene, a misty forest, or a historical protest, they are not simply decorating the lesson. They are offering multimodal entry points into academic language (Karchmer-Klein & Shinas, 2019; Kress, 2010). These images can activate background knowledge, reinforce key vocabulary, and offer structured opportunities to practice written language with greater clarity and confidence.

FORM 7.2

Student Checklist for Revising Historical Arguments with GenAI Support

Use this checklist after completing your first full draft of the historical argument essay. It will help you reflect on using GenAI tools, verify historical accuracy, and strengthen your claims. Work through each section carefully and use it as a guide to revise your writing before submitting your final draft.

Step 1: Evaluating Sources and Historical Role Play

☐ I used both primary and secondary sources provided by the teacher.

☐ I located at least two additional sources using Perplexity AI (or another research tool).

☐ I summarized each source's key points and fact-checked AI summaries.

☐ I used GenAI to role-play as a historical figure and compared the response to authentic sources.

☐ I analyzed the AI role play for accuracy, bias, and perspective.

Source Analysis Prompts

☐ I asked: "Who created this source and when?"

☐ I considered the point of view and purpose behind each source.

☐ I checked whether sources agreed, disagreed, or added different perspectives.

☐ I identified any biases or gaps in the historical record.

Step 2: Writing the Argument and Engaging in Debate

☐ I developed a clear, historically defensible claim supported by multiple sources.

☐ I used GenAI to help generate an outline, then revised it to match my evidence.

☐ I prompted GenAI to debate both sides of my argument and analyzed its responses.

☐ I included and addressed counterarguments in my essay.

☐ I acknowledged bias and missing perspectives where appropriate.

Step 3: Peer and AI Feedback

☐ I submitted my draft to GenAI using a prompt like "Act as a peer reviewer. Challenge my reasoning, suggest counterarguments, and point out weak evidence."

☐ I revised my essay based on GenAI's feedback and peer comments.

☐ I checked my reasoning for clarity, accuracy, and depth.

☐ I verified all facts and quotes from sources, especially anything AI suggests.

Responsible Use of AI in Historical Writing

☐ I fact-checked all AI-generated claims against credible historical sources.

☐ I did not copy any AI-generated writing directly into my essay without revision.

☐ I treated AI like a discussion partner, not a historian.

☐ My final draft reflects my thinking, analysis, and historical interpretation.

TABLE 7.3. Using Image Generators for Literary Analysis and Creative Writing

Discipline	English language arts
Introduction	Today's students encounter meaning across multiple modes, not just through printed text but through digital images, audio, and video. When used thoughtfully, generative AI image tools can support literary analysis and creative writing by helping students visualize abstract concepts, experiment with tone and symbolism, and enhance their descriptive detail.
Objective	Students will use AI-generated images to deepen their understanding of literary themes, symbolism, and descriptive writing. Through image analysis, creative storytelling, and comparative writing, students will connect visual interpretations with textual evidence and expand their descriptive language skills.
Evidence-informed strategies	• Digital multimodal composition (Karchmer-Klein & Shinas, 2019; Kress, 2010; Smith et al., 2021) • Using visuals to support writing (Lewis et al., 2014)
Standards	Common Core State Standards • Reading: CCRA.R.1, R.2, R.4: Citing textual evidence, analyzing themes, and interpreting word meanings. • Writing: CCRA.W.2, W.3, W.4, W.5: Writing analytical and narrative texts, organizing ideas, and revising. • Speaking and Listening: CCRA.SL.1, SL.5: Engaging in discussions and using multimedia to enhance communication.
AI tools	• DALL·E or Midjourney: Used to generate images based on literary themes, character ideas, or symbolic scenes. • ChatGPT or Claude AI: Used to brainstorm image prompts, provide writing feedback, and support comparative analysis.
Step 1	Analyzing literature through AI-generated visuals • Students select a literary symbol, motif, or scene from a novel or short story. • Using an AI image generator, students create a visual interpretation of that concept. • Example prompt: "Create an image that represents loneliness in *Of Mice and Men* (Steinbeck, 1937), using only symbolic elements." • Students compare the AI image to the author's description and analyze the similarities and differences. Student writing task: • Write a paragraph comparing the AI-generated image with the literary description. • Include textual evidence and discuss how the image shaped or deepened your interpretation of the theme.
Step 2	Descriptive writing with AI-generated images • Students generate a creative or abstract image to use as a writing prompt. • Example prompt: "Generate an eerie, foggy landscape with an abandoned house and a glowing lantern." • Students write a one-page descriptive scene inspired by the image, focusing on mood, tone, and vivid language.

(continued)

TABLE 7.3. *(continued)*

Step 3	Character portraits and perspective writing • Students generate an image of a character based on a prompt. • Example prompt: "Generate a portrait of a Victorian-era woman with a secret." • Students write from that character's point of view—a diary entry, internal monologue, or first-person narrative. • Students are encouraged to incorporate historical or thematic context in their writing (e.g., class, gender, freedom, secrecy).
Reminder	AI hallucinations in literary analysis • AI-generated images are created from patterns, not literary understanding. • Students must always compare the GenAI's interpretation to the actual text. • AI should serve as inspiration, not a replacement for literary thinking or interpretation.

For example, students may describe actions, settings, or emotions in AI-generated scenes, using the visuals to support sentence-level writing development. Teachers can scaffold this work with sentence starters (e.g., "In the image, I see . . ." or "The person is holding . . ."), helping students build grammatically accurate sentences. Image sequences can support narrative writing or explanatory writing by providing visual cues for time order, process, or cause and effect. Even AI-generated infographics or labeled diagrams, such as the parts of a volcano or types of government systems, can serve as the basis for short explanatory paragraphs that promote both content understanding and academic language use (Zwiers, 2014).

When used intentionally, GenAI image tools offer more than visual appeal. Paired with teacher modeling, guided writing routines, and peer interaction, they can foster writing fluency, expand vocabulary, and increase MLLs' sense of agency and confidence as writers. In this way, GenAI supports a multimodal and inclusive approach to writing instruction that honors linguistic diversity and recognizes that meaning-making extends beyond the printed word (Leu et al., 2013).

AI-Enhanced Writing: Strategies for Every Classroom

While the detailed AI-driven writing lessons in this chapter offer in-depth explorations of GenAI's role in supporting complex disciplinary writing, the following mini-lessons are designed to showcase a broader range of practical, classroom-ready applications. Writing takes many forms across disciplines—from persuasive pitches in business to justification in mathematics—and these shorter lessons illustrate how GenAI can be integrated into diverse contexts without requiring major curricular overhauls.

Each lesson follows the same streamlined format, allowing educators to adopt or adapt the ideas with minimal preparation:

- *A writing strategy tailored to the discipline:* A brief overview of the disciplinary writing focus, grounded in relevant research.
- *AI tool(s) used:* A quick description of how GenAI supports the task whether through content generation, analysis, visualization, or revision.
- *Steps:* Overview of how to integrate strategy into instruction.
- *Classroom example:* A specific scenario showing what it might look like with students in action.

These strategies are intended to equip teachers, coaches, and instructional leaders with a flexible toolkit for embedding GenAI into everyday writing practice, encouraging students to write with clarity, curiosity, and disciplinary purpose.

Mini-Lesson—Business: Writing a Persuasive Pitch with GenAI

Writing Strategy

Strong business writing requires an understanding of market conditions and persuasive positioning. Research suggests that analyzing competitors enhances the clarity and impact of business proposals by helping students ground their ideas in real-world contexts (Barringer & Ireland, 2018). In this lesson, AI supports students as they generate market research, competitor comparisons, and pitch frameworks to strengthen their business cases.

AI Tool(s)

- *AI research generator* (e.g., ChatGPT, Claude, Perplexity AI)—for identifying competitors, market trends, and gaps.
- *AI presentation generator* (e.g., Canva AI, Tome)—for structuring and visualizing the pitch in a slide deck format.

Implementation

- *Choose a business idea:* Students propose a start-up or product concept.
- *Use AI for competitor analysis:* Students prompt AI to identify competitors, pricing models, and market opportunities.
- *Structure a persuasive pitch:* AI suggests persuasive language, pitch structure, and compelling hooks.
- *Create a slide deck:* Students use AI tools to generate visuals and organize the presentation.
- *Revise for clarity and impact:* Students review AI-generated feedback and revise their pitch accordingly, incorporating peer review as well.

Classroom Example

In a "Shark Tank"-style classroom activity, students develop business ideas and use AI to identify competitors and refine their market positioning. After generating an initial pitch with AI support, they receive AI and peer feedback, revise their proposals, and present them to a panel of classmates or guest judges. The process helps students combine creativity, research, and communication—core skills in business writing.

Mini-Lesson—Math: Writing Mathematical Justifications with GenAI

Writing Strategy

Mathematical justification requires students to explain why a solution works, not just how. Research shows that writing about reasoning enhances conceptual understanding and supports students' ability to justify their thinking (Mastroianni, 2013; Schoenfeld, 1992). GenAI tools can help students compare solutions and structure clearer, more logical written justifications.

AI Tool(s)

- *AI math solver* (e.g., Wolfram Alpha, Photomath)—generates step-by-step solutions for comparison.
- *AI writing assistant* (e.g., ChatGPT, Grammarly)—supports sentence structure and clarity.

Implementation

- Introduce the concept of justification and its value in mathematical thinking.
- Pose a word problem for students to solve independently.
- Have students compare their solution to an AI-generated explanation.
- Students use an AI writing tool to revise their justification.
- Conduct peer review and reflection on clarity and logic.

Classroom Example

In a seventh-grade class, students solve a perimeter word problem, use an AI math tool to compare approaches, and revise their written justifications. Pairs exchange their explanations, giving feedback on clarity and logic, reinforcing mathematical communication.

Mini-Lesson—Environmental Science: Writing a Scientific Proposal with GenAI

Writing Strategy

Research has shown that explicit instruction in written language will improve scientific thinking (Hand et al., 2018). Specifically, scientific proposal writing strengthens students' evidence-based reasoning and communication skills. GenAI tools can scaffold proposal organization and help visualize restoration outcomes.

AI Tool(s)

- *AI research assistant* (e.g., Elicit, Consensus)—summarizes scientific studies.
- *AI image generator* (e.g., DALL·E, Midjourney)—produces before-and-after ecosystem visuals.

Implementation

- Students choose a local or global ecosystem facing environmental degradation.
- Use AI to gather scientific research on similar restoration efforts.
- Draft a structured restoration proposal with AI-assisted outlines.
- Generate visual models of restored ecosystems using AI images.
- Present proposals, justifying strategies using scientific evidence.

Classroom Example

Students in an AP environmental science class design a plan to restore coral reefs. Using AI tools, they collect research, visualize restored ecosystems, and defend their approach in presentations using evidence and reasoning.

Mini-Lesson—Foreign Language: Writing Dialogues with AI Role-Play Partners

Writing Strategy

Writing and speaking reinforce each other in language acquisition (Akki & Larouz, 2021; Rokni & Seifi, 2014). GenAI enables interactive role play and real-time feedback, helping students improve fluency, vocabulary, and writing skills.

AI Tool(s)

- *AI chatbot role play* (e.g., FluentPal, AILingoPlay)—simulates conversational partners.

- *AI writing assistant* (e.g., Grammarly, DeepL Write)—supports grammar and sentence structure.
- *AI voice generator* (e.g., Murf AI, Speechify)—improves pronunciation through spoken output.

Implementation

- Students choose a real-world scenario (e.g., ordering food).
- Draft a dialogue using key vocabulary.
- Use AI to simulate an interactive conversation.
- Revise for clarity and fluency.
- Practice and perform in class.

Classroom Example

In Spanish class, students draft a restaurant dialogue, interact with an AI chatbot, revise based on feedback, and then perform live in pairs, practicing both writing and speaking for fluency.

Teacher Note

Review AI role-playing tools in advance for age appropriateness, educational alignment, and safety. Ensure students are guided in evaluating AI-generated content for relevance and accuracy.

Conclusion: Shifting Your Mindset about GenAI and Writing

This chapter reimagined how GenAI intersects with writing instruction across disciplines, inviting educators to shift their mindset from seeing AI as a shortcut to recognizing it as a dual-purpose tool: one that can both generate content and serve as an interactive writing partner.

On one hand, GenAI offers powerful opportunities to generate ideas, outlines, models, and even first drafts, helping students overcome barriers like writer's block or uncertainty about disciplinary conventions. On the other hand, its real instructional power emerges when students use it interactively—to test arguments, ask for clarification, get feedback, and revise with intention. In this mode, GenAI becomes a dialogical partner that prompts deeper thinking and supports metacognition, rather than replacing it.

For educators, coaches, and leaders, the challenge is not whether to allow AI in the writing process, but how to integrate it meaningfully, ensuring students remain critical thinkers and decision makers. Writing in an AI-augmented world still demands voice, evidence, structure, and discipline-specific reasoning. What changes is the pathway students take to get there and the support they receive along the way.

By designing writing instruction that leverages AI's generative capacity and interactive potential, we can help students become not just better writers but also more reflective, flexible, and independent communicators.

Teacher Reflection Questions

Use the prompts below to reflect on how GenAI might enhance, complicate, or transform your current approach to writing instruction and how you can help students maintain voice, agency, and authenticity in the writing process.

1. How do I currently support students through the stages of the writing process, from brainstorming to revision to the final product? Where might GenAI offer meaningful scaffolding without replacing student thinking?
2. How do I help students find and maintain their voice in writing? How can GenAI be used to support students' expression rather than diminish their originality?
3. What concerns do I have about students overrelying on GenAI to generate writing? What instructional strategies can I use to promote the intentional and ethical use of AI in writing?
4. How can I design writing activities where GenAI functions as a collaborator or feedback partner rather than a shortcut? What prompts, tools, or supports might help students engage in this kind of dialogue?

ETHICAL DILEMMA AND DISCUSSION PROMPTS

Ethical Dilemma: Who's the Author Now?

Mrs. Knox is teaching an 11th-grade interdisciplinary writing seminar focused on social change. Students are tasked with writing an op-ed article on a current issue they care deeply about. They're encouraged to use GenAI as a brainstorming and revision tool—but must maintain their voice, provide personal insights, and cite all sources.

One student, Maya, is passionate about the topic of mental health in schools. She uses GenAI to generate counterarguments, structure her reasoning, and help her frame an emotionally resonant conclusion. She also uses an AI image generator to create a visual to accompany her article—a powerful, stylized portrait of a student looking overwhelmed in a crowded hallway. Her final piece is exceptional. The voice is clear. The message is compelling. It even gets featured in the school newsletter.

But when Mrs. Knox talks with Maya about her process, she shares that the entire essay was built through iterative prompting and revision with GenAI. She fed the AI rough ideas and fragments, asked it to reword key phrases, tested different tones for her introduction, and even asked it to suggest analogies that might "hit harder" with the audience. The end result is deeply aligned with her intent, but nearly every sentence has been reshaped, restructured, or rewritten through her dialogue with the GenAI tool.

Discussion Prompts

1. What does authorship mean in the age of GenAI?
2. Should teachers assess the final product, the writing process, or both?
3. When does revision with GenAI become outsourcing?

PART III

How Do We Prepare Students for an AI-Infused Workforce and Higher Education?

Chapter 8

Reimagining Teaching in the Age of GenAI

PREPARING EDUCATORS FOR THE PRESENT AND FUTURE

> AI has become a big part of my day-to-day, especially regarding content creation and marketing strategy. So, what's the most valuable skill I've developed? It all comes down to prompt engineering—if you don't give clear direction, you'll waste time sifting through irrelevant or mediocre outputs.
>
> —ZACH BEERGER, marketing

> The most valuable skills for someone on my team regarding AI would include the ability to critically evaluate AI-generated outputs, effectively prompt AI tools for optimal results, and integrate AI-driven insights into our various initiatives. Potential candidates who can harness AI to improve accuracy, speed, and strategic decision making in their work will have a strong competitive advantage.
>
> —EVAN MILLMAN, cybersecurity

> AI in graphic design is a complex and tricky topic. Generating AI images based on existing artwork raises legitimate ethical and copyright issues. However, AI tools like generative fill enhance workflow efficiency. Many designers I know believe that understanding AI technology is essential to leverage its benefits and ensure proper safeguards and oversight in its use.
>
> —KATHERINE CONROY, graphic design

These voices from marketing, cybersecurity, and graphic design all point to a common truth: AI is not a future skill. It is a present-day professional necessity. Success in today's workforce hinges on technical proficiency, problem solving, critical thinking, and applying GenAI tools responsibly and strategically.

This transformation is not speculative. According to the *2025 Future of Jobs Report* by the World Economic Forum, digital advancements and AI will be among the most powerful forces shaping the global economy in the next 5 years. By 2030, 60% of employers expect AI and digital access to alter their businesses fundamentally. In turn, AI fluency and technological literacy are becoming some of the fastest-growing and most in-demand professional skills.

Yet, in many K–12 schools, GenAI is still seen as an add-on, interesting but not essential. This disconnect risks students graduating unprepared for higher education and an increasingly AI-infused workforce. But GenAI literacy is not just about knowing how to use tools. It's about knowing how to use them well.

Recent missteps in professional fields offer a clear reminder of this. In one case, a pro se litigant was fined $10,000 for submitting a ChatGPT-generated reply brief that cited fictitious case law (Fawbush, 2024). In another case, two attorneys were sanctioned for producing legal filings with fabricated references (CBS News, 2023). In Alaska, the state education commissioner used AI to generate policy language and cited nonexistent academic studies on the official Department of Education (2025) website ahead of a Board of Education meeting (Stremple, 2024). In every case, those involved claimed they did not realize GenAI tools could "hallucinate." Their excuse reveals a common gap: the assumption that fluency with digital tools is the same as understanding how to use them critically and responsibly.

These incidents underscore the need for students to learn how to engage with AI critically and ethically. And teachers must be equipped to guide them with clarity, confidence, and curiosity. This chapter explores two interconnected dimensions of teaching in the age of GenAI. First, it examines how educators can design learning experiences that immerse students in real-world applications of GenAI through simulations, creative production, and interdisciplinary projects. These classroom practices do not just introduce AI as a tool; they help students understand how it shapes the professions they may one day enter.

Second, the chapter outlines key considerations for supporting teachers' professional growth in this evolving landscape. Like marketers, designers, and cybersecurity professionals, educators need opportunities to use GenAI efficiently, ethically, and reflectively. Instructional planning, assessment, and classroom communication can be reshaped in thoughtful, creative ways that make instructional tasks more efficient, and educators should be empowered to lead that work, not simply respond to it.

While not an exhaustive road map, this chapter offers a starting point to guide teachers and school leaders as they engage with GenAI in meaningful, future-focused ways.

Bridging High School GenAI Learning to Real-World Applications

Practicing Professional Communication with GenAI

Professional communication is one of the most direct ways GenAI skills translate into real-world readiness. Whether preparing for college admissions interviews, internships, or job applications, students must be able to articulate their ideas clearly, confidently, and with professional polish—an essential skill in nearly every career field.

GenAI tools provide students with a low-stakes, highly personalized environment to develop those skills. Platforms like ChatGPT offer immediate feedback on clarity, tone, pacing, and word choice, allowing students to refine their communication through iteration. This kind of sustained, responsive practice is especially effective; research shows that repeated engagement with AI-generated feedback improves communication skills over time (Demszky et al., 2023).

Leigh Hibbard, a doctoral student at the University of Delaware and experienced high school English and public speaking teacher, designed the following lesson (see Table 8.1) to demonstrate how GenAI can serve as a personal coach for public speaking. In this activity, students deliver a short speech to ChatGPT, which then:

- Counts the number of filler words (e.g., *um*, *like*)
- Asks a follow-up question to assess depth and clarity
- Recommends three discipline-specific terms to strengthen the revision

Students receive actionable, personalized feedback and are guided through multiple rounds of reflection and revision. By engaging in this GenAI-supported dialogue, they build fluency, refine professional vocabulary, and practice thinking on their feet in response to AI-generated questions. The experience is designed to feel authentic and relevant, bridging classroom instruction with real-world expectations for professional communication.

To support independent learning and reinforce skill development, students also complete a checklist (see Form 8.1) that helps them track their progress in areas such as filler-word reduction, vocabulary enhancement, and interview confidence. This checklist turns self-assessment into part of the learning process, giving students a concrete way to reflect on their growth and prepare for future speaking opportunities in school, in college, and in the workforce.

GenAI Tools for Simulated Career Experience and Creative Application

GenAI does not just support academic content—it reshapes what students *experience* in the classroom. When used well, GenAI tools allow students to step into authentic roles, experiment with real-world challenges, and practice the kinds of thinking required in today's evolving workforce. This is more than digital literacy—it's professional literacy.

Immersive Simulations: Stepping into Professional Roles

Simulation is one of the most powerful uses of AI in education (Weinstein et al., 2025). Rather than reading about what a researcher, engineer, or diplomat does,

TABLE 8.1. AI as a Personalized Tutor for Public Speaking and Job Interview Preparation

Discipline	Public speaking
Objective	Students will use AI as a personalized speech coach to improve their public speaking and job interview skills by: • Reducing filler words and improving fluency • Incorporating discipline-specific vocabulary for professional communication. • Practicing responses to real-world interview questions. • Developing confidence in answering audience or interviewer questions.
Evidence-informed strategies	• AI-generated feedback (Demszky et al., 2023): Can accelerate learning by providing real-time corrections and personalized guidance
Standards	• Common Core Math Practice Standards: Make sense of problems and persevere in solving them • Common Core ELA in Mathematics: Interpret and analyze mathematical text and symbols in word problems
AI tools	• ChatGPT (or similar AI chatbot): Provides real-time speech feedback, filler word tracking, and professional vocabulary suggestions • AI-powered interview simulators (e.g., Yoodli, Interview Warmup by Google): Generates and evaluates mock job interview responses
Step 1	Baseline speech recording • Students write a short speech or professional introduction related to their field of interest (e.g., a scientist explaining their research, a business student pitching an idea). • They record themselves delivering the speech without AI assistance using a speech-to-text tool. • AI transcribes the speech and provides quantitative feedback (e.g., filler word count, clarity, pacing). AI-assisted self-assessment • After reviewing the AI feedback, students reflect on: • What are my most common filler words? • Where did I struggle with clarity or confidence? • Did I use strong discipline-specific vocabulary?

Step 2	AI-generated vocabulary and refinement
	• Students input their speech into ChatGPT, asking for:
	  ○ A revised version with stronger disciplinary vocabulary
	  ○ A breakdown of jargon or key terms used in professional settings
	• AI provides alternative word choices and explanations, helping students refine their speaking style.
	• Student task
	• Rewrite the speech, incorporating at least three discipline-specific terms provided by AI.

(continued)

TABLE 8.1. *(continued)*

Step 3	AI-enhanced practice round • Students rerecord their speech with the revised vocabulary. • AI again analyzes fluency, filler words, and word choice to show progress. • Students compare their first and second recordings, noting improvements. Teacher discussion • How did AI help refine their delivery? • Did their confidence improve?
Step 4	Job interview simulation • Students use an AI interview simulator (e.g., Interview Warmup by Google) to practice answering common job interview questions. • AI generates follow-up questions based on student responses, mimicking a real interview. • Students engage in a back-and-forth conversation with AI, focusing on: ○ Concise, professional responses ○ Clear articulation and confidence ○ Using discipline-specific terminology appropriately Peer feedback • Students pair up and role-play as interviewers, using AI-generated questions to challenge each other.
Assessment criteria	• Speech improvement: Student demonstrates progress in fluency, confidence, and vocabulary use between recordings. • AI engagement: Student effectively uses AI for feedback, revision, and self-assessment. • Interview preparedness: Student confidently answers AI-generated questions using clear, professional language.

students can inhabit those roles in AI-powered environments. In Labster, for example, students take on the role of a biochemist or forensic analyst in a virtual science lab, testing hypotheses, recording data, and seeing the consequences of their decisions. In AI4Mars, developed by NASA and Google, students help classify Martian terrain by training an AI model, contributing to real planetary science. ImmerseMe lets students negotiate business deals or order meals in a foreign language, mirroring global professional interactions. These tools build technical fluency, decision making, context awareness, and communication under pressure—core career-ready skills.

Creative Production: Using GenAI Like a Professional

Beyond simulations, students can use GenAI tools to create original work in ways that mirror professional processes. In digital storytelling, tools like Runway ML allow students to design animated sequences, generate short films, or visually communicate abstract ideas. In historical inquiry, D-ID brings historical figures to life through AI-generated avatars, letting students script interviews or role-play debates. Histograph helps students visualize historical patterns and timelines in dynamic, AI-supported formats. And in writing-intensive classes, Sudowrite acts

FORM 8.1

GenAI Public Speaking and Interview Prep Guide

Use this guide to practice public speaking and prepare for job interviews using GenAI tools.

☑ Step-by-Step Guide

1. Write and record (baseline)
   - Write a short speech or introduction about a career you are interested in.
   - Record yourself reading it.
   - Paste the audio of your speech into ChatGPT or record it directly into the chatbot using the built-in microphone.
2. Evaluate and feedback
   - Prompt ChatGPT to analyze your speech and ask it to provide feedback:
     - How many filler words did I use (*and*, *um*, *like*, etc.)?
     - Was my voice clear and confident?
     - Did I use discipline-specific vocabulary?

   Notes:

3. Revise with AI help
   - Paste the original speech into ChatGPT.
   - Ask: "Can you revise this speech using better discipline-specific vocabulary for a career in [insert career]?"
   - Choose and list at least three new terms from the AI response to add to your speech:
4. Practice again
   - Rerecord your speech using the new vocabulary.
   - Ask ChatGPT: "How can I improve this version?" Add specifics based on the feedback from the first evaluation.
   - Compare the feedback with your first speech:
     What has improved?

     What still needs to improve?

5. Job interview practice
   - Use ChatGPT or another GenAI tool of your choice to practice interviewing.
   - Paste the following chain-of-thought prompt into the tool. Be sure to fill in the blanks!
     "Act as a job interviewer for someone applying to be a [insert career]. This position requires [provide a three to five sentence description]. Ask me five common interview questions, one at a time. After each of my answers, provide me with feedback on my clarity, confidence, and vocabulary. You can also tell me how many filler words I used. Then ask a follow-up question."

as a creative partner offering feedback, suggesting vocabulary, and prompting students to develop ideas more fully. In each of these cases, students are not passively receiving information; they are crafting, revising, and producing work that reflects both disciplinary thinking and real-world practices.

Critical Thinking through Problem Solving and Debate

GenAI can also stretch students' reasoning and challenge their ethical judgment. Tools like the United Nations AI Challenge ask students to use AI to address urgent global issues, such as food insecurity or climate change, by proposing solutions grounded in data and context. MIT's Moral Machine simulates autonomous vehicles' complex decisions, inviting students to grapple with questions of fairness, value, and impact. Pol.is enables students to explore public policy arguments using machine learning to visualize areas of consensus and disagreement. And student-created AI escape rooms combine storytelling, logic, and systems thinking into game-based problem-solving experiences. These kinds of GenAI applications are not just about content; they foster the kind of civic reasoning and ethical reflection students will need as future leaders.

Real-World Thinking, Powered by GenAI

Educators do not need to master every AI tool to begin. What matters is giving students opportunities to explore GenAI in ways that mirror the world they're stepping into. Whether simulating a medical lab, designing an AI-assisted presentation, or solving global challenges, these experiences build confidence, creativity, and critical literacy. The following tools can support those efforts and help bring GenAI learning to life.

Quick Reference: Tools to Support This Work

Educators can explore the following tools to support immersive, creative, and critical thinking experiences with GenAI. These tools do not replace instruction. They expand what students can do, experience, and create.

Immersive Simulations

Students take on professional roles in realistic, AI-enhanced environments.

- *Labster:* Virtual science labs simulating careers in medicine, forensics, and biotech
- *AI4Mars* (NASA + Google): Students train AI to classify Martian terrain
- *ImmerseMe:* Language immersion with real-world role-playing (e.g., business deals, travel)

Creative and Disciplinary Production

Students use GenAI to write, design, and create with disciplinary depth.

- *Runway ML:* AI-generated video and animation for digital storytelling
- *D-ID:* Create AI avatars of historical figures for interviews or narrative role plays
- *Histograph:* Build AI-supported historical timelines and pattern analysis
- *Sudowrite:* Creative writing support tool for brainstorming, drafting, and revising

Critical Thinking, Debate, and Problem Solving

Students engage with ethical dilemmas, civic reasoning, and global challenges.

- *United Nations AI Challenge:* Solve real-world problems using AI-supported innovation
- *MIT Moral Machine:* Explore ethical decision-making in autonomous vehicle scenarios
- *Pol.is:* Analyze public debates using AI-generated argument mapping
- *AI-Powered Escape Rooms:* Students design interactive, AI-enhanced problem-solving games

To make experiences like these possible, educators need time, support, and professional development to explore GenAI as learners and leaders. The second half of this chapter turns to that question.

Professional Development for GenAI Integration: Equipping Educators for the Future

Most conversations about GenAI in schools begin with students. But preparing students for an AI-powered world depends entirely on whether their teachers have been given the time, space, and support to understand these tools themselves.

I introduced Melissa Rapp in Chapter 7 as one of the most experienced teachers I know when it comes to integrating GenAI into instruction. When I asked her if her school district had provided any professional development on GenAI, her answer reflected what many educators are experiencing:

> I received a little PD [professional development] at my school 2 years ago on ChatGPT when AI was really new. It was on what it was and how it could be used. I learned [how to integrate it into my instruction] through research and online communities that I am a part of. I have also researched on my own and tested out a few sites for

> efficacy before proceeding with the GenAI tools in my teaching. (M. Rapp, personal communication, February 24, 2025)

Melissa's story is not unique. While GenAI is becoming more prominent in education, formal support for teachers remains rare (Irwin, 2024). Many educators are left to navigate integration on their own, relying on trial and error, social media networks, and personal experimentation. These efforts are often resourceful and inspiring, but they shouldn't have to be solo.

Ethan Mollick and colleagues at the Wharton School describe AI as a "jagged frontier" (Dell'Acqua et al., 2023) because it is astonishingly advanced in some areas and surprisingly erratic in others. GenAI can summarize complex research, design creative lessons, and analyze student writing. But it also miscounts, fabricates sources, and speaks with confident inaccuracy. This tension between power and unpredictability is exactly why professional development on GenAI must be active, not theoretical. Teachers cannot learn these tools by watching a slide deck. They need space to experiment, push boundaries, and encounter their brilliance and blind spots firsthand.

Too often, professional learning around technology is built around compliance or vague overviews. When it lacks relevance or immediacy, teachers disengage not because they are resistant to GenAI, but because the training never meets them where they teach. For professional development to be effective, it must be:

- *Hands-on and exploratory:* Teachers need time to experiment with AI tools, observe how responses change with different prompts, and experience the jagged frontier firsthand.
- *Rooted in real classroom scenarios:* Instead of generic AI overviews, training should let teachers apply AI to their own lesson planning, grading, and content creation.
- *Time allocated for failure as much as success:* Teachers should be encouraged to find AI's flaws, debunk AI myths, and learn how to fact-check and refine outputs.
- *Collaborative, not isolated:* AI training works best when teachers can discuss findings with peers, problem solve together, and build confidence through shared discoveries.

I have presented enough technology-focused professional development (PD) sessions to learn this: the best way to overcome fear is not through a presenter explaining what GenAI can do but by teachers experiencing it for themselves. My role is to guide them into that space—to create a setting where they can explore, experiment, and encounter "the jagged frontier" with support and curiosity. Only then can they move from hesitation to confidence, and from confusion to creativity.

Models That Work: Designing Effective PD for GenAI Integration

Educators do not need another slideshow about what AI *might* do. They need meaningful, hands-on opportunities to explore what GenAI *can do in their classrooms, with their students, right now.* The PD models below reflect what teachers consistently say they want: time to experiment, space to collaborate, and support that honors their expertise. These approaches can be adapted across contexts and grade levels, offering flexible entry points for schools just beginning or deepening their journey into AI-integrated learning.

AI-Powered Lesson Study Groups

Why It Works

Teachers learn best by doing and some by doing together. Lesson study groups (Zepeda, 2019) bring educators into small teams where they co-design AI-infused lessons, try them out in real classrooms, reflect on what happened, and revise. This continuous cycle of inquiry makes AI integration a *teaching practice*, not a tech add-on.

What It Looks Like

Imagine a team of three teachers—an English teacher, a science teacher, and a social studies teacher—meeting during a common prep period. Their goal? To create a cross-disciplinary unit where students use GenAI to simulate a historical trial, generate courtroom arguments, and analyze scientific evidence. They each pilot the activity in different ways, gather student feedback, and refine their approach in a follow-up session.

Why It Matters

Lesson study builds shared ownership, deepens content alignment, and helps teachers see AI as a flexible tool that supports their instructional goals—not something separate from what they already do well.

Peer Coaching and AI Mentorship Programs

Why It Works

Not every teacher needs to become an AI expert, but every school has teachers already exploring GenAI who can help others begin. Peer coaching (Zepeda, 2019) puts those early adopters in leadership roles, creating a trusted, teacher-led structure for learning and growth.

What It Looks Like

A school identifies three teachers who've been using GenAI tools in thoughtful, curriculum-aligned ways. One becomes a mentor for a group of new AI explorers in the English department. Another teacher leads monthly "PD Rounds," where teachers observe a real lesson using AI and debrief with guiding questions. A third co-teaches a lesson on prompt engineering with a colleague, modeling how GenAI can support writing instruction.

Why It Matters

Teachers learn best from other teachers. These models foster a culture of experimentation and collegial trust, essential ingredients for any innovation to take root.

AI Learning Labs and Sandbox Experiences

Why It Works

Teachers often feel pressure to "get it right" when using new tech for the first time. Sandbox PD (Sreenivasan, 2024) removes that pressure. It provides a safe, low-stakes space to play, test ideas, and discover what GenAI can (and can't) do—before bringing it into the classroom.

What It Looks Like

A district creates an "AI Playground" during a PD day where teachers rotate through stations—one for experimenting with image generators, another for designing writing prompts with ChatGPT, a third for exploring bias in AI-generated search results. No one has to leave with a polished product. The goal is to experience the tools and ask good questions together.

Why It Matters

The jagged frontier of AI can feel intimidating. Giving teachers time to explore, laugh, and tinker with AI tools *as learners* breaks down fear and builds curiosity.

Micro-Credentials and Certification Programs

Why It Works

Some teachers want a structured pathway to develop GenAI expertise over time. Micro-credentials and certifications (Carbaugh et al., 2022) offer focused, self-paced learning that results in recognized, portable professional development.

What It Looks Like

A teacher completes the International Society for Technology in Education (ISTE) AI Educator Certification, gaining foundational knowledge in ethical AI use, prompt design, and classroom applications. Another chooses a micro-credential through AI for Education, found at https://www.aiforeducation.io, focused on using GenAI to train educators to train other educators. These credentials give teachers something tangible to add to their portfolios and confidence to share their learning with peers.

Why It Matters

Not all PD needs to happen in a room full of people. Certification pathways give teachers autonomy, direction, and credibility as they grow their expertise.

Try It Out Action Steps for Educators and School Leadership

Integrating GenAI into instruction does not require a complete overhaul. The most effective changes begin with small, intentional shifts. Think of them as experiments that help teachers build confidence, spark curiosity, and start seeing GenAI as part of their instructional toolkit rather than replacing it.

The action steps below are designed to support both individual educators and school leadership in moving forward. These steps are not about mastering every AI tool. They are about creating the right conditions at the classroom and system level for exploration, learning, and long-term impact.

Action Steps for Individual Educators

Experiment in Low-Stakes Settings

Teachers do not need to wait for formal PD to begin exploring GenAI. The best first step is simply choosing one tool, such as ChatGPT, SlidesGo, or an AI-powered assessment assistant, and trying it out. Use it to generate lesson ideas, give formative feedback on writing, or create a quick image for a slideshow. The key is to keep the stakes low. Start with curiosity, not perfection.

Try It Out

Open ChatGPT and type in a few-shot prompt: "I'm teaching a lesson on [topic] to [grade of your choice] students. Can you suggest three engaging warm-up questions that spark curiosity and don't require prior knowledge?" Use or revise one result. Time yourself: 10 minutes max. The goal is *play*, not perfection.

Build AI Literacy and Ethical Awareness

Effective GenAI use is not just technical. It is ethical and critical. Teachers must understand how these tools are built; how they generate responses; and where bias, misinformation, or hallucination may emerge. AI tools can reinforce stereotypes, cite nonexistent sources, or confidently present misleading summaries. Educators need space to explore these issues before introducing GenAI into the classroom. Resources like the ISTE AI Exploration Network (*https://iste.org/ai*), AI4K12 (*https://ai4k12.org*), and AIandYou (*https://aiandyou.org*) offer accessible guidance on ethical use, transparency, and data literacy in ways that connect to the K–12 context.

Try It Out

Choose one of the following ethical inquiry tasks to explore in a staff meeting, professional learning community (PLC), or on your own:

- *Run a hallucination test:* Ask ChatGPT or another GenAI tool to generate five sources on a topic you teach. Check if the citations are real. What do you notice about how confidently misinformation is presented?
- *Prompt for bias:* Ask your GenAI tool "Write a paragraph describing a scientist," or "Create a story about a successful business leader." Then reflect: Who's represented? Who's missing? How might this shape student understanding?
- *Facilitate an "AI on trial" discussion:* Tell colleagues or students that "AI should never be used for grading student work." Split into two sides and have AI generate arguments for each. Then discuss what feels valid, where AI might be misleading, and what your personal stance is.

Each of these helps build the critical thinking muscles educators will need to lead GenAI conversations with students, not just follow them.

Design One AI-Enhanced Lesson or Activity

Apply what you've learned in a focused way. Identify a single lesson where GenAI could support student learning—perhaps by enhancing writing revision in ELA, helping students simulate a historical debate, or supporting multilingual learners with image generation. Try it out, ask students for feedback, and reflect on what worked. You don't have to transform your whole unit—just start with one meaningful moment.

Try It Out

Pick one existing lesson and ask ChatGPT: "I teach [subject]. I want students to [learning goal]. What are two ways GenAI tools could support this without doing the thinking for them?" Review the suggestions. Try one. Debrief with students about what GenAI helped with and what they still had to do themselves.

Action Steps for Schools and Leadership

Support Ongoing AI Professional Development

Teachers need structured time and support to explore GenAI tools. Schools can offer PD in many formats: full-day workshops, after-school sandbox labs, informal peer coaching, or embedded planning time. The most important thing is to create opportunities for teachers to practice, talk, and iterate together. Providing integration guides, sample lessons, and prompt banks can reduce the cognitive load of starting from scratch.

Try It Out

Block off one department meeting or PLC to explore GenAI. Offer teachers a single question: "What is one classroom task, like drafting an exit ticket or giving feedback on writing, that GenAI could help you with?" Provide time for them to test it out, then reflect. Capture their findings in a shared document or "Go for It: GenAI" wall.

Create a Schoolwide AI Integration Plan

Just as schools plan for literacy or STEM across grade levels, they should begin building a shared road map for AI integration. This includes aligning GenAI use with curriculum objectives, developing policies on responsible use and data privacy, and naming clear goals for student learning. Involving teachers in this process is essential because they are the ones who will bring the plan to life in classrooms.

Try It Out

Block off one department meeting or PLC to explore GenAI. Offer teachers a single question: "What's one classroom task—like drafting an exit ticket or giving feedback on writing—that GenAI could help you with?" Provide time for them to test it out, then reflect. Capture their findings in a shared document or "Go for It: GenAI" wall.

Encourage Cross-Disciplinary Collaboration

Some of the most creative GenAI learning experiences come from interdisciplinary design. School leaders can foster this by creating AI lesson study teams or PLCs where teachers from different content areas co-design learning experiences. A science teacher and an art teacher might collaborate on an AI-powered public health campaign. A world language teacher and a social studies teacher might use GenAI to simulate an international summit.

Try It Out

Kick off a 3-week "AI Collab Sprint" where teams of two to three teachers co-design one AI-powered lesson that integrates at least two disciplines. Provide flexible formats (shared doc, idea board, brief share-out), and celebrate finished prototypes even if they are in rough form.

Foster a Culture of Inquiry and Experimentation

Perhaps most important, schools should treat GenAI not as a threat or a trend but as a tool for inquiry. Encourage teachers to ask hard questions about AI bias and hallucinations. Invite them to reflect on how AI might reshape assessment or feedback. Position AI not as a shortcut but as a new lens through which students can think more deeply, write more effectively, and solve more creatively.

Try It Out

Start a monthly "AI & Coffee" series where teachers can bring wins, messes, questions, and demos. No pressure, no agenda. Just community learning. Kick off the first session by asking: "What did AI do this month that surprised you for better or worse?"

Conclusion

The most transformative force in GenAI integration will not be the next algorithm. It will be educators. The tools will continue to evolve, and some will become essential, while others will fade. But what remains constant is the role of the teachers. They will design the questions, curate the contexts, and model how to think critically and ethically in the face of complexity. GenAI may generate answers, but it cannot generate wisdom. That work still belongs to educators.

Too often, the narrative around AI in education is one of replacement or resistance. But the real story is one of imagination. Teachers are already exploring what is possible: designing inquiry projects with AI-generated prompts, helping MLLs tell richer stories using image generators, challenging students to critique AI-generated historical summaries, and asking better and better questions. This is what it means to teach in the age of GenAI—to know how to ask:

- Does this tool deepen learning?
- Does it support student agency and growth?
- What kind of thinking does it encourage or discourage?

When schools empower teachers with time, trust, and professional learning, GenAI becomes a tool for reflection, creativity, and connection. Marissa Bongo, a high school social studies teacher with 18 years of experience, captures this well:

> A 21st-century educator needs to be a strong critical thinker who knows how to use AI, adapt to changes in the technology, evaluate AI outputs for accuracy and bias, and model for students how to implement generative AI within the guardrails of policies that maintain ethics and academic honesty. (M. Bongo, personal communication, May 30, 2025)

This is the kind of educator we need—not one who is perfect with AI but one who is willing to lead through uncertainty, experiment with integrity, and shape a future where students are empowered, not automated. The real challenge of GenAI in education is not technical. It is human. And the future will be built not by tools but by teachers.

Teacher Reflection Questions

Use the prompts below to reflect on your own professional development journey as you consider how to integrate GenAI into your teaching practice.

1. How confident do I feel in my current understanding of GenAI tools? What experiences or gaps in knowledge are shaping that confidence?
2. How does my school or district currently approach GenAI? Are clear expectations, support systems, or collaborative opportunities in place?
3. What concerns (ethical, pedagogical, or logistical) do I still have about using GenAI in the classroom? How might I begin to address those concerns through experimentation, discussion, or professional learning?
4. What steps can I take to advocate for meaningful, hands-on GenAI PD in my school or district? How might I support and collaborate with colleagues who are hesitant or still learning?

ETHICAL DILEMMA AND DISCUSSION PROMPTS

Ethical Dilemma: When One Teacher Embraces GenAI and the System Does Not

Ms. Rivera, a high school teacher, has spent months learning how to integrate GenAI tools into her classroom. She uses them thoughtfully and enjoys designing writing prompts that encourage students to compare their own ideas with AI responses, building lessons around prompt engineering and source evaluation, and holding classroom discussions about the ethical use of these tools. Her students are engaged and report feeling more confident navigating AI in their learning.

However, Ms. Rivera begins to face pushback. Some colleagues accuse her of encouraging "cheating." An administrator warns her not to mention AI during back-to-school night, citing concerns about parent reactions. Meanwhile, other teachers avoid the topic altogether, leading students to receive mixed messages across classes, leaving them unsure about when, how, or even if they can use AI tools for schoolwork. Ms. Rivera believes students need clear, consistent guidance if they are to learn to use AI responsibly. But without institutional support, she feels isolated. Should she continue using the tools in her teaching? Should she push for schoolwide policies? And how can schools create a culture where ethical AI use is not just permitted but supported?

Discussion Prompts

1. How can schools support teachers who are willing to innovate with AI while addressing concerns from parents, colleagues, or leadership?
2. What are the risks of giving students inconsistent or unclear messages about using AI tools in school?
3. When is it appropriate for an individual teacher to take initiative, and when is schoolwide alignment necessary?
4. What PD or leadership support is needed to ensure all students receive ethical, informed guidance around AI?

References

AI for Education. (n.d.). GenAI Chatbot Prompt Library for Educators. Retrieved July 20, 2025, from www.aiforeducation.io/prompt-library

Akgun, S., & Greenhow, C. (2022). Artificial intelligence in education: Addressing ethical challenges in K–12 settings. *AI and Ethics, 2*, 431–440.

Akki, F., & Larouz, M. (2021). Speaking and writing interconnections: A systematic review. *Journal of Translation and Language Studies, 2*(2), 19–33.

AlMakinah, R., Goodarzi, M., Tok, B., & Canbaz, M. A. (2024). Mapping artificial intelligence bias: A network-based framework for analysis and mitigation. *AI and Ethics, 5*, 1995–2014.

Barringer, B. R., & Ireland, R. D. (2018). *Entrepreneurship: Successfully launching new ventures* (6th ed.). Pearson.

Bazerman, C., Applebee, A. N., Berninger, V. W., Brandt, D., Graham, S., Matsuda, P. K., et al. (2017). Taking the long view on writing development. *Research in the Teaching of English, 51*(3), 351–360.

Bean, T., & Rigoni, N. (2001). The impact of a multicultural young adult novel on intergenerational dialog discussion journals. *Reading Research Quarterly, 36*, 232–248.

Boussioux, L., Lane, J. N., Zhang, M., Jacimovic, V., & Lakhani, K. R. (2024). The crowdless future? Generative AI and creative problem-solving. *Organization Science, 35*(5), 1589–1607.

Bransford, J. D., & Stein, B. S. (1984). *The IDEAL problem solver: A guide for improving thinking, learning, and creativity*. Freeman.

Brookfield, S. D. (2012). *Teaching for critical thinking: Tools and techniques to help students question their assumptions*. Jossey-Bass.

Burleigh, C. L., & Wilson, A. M. (2022). Mobile technology acceptable use policies and teaching in high school classrooms: Do boundaries exist? *International Journal of Multidisciplinary and Current Educational Research, 4*(1), 71–86. www.ijmcer.com

Carbaugh, E. M., McCullough, L., Raftery, M., & Linaburg, E. (2022, August 9). How microcredentials can save professional learning. *ASCD Blog.* www.ascd.org/blogs/how-microcredentials-can-save-professional-learning

Carle, E. (1981). *The very hungry caterpillar.* Philomel Books.

Cartwright, K. B. (2023). *Executive skills and reading comprehension: A guide for educators* (2nd ed.). Guilford Press.

CBS News. (2023, June 23). Lawyers fined for filing bogus case law created by ChatGPT. *CBS News.* www.cbsnews.com/news/chatgpt-judge-fines-lawyers-who-used-ai

Choi, I., & Lee, K. (2009). Designing and implementing a case-based learning environment for enhancing ill-structured problem solving: Classroom management problems for prospective teachers. *Educational Technology Research and Development, 57*(1), 99–129.

Chun, C. W. (2009). Critical literacies and graphic novels for English-language learners: Teaching Maus. *Journal of Adolescent and Adult Literacy, 53,* 144–153.

Cisneros, S. (1983). *The house on Mango Street.* Vintage Books.

Clarke, L. W., & Whitney, E. (2009). Walking in their shoes: Using multiple-perspective texts as a bridge to critical literacy. *The Reading Teacher, 62*(6), 530–534.

Coiro, J. (2021). Toward a multifaceted heuristic of digital reading to inform assessment, research, practice, and policy. *Reading Research Quarterly, 56*(1), 9–31.

Coiro, J., & Dobler, E. (2007). Exploring the online reading comprehension strategies used by sixth-grade skilled readers to search for and locate information on the internet. *Reading Research Quarterly, 42*(2), 214–257.

Cope, B., & Kalantzis, M. (2015). *A pedagogy of multiliteracies: Learning by design.* Palgrave Macmillan.

Croteau, J. (2024). 300 best AI prompts for K–12 teachers. *We Are Teachers.* www.weareteachers.com/ai-prompts/#how-to

Cullinan, M. (2024). Surveying the perspectives of middle and high school educators who use role-playing games as pedagogy. *International Journal of Role-Playing, 15,* 127–141.

Dang, H., Mecke, L., Lehmann, F., Goller, S., & Buschek, D. (2022). How to prompt? Opportunities and challenges of zero- and few-shot learning for human-AI interaction in creative applications of generative models. In *Proceedings of the CHI Conference on Human Factors in Computing Systems, Workshop on Generative AI and HCI (GenAICHI 2022).*

De La Paz, S., & Graham, S. (2002). Explicitly teaching strategies, skills, and knowledge: Writing instruction in middle school classrooms. *Journal of Educational Psychology, 94*(4), 687–698.

Dell'Acqua, F., McFowland, E., Mollick, E., Lifshitz-Assaf, H., Kellogg, K. C., Rajendran, S., et al. (2023). *Navigating the jagged technological frontier: Field experimental evidence of the effects of AI on knowledge worker productivity and quality* (Harvard Business School Working Paper No. 24-013). Harvard Business School. www.hbs.edu/ris/Publication%20Files/24-013_d9b45b68-9e74-42d6-a1c6-c72fb70c7282.pdf

Demszky, D., Liu, J., Hill, H. C., Jurafsky, D., & Piech, C. (2023). Can automated feedback improve teachers' uptake of student ideas? Evidence from a randomized controlled trial in a large-scale online course. *Educational Evaluation and Policy Analysis, 46*(3), 483–505.

Diliberti, M. K., Schwartz, H. L., Doan, S., Shapiro, A., Rainey, L. R., & Lake, R. J. (2024). *Using artificial intelligence tools in K–12 classrooms*. RAND. www.rand.org/pubs/research_reports/RRA956-21.html

Dobbs, C. L., Ippolito, J., & Charner-Laird, M. (2016). Layering intermediate and disciplinary literacy work: Lessons learned from a secondary social studies teacher team. *Journal of Adolescent and Adult Literacy, 60*(2), 131–139.

Drucker, P. F. (1994). The age of social transformation. *Atlantic Monthly*, pp. 53–80.

Duffy, G. G. (2014). *Explaining reading: A resource for teaching concepts, skills, and strategies* (3rd ed.). Guilford Press.

Dumper, K., Jenkins, W., Lacombe, A., Lovett, M., & Perimutter, M. (n.d.). *Introductory psychology*. Washington State University. https://opentext.wsu.edu/psych105

Dwyer, C. P. (2023). An evaluative review of barriers to critical thinking in educational and real-world settings. *Journal of Intelligence, 11*(105), 1–17.

The Economist. (2021, January 9). Wikipedia is 20, and its reputation has never been higher. www.economist.com/international/2021/01/09/wikipedia-is-20-and-its-reputation-has-never-been-higher

Ennis, R. H. (1987). A taxonomy of critical thinking dispositions and abilities. In J. B. Baron & R. J. Sternberg (Eds.), *Teaching thinking skills: Theory and practice* (pp. 9–26). W H Freeman/Times Books/Henry Holt.

Ericsson, K. A., & Simon, H. A. (1993). *Think aloud protocols* (rev. ed.). MIT Press.

Facione, P. A. (1990). *Critical thinking: A statement of expert consensus for purposes of educational assessment and instruction—Research findings and recommendations* (The Delphi Report). California Academic Press.

Faggella-Luby, M., & Wardwell, M. (2011). RTI in a middle school: Findings and practical implications of a tier 2 reading comprehension study. *Learning Disability Quarterly, 34*(1), 35–49.

Fawbush, J. F., Esq. (2024, February 16). *Pro se litigant fined 10k for filing AI-generated reply brief*. FindLaw. www.findlaw.com/legalblogs/practice-of-law/pro-se-litigant-fined-10k-for-filing-ai-generated-reply-brief

Fisher, D., & Frey, N. (2014). Content area vocabulary learning. *The Reading Teacher, 67*(8), 594–599.

Fisher, M. (2019). The case for metacognitive reflection: A theory integrative review with implications for medical education. *Medical Education, 53*(5), 441–452.

Fitzgerald, F. S. (1925). *The great Gatsby*. Scribner's.

Flower, L., & Hayes, J. R. (1981). A cognitive process theory of writing. *College Composition and Communication, 32*(4), 365–387.

Frey, R. F., Brame, C. J., Fink, A., & Lemons, P. P. (2022). Teaching discipline-based problem solving. *CBE—Life Sciences Education, 21*(2).

Fuchs, D., Fuchs, L. S., Mathes, P. G., & Simmons, D. C. (1997). Peer-assisted learning strategies: Making classrooms more responsive to diversity. *American Educational Research Journal, 34*(1), 174–206.

Gee, J. P. (2007). *What video games have to teach us about learning and literacy* (2nd ed.). Palgrave Macmillan.

Giri, V., & Paily, M. U. (2020). Effect of scientific argumentation on the development of critical thinking. *Science and Education 29*, 673–690.

Glazewski, K. D., & Hmelo-Silver, C. E. (2019). Scaffolding and supporting the use of information for ambitious learning practices. *Information and Learning Sciences, 120*(1/2), 39–58.

Goldman, S. R., Britt, M. A., Brown, W., Cribb, G., George, M., Greenleaf, C., et al. (2016). Disciplinary literacies and learning to read for understanding: A conceptual framework for disciplinary literacy. *Educational Psychologist, 51*(2), 219–246.

Goldstein, D. (2023, September 19). Comparing online and AI-assisted learning: A student's view. *Education Next.* www.educationnext.org/comparing-online-ai-assisted-learning-students-view-khan-academy-khanmigo

Gonsalves, C. (2024). Generative AI's impact on critical thinking: Revisiting Bloom's taxonomy. *Journal of Marketing Education, 1*(1), 1–16.

Graham, S., MacArthur, C. A., & Hebert, M. A. (Eds.). (2018). *Best practices in writing instruction* (3rd ed.). Guilford Press.

Graham, S., & Perin, D. (2007). *Writing next: Effective strategies to improve writing of adolescents in middle and high schools.* Alliance for Excellent Education.

Hand, B., Park, S., & Suh, J. (2018). Examining teachers' shifting epistemic orientations in improving students' scientific literacy through adoption of the Science Writing Heuristic approach. In C. V. Johnson, E. A. Shanahan, & G. P. Demoiny (Eds.), *Global developments in literacy research for science education* (pp. 339–355). Springer.

Handford, M., & Gee, J. P. (Eds.). (2023). *The Routledge handbook of discourse analysis* (2nd ed.). Routledge.

Hobbs, R. (2010). *Digital and media literacy: A plan of action.* Aspen Institute.

Irwin, S. (2024, March 22). Survey report: The state of AI for teachers. *EdTech Evolved.* www.esparklearning.com/blog/survey-report-the-state-of-ai-for-teachers

Johnson, A. (2023). ChatGPT in schools: Here's where it's banned—and how it could potentially help students. *Forbes.* www.forbes.com/sites/ariannajohnson/2023/01/18/chatgpt-in-schools-heres-where-its-banned-and-how-it-could-potentially-help-students

Juuzt AI. (n.d.). *Fewshot prompt framework.* Author. Retrieved July 21, 2025, from www.juuzt.ai/knowledge-base/prompt-frameworks/the-few-shot-framework

Karchmer, R. A. (2001). Teachers on a journey: Thirteen teachers report how the Internet influences literacy instruction in their K–12 classrooms. *Reading Research Quarterly, 36*(4), 442–466.

Karchmer-Klein, R. (2020). *Improving online teacher education: Digital tools and evidence-based practices.* Teachers College Press.

Karchmer-Klein, R., Boulden, L., & McDonald, M. (2022). *Next-level digital tools and teaching: Solving six major instructional challenges—K–12.* Teachers College Press.

Karchmer-Klein, R., Hibbard, L., & Li, M. (in press). Holistic approaches to digital literacies in secondary classrooms. In E. A. Baker (Ed.), *Research handbook on digital literacies,* Elgar.

Karchmer-Klein, R., & Shinas, V. (2019). Adolescents' navigation of linguistic and nonlinguistic modes in a digital narrative. *Journal of Research in Reading, 42*(3–4), 469–484.

Kastberg, S., & Leatham, K. (2005). Research on graphing calculators at the secondary level: Implications for mathematics teacher education. *Contemporary Issues in Technology and Teacher Education, 5*(1), 25–37. https://citejournal.org/wpcontent/uploads/2016/04/v5i1mathematics1.pdf

Keck, J. (2023, May 2). Reverse engineer the problem. *Medium.* https://medium.com/@chivarse/reverse-engineer-the-problem-eedb72fd2be

Knoth, N., Tolzin, A., Janson, A., & Leimeister, J. M. (2024). AI literacy and its implications for prompt engineering strategies. *Computers and Education: Artificial Intelligence, 6*, Article 100225.

Kolb, D. A. (1984). *Experiential learning: Experience as the source of learning and development.* Prentice Hall.

Konieczny, P. (2016). Teaching with Wikipedia in a 21st-century classroom: Perceptions of Wikipedia and its educational benefits. *Journal of the Association for Information Science and Technology, 67*(7), 1523–1534.

Kress, G. (1998). Visual and verbal modes of representation in electronically mediated communication: The potentials of new forms of text. In I. Snyder (Ed.), *Page to screen: Taking literacy into the electronic era* (pp. 53–79). Routledge.

Kress, G. (2010). *Multimodality: A social semiotic approach to contemporary communication.* Routledge.

Kuhn, D. (2019). Critical thinking as discourse. *Human Development, 62*(3), 146–164.

Lee, H. (1960). *To kill a mockingbird.* J. B. Lippincott.

Lent, R. C. (2016). *This is disciplinary literacy: Reading, writing, thinking, and doing . . . content area by content area.* Corwin.

Leu, D. J., Kinzer, C. K., Coiro, J., Castek, J., & Henry, L. A. (2013). New literacies: A dual-level theory of the changing nature of literacy, instruction, and assessment. In D. E. Alvermann, N. J. Unrau, & R. B. Ruddell (Eds.), *Theoretical models and processes of literacy* (6th ed., pp. 1150–1181). International Reading Association.

Levine, S., Beck, S. W., Mah, C., Phalen, L., & Pittman, J. (2025). How do students use ChatGPT as a writing support? *Journal of Adolescent and Adult Literacy, 68*, 445–457.

Lewis, K., Walpole, S., & McKenna, M. C. (2014). *Cracking the common core: Choosing and using texts in grades 6–12.* Guilford Press.

Lewis, W. E., & Strong, J. Z. (2020). *Literacy instruction with disciplinary texts: Strategies for grades 6–12.* Guilford Press.

Li, W., Yu, J., Zhang, Z., & Liu, X. (2022). Dual coding or cognitive load? Exploring the effect of multimodal input on English as a foreign language learners' vocabulary learning. *Frontiers in Psychology, 13*, Article 834706.

Lo, L. S. (2023). The CLEAR path: A framework for enhancing information literacy through prompt engineering. *Journal of Academic Librarianship, 49*(4).

Lukpat, A. (2023). ChatGPT banned in New York City public schools over concerns about cheating, learning development. *Wall Street Journal.* www.wsj.com/articles/chatgpt-banned-in-new-york-city-public-schools-over-concerns-about-cheating-learning-development-11673024059

MacArthur, C. A., Graham, S., & Fitzgerald, J. (Eds.). (2025). *Handbook of writing research* (3rd ed.). Guilford Press

Malin, J. R., Brown, C., Ion, G., van Acheren, I., Bremm, N., Luzmore, R., et al. (2020). World-wide barriers and enablers to achieving evidence-informed practice in education: What can be learnt from Spain, England, the United States, and Germany? *Humanities and Social Science Communication, 7*(99).

Mastroianni, M. P. (2013). Writing in mathematics. In A. N. Applebee & J. A. Langer (Eds.), *Writing instruction that works: Proven methods for middle and high school classrooms* (pp. 71–93). Teachers College Press.

McConachie, S. M., & Petrosky, A. R. (2010). *Content matters: A disciplinary literacy approach to improving student learning.* Jossey-Bass.

McDonell Area Catholic Schools. (2024). *Acceptable use policy for AI technology policy document.* www.mcdonellareacatholicschools.org/editoruploads/files/MACS%20Acceptable%20Use%20Policy%20for%20AI%20Technology.pdf

McKenna, M. C., & Stahl, K. A. D. (2009). *Assessment for reading instruction* (2nd ed.). Guilford Press.

Mehta, J., & Fine, S. (2019). *In search of deeper learning: The quest to remake the American high school.* Harvard University Press.

Microsoft. (2023, November). *AI in education: A Microsoft special report.* Author. https://cdndynmedia1.microsoft.com/is/content/microsoftcorp/microsoft/final/en-us/microsoft-product-and-services/microsoft-education/downloadables/AI-in-Education-A-Microsoft-Special-Report.pdf

Mishra, P., Oster, N., & Henriksen, D. (2024). *Generative AI, teacher knowledge and educational research: Bridging short- and long-term perspectives. TechTrends, 68*(2), 205–210.

Moje, E. B. (2015). Doing and teaching disciplinary literacy with adolescent learners: A social and cultural enterprise. *Harvard Educational Review, 85*(2), 254–278.

Mok, A. (2023, June 24). Jobs are now requiring experience with ChatGPT—and they'll pay as much as $800,000 a year for the skill. *Insider.* www.businessinsider.com/jobs-roles-companies-want-ai-chatgpt-experience-salary-2023-6

MonteSano, C. (2011). Beyond reading comprehension and summary: Learning to read and write in history by focusing on evidence, perspective, and interpretation. *Journal of Curriculum Inquiry, 41*(2), 212–249.

MonteSano, C., & Thomson, S. (2022). "It's not that simple": Re-thinking historical writing tasks based on insights from disciplinary experts. *The History Teacher, 55*(3), 391–418.

Mouza, C., Pan, Y.-C., Yang, H., & Pollock, L. (2020). A multiyear investigation of student computational thinking concepts, practices, and perspectives in an after-school computing program. *Journal of Educational Computing Research, 58*(5), 1029–1056.

National Governors Association Center for Best Practices & Council of Chief State School Officers. (2010). *Common Core State Standards.* Authors. www.corestandards.org

National Research Council. (2013). *Next Generation Science Standards: For states, by states.* National Academies Press. www.nextgenscience.org

The New London Group. (1996). A pedagogy of multiliteracies: Designing social futures. *Harvard Educational Review, 66*(1), 60–92.

Newman, P. M., & DeCaro, M. S. (2019). Learning by exploring: How much guidance is optimal? *Learning and Instruction, 62*, 49–63.

Nguyen, T. N. N., Tran, T. T., Nguyen, N. H. A., Lam, H. P., Nguyen, H. M. S., & Tran,

N. A. T. (2025). The benefits and challenges of AI translation tools in translation education at the tertiary level: A systematic review. *International Journal of TESOL & Education, 5*(2), 132–148.

Oliveri, M. E., Lawless, R., & Molloy, H. (2017). *ETS GRE® board research report: ETS GRE®–17-03, ETS RR–17-06*. Educational Testing Service. https://files.eric.ed.gov/fulltext/EJ1168401.pdf

Omeokwe, A. (2023, October 16). AI could spur an economic boom. Humans are in the way. *Wall Street Journal*. www.wsj.com/tech/ai/ai-could-spur-an-economic-boom-humans-are-in-the-way-3f13182c

Palacio, R. J. (2016). *Wonder*. Knopf.

Palatucci, M., Pomerleau, D., Hinton, G. E., & Mitchell, T. M. (2009). Zero-shot learning with semantic output codes. *Advances in Neural Information Processing Systems, 22*, 1410–1418. https://proceedings.neurips.cc/paper_files/paper/2009/file/fe73f5b6f-6c3f11df1ce5d604f7bb95e-Paper.pdf

Pew Research Center. (2024). *Teens and social media fact sheet*. Author. www.pewresearch.org/internet/fact-sheet/teens-and-social-media-fact-sheet

Pólya, G. (1993). *How to solve it: A new aspect of mathematical method* (2nd ed.). Princeton University Press.

Powell, S. R., Hebert, M. A., & Hughes, E. M. (2021). How educators use mathematics writing in the classroom: A national survey of mathematics educators. *Reading and Writing, 34*, 417–447.

Price, L., & Kirkwood, A. (2014). Informed design of educational technology for teaching and learning? Towards an evidence-informed model of good practice. *Technology, Pedagogy and Education, 23*(3) 325–347.

Pytash, K. E., & Morgan, D. N. (2014). Using mentor texts to teach writing in science and social studies. *The Reading Teacher, 68*(2), 93–102.

Reuters. (2023). *Top French university bans use of ChatGPT to prevent plagiarism*. Author. www.reuters.com/technology/top-french-university-bans-use-chatgpt-prevent-plagiarism-2023-01-27

Reynolds, D., & Fisher, W. (2022). What happens when adolescents meet complex texts? Describing moments of scaffolding textual encounters. *Literacy, 56*(4), 277–287.

Rokni, S. J. A., & Seifi, A. (2014). Dialog journal writing and its effect on learners' speaking accuracy and fluency. *Study in English Language Teaching, 2*(1), 28–37.

Sampson, V., & Blanchard, M. R. (2012). Science teachers and scientific argumentation: Trends in views and practice. *Journal of Research in Science Teaching, 49*, 1122–1148.

San Gabriel Unified School District. (2024, July). *Responsible use guidelines for generative AI tools*. www.sgusd.k12.ca.us/apps/pages/index.jsp?pREC_ID=2594534&type=d&uREC_ID=413700

Scharff, L., Draeger, J., Verpoorten, D., Devlin, M., Dvorakova, L. S., Lodge, J. M., & Smith, S. (2017). Exploring metacognition as support for learning transfer. *Teaching and Learning Inquiry, 5*(1), 78–92.

Schoenfeld, A. (1985). Metacognitive and epistemological issues in mathematical understanding. In E. A. Silver (Ed.), *Teaching and learning mathematical problem solving: Multiple research perspectives* (pp. 361–380). Erlbaum.

Schoenfeld, A. H. (1992). Learning to think mathematically: Problem solving, metacognition, and sense-making in mathematics. *Journal of Mathematical Behavior, 10*(3), 209–226.

Seixas, P., & Morton, T. (2013). *The big six historical thinking concepts.* Nelson Education.

Shakespeare, W. (2011). *Romeo and Juliet* (B. A. Mowat & P. Werstine, Eds.). Simon & Schuster.

Shanahan, T. (2015, May 17). Vocabulary teaching. *Shanahan on literacy.* www.shanahanonliteracy.com/blog/vocabulary-teaching

Shanahan, T., & Shanahan, C. (2008). Teaching disciplinary literacy to adolescents: Rethinking content-area literacy. *Harvard Educational Review, 78*(1), 40–59.

Sillito, D. (2022, July 20). Teens shun traditional news channels for TikTok and Instagram, Ofcom says. *BBC News.* www.bbc.com/news/entertainment-arts-62238307

Smith, B. E., Pacheco, M. B., & Khorosheva, M. (2021). Emergent bilingual students and digital multimodal composition: A systematic review of research in secondary classrooms. *Reading Research Quarterly, 56*(1), 33–52.

Sprague, Z., Yin, F., Rodriguez, J. D., Jiang, D., Wadhwa, M., Singhal, P., et al. (2024). To CoT or not to CoT? Chain-of-thought helps mainly on math and symbolic reasoning. *arXiv.* https://arxiv.org/abs/2409.12183

Sreenivasan, A. (2024, December 6). *Assessing readiness: How sandbox training environments enhance skill validation and practice.* Nuvepro. nuvepro.com/assessing-readiness-how-sandbox-training-environments-enhance-skill-validation-and-practice

Stahl, K. A. D., Flanigan, K., & McKenna, M. C. (2020). *Assessment for reading instruction* (4th ed.). Guilford Press.

Steinbeck, J. (1937). *Of mice and men.* Covici Friede.

Stremple, C. (2024, October 28). *False citations show Alaska education official relied on generative AI, raising broader questions.* Alaska Beacon. https://alaskabeacon.com/2024/10/28/alaska-education-department-published-false-ai-generated-academic-citations-in-cell-policy-documentTam, D., Mascarenhas, A., Zhang, S., Kwan, S., Bansal, M., & Raffel, C. (2023). Evaluating the factual consistency of large language models through news summarization. *Findings of the Association for Computational Linguistics,* 5220–5255.

Tarrant, G. (2023). Generative AI is already changing white-collar work as we know it. *The Wall Street Journal.* www.wsj.com/articles/generative-ai-is-already-changing-white-collar-work-as-we-know-it-58b53918

U.S. Department of Education. (2025, January 14). *Root cause analysis in action.* Retrieved May 5, 2025, from www.ed.gov/teaching-and-administration/lead-and-manage-my-school/state-support-network/ssn-resources/root-cause-analysis-in-action

U.S. Department of Education, Office of Educational Technology. (2024). *A call to action for closing the digital access, design, and use divides: 2024 National Educational Technology Plan* (ERIC Publication No. ED641164) (113 pp.). Author.

Walpole, S., McKenna, M. C., & Philippakos, Z. A. (2011). *Differentiated literacy instruction in grades 4 and 5: Strategies and resources.* Guilford Press.

Wei, J., Wang, X., Schuurmans, D., Bosma, M., Ichter, B., Xia, F., et al. (2022). Chain-of-thought prompting elicits reasoning in large language models. *Advances in Neural Information Processing Systems, 35,* 24824–24837.

Weinstein, A., Brotspies, H. V., & Gironda, J. T. (2025, April 14). Do your students know how to analyze a case with AI—and still learn the right skills? A framework for using GenAI to support, not replace, students' critical thinking. *Harvard Business: Inspiring Minds.* https://hbsp.harvard.edu/inspiring-minds/framework-analyze-cases-using-ai-enhance-decision-making-skills

Werderich, D. E. (2006). The teacher's response process in dialogue journals. *Reading Horizons: A Journal of Literacy and Language Arts, 47* (1). Retrieved from https://scholarworks.wmich.edu/reading_horizons/vol47/iss1/4

White, S., Groom-Thomas, L., & Loeb, S. (2022). *Undertaking complex but effective instructional supports for students: A systematic review of research on high-impact tutoring planning and implementation* (Ed Working Paper No. 22-652). Annenberg Institute at Brown University.

Wilhelm, J. D. (2016). *"You gotta BE the book": Teaching engaged and reflective reading with adolescents* (3rd ed.). Teachers College Press.

Wilson, J. (2019). Assessing writing. In S. Graham, C. A. MacArthur, & M. Hebert (Eds.), *Best practices in writing instruction* (3rd ed., pp. 333–360). Guilford Press.

Wineburg, S. (1991). Historical problem solving: A study of the cognitive processes used in the evaluation of documentary and pictorial evidence. *Journal of Educational Psychology, 83*(1), 73–87.

Wineburg, S. (2018). *Why learn history (when it's already on your phone?).* University of Chicago Press.

Wineburg, S., & McGrew, S. (2019). Lateral reading and the nature of expertise: Reading less and learning more when evaluating digital information. *Teachers College Record, 121*(11), 1–40.

Witzel, B. S., Mercer, C. D., & Miller, M. D. (2003), Teaching algebra to students with learning difficulties: An investigation of an explicit instruction model. *Learning Disabilities Research & Practice, 18*. 121–131.

World Economic Forum. (2025). *The future of jobs report 2025.* Author. https://reports.weforum.org/docs/WEF_Future_of_Jobs_Report_2025.pdf

Wu, Y., & Schunn, C. D. (2021). The effects of providing and receiving peer feedback on writing performance and learning of secondary school students. *American Educational Research Journal, 58*(3), 492–526.

Zepeda, S. J. (2019). *Professional development: What works* (3rd ed.). Routledge.

Zusak, M. (2005). *The book thief.* Knopf Books for Young Readers.

Zwiers, J. (2014). *Building academic language: Meeting Common Core standards across disciplines, grades 5–12* (2nd ed.). Jossey-Bass.

Index

Note. *f* or *t* following a page number indicates a figure or a table.

D

E

N

O

P

Q

R